DIS COVER BRIXY

24. Juli 2014

Für Brinta und Axel!
Vom Brixy
Alles Liebe und Gute
und wie du job...!

DIS COVER BRIXY

Herausgegeben von | **Edited by**
Jürgen Krieger

Essays von | **by**
Volker Lehmkuhl, Ulrike Lorenz, Reinhard Spieler, Werner Tammen, Christoph Tannert

Interview von | **by**
Melanie Klier

BRAUS

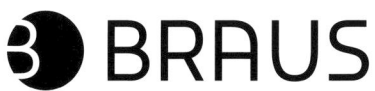

Für meine Eltern
Tienchen und Paul

For my parents
Tienchen and Paul

Ich bin ins Unbekannte aufgebrochen.
Habe das Unvermutete zugelassen.
Auf der Suche nach einer künstlerischen Essenz.

I set out into the unknown.
Allowed the unexpected to occur.
In search of an artistic essence.

INHALT | CONTENTS

Werner Tammen
Virtuose im Leinwandgeviert – Dietmar Brixy
16 **Virtuoso of the Canvas – Dietmar Brixy**

Ulrike Lorenz
Gesamtkunstwerk und Großkraftwerk
31 **The Gesamtkunstwerk and the Power Station**

Melanie Klier
Ein kurzer Gedankenaustausch mit Dietmar Brixy
49 **A Brief Exchange of Ideas with Dietmar Brixy**

Christoph Tannert
Brixy auf Entdeckungstour
78 **Brixy on a Voyage of Discovery**

Reinhard Spieler
Brixy im Paradies-Labor
144 **Brixy's Laboratory of Paradise**

Volker Lehmkuhl
Inspiration inbegriffen
186 **Inspiration Included**

195 Biografie | **Biography**
197 Ausstellungen | **Exhibitions**
200 Autoren | **Authors**

Alle abgebildeten Werke: Öl auf Nessel
mit Ausnahme der Sonderedition

All works shown: oil on nettle
with the exception of the collector's edition

VIRTUOSE IM LEINWANDGEVIERT: DIETMAR BRIXY

Werner Tammen

Man ist überrascht: Der Weg des auswärtigen Besuchers vom Mannheimer Bahnhof durch die nicht gerade anheimelnde Nachkriegsarchitektur hinaus zum Studio des Malers Dietmar Brixy ist das Eine.
Das Andere: Angekommen im industriellen, majestätischen Schatten des Mannheimer Großkraftwerks am verwachsenen und verschlossen wirkenden Stahltor des Brixy Anwesens wächst die Neugierde. Mit elektronischem Türsummer eingelassen, verharrt man unwillkürlich beim ersten Anblick des sich darbietenden, imposanten neogotischen – 1903 erbauten – alten Abwasserpumpwerk Neckarau.

Erlebt und erfasst man Schritt für Schritt das ganze einmalige, geschlossene Ensemble von gestalteter, von Künstlerhand geschaffener Botanik außen und sensibel saniertem, kulturellen Ort der Malerei und des Lebens innen, fragt man sich unwillkürlich – nachdem man kurz in Gedanken bei Emil Nolde in Seebüll/Schleswig-Holstein eingekehrt ist – nach der Künstlerpersönlichkeit und der Motivation für dieses außergewöhnliche Gestaltungsengagement. Ein abgeschirmter Schutzraum scheinbar – und dennoch kommunikative Insel und Ort der Kontemplation.

In dem hier nun vorliegenden fulminanten Katalog beschäftigen sich aus unterschiedlichen Positionen namhafte AutorenInnen wie Dr. Ulrike Lorenz (Direktorin Kunsthalle Mannheim), Dr. Melanie Klier (Kunstbuchautorin, München), Dr. Reinhard Spieler (Direktor Sprengel-Museum, Hannover),

VIRTUOSO OF THE CANVAS: DIETMAR BRIXY

It comes as a surprise. First, there is the journey that the visitor from other parts must undertake: it leads from Mannheim's main station through postwar architecture, which can hardly be described as homey, to the painter Dietmar Brixy's studio.
The Other. The visitor's curiosity increases upon arrival at the overgrown and locked-looking steel gate to Brixy's property in the majestic industrial shadow of Mannheim's power station. Buzzed in by an electric gate opener, the visitor will involuntarily pause when the imposing old, neo-Gothic wastewater pumping station of Neckarau, built in 1903, first appears.

This sense of surprise does not fade. Step by step, one experiences and grasps the entirety of the unique and cohesive ensemble of the botanical elements outside, designed and created by an artist's hand, and the sensitively restored cultural painting and living space inside. One cannot help but wonder, after a brief mental sojourn with Emil Nolde in Seebüll/Schleswig-Holstein, about the artist and the motivation for this extraordinary creative commitment. It appears to be a shielded sanctuary, and yet it is a communicative island and place of contemplation.

In this splendid catalogue, renowned authors such as Dr. Ulrike Lorenz (Kunsthalle Mannheim), Dr. Melanie Klier (author of art books, Munich), Dr. Reinhard Spieler (director of the Sprengel-Museum, Hannover), Christoph Tannert (Künstlerhaus Bethanien, Berlin) and Volker Lehmkuhl (specialist journalist) consider the special art space and the artistic work of Dietmar Brixy from a variety of angles.

The author Volker Lehmkuhl describes in a highly informative and engaging manner, the history and the conversion of the listed building that the

Christoph Tannert (Künstlerischer Leiter Künstlerhaus Bethanien, Berlin) sowie Volker Lehmkuhl (Fachjournalist) mit dem besonderen Kunstort und dem künstlerischen Werk Dietmar Brixys.

Der Autor Volker Lehmkuhl beschreibt sehr informativ und anregend die Historie des denkmalgeschützten Umbaus, den der Künstler Dietmar Brixy zusammen mit dem Speyerer Architekten Mathias Henrich vor zehn Jahren realisiert hat. Brixy, der das Bauwerk Mitte 2001 erwarb, verbrachte seine Kindheit in der Nachbarschaft. Als kreativen Menschen faszinierten ihn schon immer die besondere Lage und die Einzigartigkeit dieses Bauwerks. Wie von Künstlerhand an Unorten „…aus der anachronistischen Sehnsucht nach einem mythischen Ort inmitten der greifbaren Schönheit der Natur…" (Ulrike Lorenz) ein wahres Paradies erschaffen werden kann, lässt sich hier nun auf überwältigende Weise besichtigen und man kann im Nachhinein dem Künstler und allen Unterstützern zu diesem Kultur Ort nur herzlich gratulieren.

„Keine Abwässer wälzen sich mehr durch die perfekt geformten unterirdischen Kanäle des Pumpwerks, vielmehr ergießt sich ein alles verschlingender Malstrom wirbelnder Farbmassen und Formfragmente über die Oberflächen überlebensgroßer Leinwände", vermerkt Ulrike Lorenz sprachgewaltig über dieses neugotische Baudenkmal und die Kunst Dietmar Brixys und konstatiert: „Diese Insel der Seligen, abgeschirmt vom Alltag und dennoch porös für die Welt, ist Ausgangs- wie Zielpunkt eines imponierend kraftvollen Selbstentwurfs, Resonanzraum eines selbstbewussten Anspruchs auf Geltung." Und fährt fort: „Der Ort bestimmt die Malerei. Die Malerei beseelt den Ort. Pathos und Energie kennzeichnen beide. Die unnachahmliche Transformationsleistung aber, das eine aus dem anderen hervorgehen zu lassen und beides in der Schwebe zu halten, erbringt der Künstler".

Den Künstler als Leinwandvirtuosen beschreibt Christoph Tannert wie folgt: „Brixy schlemmt heftig Farbe ins Keilrahmengeviert. Er kehrt sein Innerstes nach außen. Wülste und insulare Gebilde lassen den Blick beim Abtasten der Leinwand stolpern. Die Dinge überschlagen sich. Spontan wird

artist Dietmar Brixy realized ten years ago with the architect Mathias Heinrich. Brixy, who purchased and restored the building in early 2001, spent his childhood in the neighborhood. As a creative person, he was always fascinated by the unusual location and the uniqueness of the building. It is now possible to witness in an overwhelming way how a veritable paradise can be created in a non-place by an artist's hand "… from the anachronistic longing for a mythical place in the midst of the tangible beauty of nature" (Ulrike Lorenz). In retrospect one can wholeheartedly congratulate the artist and all his supporters for this cultural space.

"No wastewater churns its way through the perfectly formed subterranean canals of the pumping station now. Instead, an all-engulfing maelstrom of swirling masses of color and fragments of form is discharged upon the surfaces of larger-than-life canvases," as Dr. Ulrike Lorenz has so eloquently remarked about Dietmar Brixy's space and art. She also notes that "This isle of the blessed, shielded from everyday life and yet porous for the world, is both the starting point and the end point of an impressively powerful creation of the self, and a space in which a self-confident claim to recognition can resonate." She continues: "The place determines the painting. The painting animates the place. Pathos and energy characterize both. The inimitable transformative achievement of causing one to grow out of the other and of keeping both up in the air, however, is effected by the artist."

Christoph Tannert describes the artist and his virtuoso paintings as follows: "Brixy slams plenty of paint onto the stretcher-frame square. He externalizes his innermost being. Bulges and insular formations cause the gaze to trip up as it feels its way across the canvas. One thing vies for space with another. Brixy spontaneously uses his hands, he streaks and circles around the painterly substance with a kneading hand and an examining eye, and spurs on the pictorial creation with his painter's hand."

Brixy handgreiflich, er schliert, er umkreist knetend und prüfend das Malstoffliche und treibt mit der Malerpranke die Bildwerdung voran."

Während Reinhard Spieler in seinem Essay „Brixy im Paradies-Labor" einen versierten Blick auf die Werkserie „Eden" wirft, untermauern hilfreich und praktisch die von Melanie Klier zusammengetragenen persönlichen Statements von Brixy dessen künstlerische Zielsetzungen und persönlichen Motivationen.

Alle Texte bündeln auch meine Erfahrungen mit dem Künstler Dietmar Brixy und beschreiben die Symbiose des besonderen Ortes mit der Künstlerpersönlichkeit aufs vortrefflichste. Die virtuose Beherrschung des malerischen Materials, das durchscheinende kenntnisreiche Zitat, die glaubhafte dialogische Verknüpfung von eigener Person mit der Reflektion von Naturphänomenen im bisherigen Gesamtwerk, ist für mich – je länger ich mich mit seinen Arbeiten und der dazu gehörenden Rezeption beschäftige – absolut stimmig.

Der Erfolg seiner künstlerischen Arbeiten rührt zum großen Teil daher, dass Brixy sich als Künstler in seinen Arbeiten immer wieder neu erfindet und weiter entwickelt, ohne dabei seine Grundüberzeugung, die der Einheit von Leben und Werk, zu verlassen.

Jedes Jahr lädt der Künstler im Herbst zur öffentlichen Präsentation seines Werkes in das Pumpwerk ein. Diese opulenten Ausstellungen (z. B. „Discover" 2012, „Achtung Brixy" 2013) haben sich von einem Geheimtipp zu einem kulturellen Pflichttermin entwickelt.

Neben seinen Werken präsentiert Brixy auch Arbeiten befreundeter Künstlerkollegen und befruchtet somit den gewünschten gemeinsamen Diskurs über die unterschiedlichen künstlerischen Auffassungen und Werke, ganz so wie es Ulrike Lorenz beschreibt: „Ort, Werk und Mensch bedingen sich gegenseitig."

Als Galerist freue ich mich sehr, den Künstler auf seinem Weg in den nationalen wie internationalen Kunstmarkt zu begleiten. Nach Ausstellungen bei anderen Galerien in der Schweiz und

In his essay "In the Laboratory of Paradise" Reinhard Spieler takes another look at the "Eden" series of paintings. The personal statements by Brixy on the subject of his artistic aims and personal motivations, collected by Melanie Klier, provide helpful and practical substantiation in the context of the various texts.

All texts also combine my experiences with the artist Dietmar Brixy, and accurately describe the symbiosis of this remarkable location with the artist's personality.

The virtuoso mastery of painterly material, the succinct and knowledgeable quotation, the credible dialogic connection of the self, and the reflection of natural phenomena in the Gesamtkunstwerk created to date – for me, all of this is entirely coherent for me as I become increasingly familiar with his work and its reception.

The success of Brixy's works of art is largely the result of the fact that he continuously reinvents himself as an artist and continues to develop in his work without abandoning his core belief in the unity of life and oeuvre.

Every year in autumn the artist invites guest to the public presentation of his works in the pumping station. These events ("Discover" in 2012 and "Achtung Brixy" in 2013) have become essential viewing.

In addition to his own works, Brixy also presents the works of his artist friends and thus fertilizes the desired joint discourse about the various artistic perceptions and works. "The place, the œuvre, and the person determine one another," explains Ulrike Lorenz in her essay.

As a gallery owner I am delighted to accompany the artist on his journey into the national and international art market. After exhibitions in Switzerland and America it was the positive reception at international art fairs in Istanbul and in Miami in 2013 in particular that confirmed the unique

Amerika bestätigte vor allem der Zuspruch bei den internationalen Messebeteiligungen unserer Galerie mit Brixy in Istanbul und Miami 2013 die besondere Strahlkraft und die universelle Sprache seiner Malerei. Ein Weg, der sicherlich seine Fortsetzung finden wird.

Heimgekehrt von diesen nationalen und internationalen Ausflügen, gefüllt mit mannigfachen Eindrücken und Erfahrungen, ist Dietmar Brixys Rückkehr ins eigene Refugium beständiges und vergewissertes Lebenselixier, was aus seinem Munde so klingt:

„Dieses Teilhabenlassen der Menschen draußen an meiner Kunstwelt hier drinnen beflügelt mich – bis ich wieder die Tore schließe für eine Zeit der Reinigung, des Inwendigwerdens."

Fast wie im Kampf mit den jahreszeitlichen Zyklen und Zeitringen der Natur, will er immer wieder neu seine malerischen Lebensringe wuchernd ins Bild setzen, andere teilhaben lassen und von diesem Leben erzählen.

Eine faszinierende Symbiose!

---

power and universal language of his painting. There can be no doubt that this is only the beginning.

When coming home from these national and international excursions, having soaked up diverse impressions and experiences, the return to his own refuge is an enduring and assured elixir:

"Allowing people 'outside' to take part in my art world 'in here' also animates me until I close the gates again for a period of purification and of focusing on that which is inside" (Dietmar Brixy)

As though in battle with nature's seasonal cycles and rings of time, his aim is to paint a sprawl of his painterly rings of life into the picture in ever new ways, to let others participate, and to speak of this life.

It is a fascinating symbiosis!

Discover, 2013
180 × 120 cm

Discover, 2012
120 × 300 cm

Discover, 2014
160 × 100 cm

Discover, 2014
je | each 40 × 50 cm

Discover, 2014
80 × 100 cm

Discover, 2014
je | each 70 × 90 cm

Ulrike Lorenz

GESAMTKUNSTWERK UND GROSSKRAFTWERK

Im Energiefeld von Malen-Wollen und Leben-Können

> „Die Totalkunst stellt die Frage: ‚WAS SOLL DAS GANZE?'
> und antwortet: *Es soll Kultur ermöglichen…*"
> Bazon Brock

Individuen handeln als Künstler, wenn aus der Einheit ihres Denkens, Wollens und Könnens eine exemplarische Vermittlung von Schöpfung und Arbeit erwächst, die Aufmerksamkeit erzwingt. Das Publikum schätzt den Künstler, der als Statthalter seiner eigenen Sehnsüchte agiert. Ein Prototyp lustvollen Begehrens im grenzüberschreitenden Energiefeld von Kunst und Leben ist Brixy: freier Maler im umhegten Paradiesgarten unter den steil aufragenden Kaminen des Großkraftwerks am Rhein in Mannheim. Ort, Werk und Mensch bedingen sich gegenseitig. Aus diesem kontextuellen Gewebe entfaltet sich ein Gesamtzusammenhang, der künstlerische Produktion und ästhetische Erfahrung in nächste Nähe rückt, wobei auf beiden Seiten Kontemplation und Exaltation in direkten Austausch treten.

1961 in einfachen Mannheimer Verhältnissen geboren, entwickelte Brixy immense kreative Kompensationsenergien aus der anachronistischen Sehnsucht nach einem mythischen Ort inmitten der greifbaren Schönheit der Natur, den er sich nach seinem inneren Bild erschuf. Im selbstverantworteten Handeln formte sich dabei während der vergangenen zwei Jahrzehnte eine erfolgreiche Künstlerbiografie. Zehn Jahre nach seinem Studium an der Kunstakademie Karlsruhe, verwirklichte Brixy in unmittelbarer Nachbarschaft zur Herkunft einen Kindheitszukunftstraum. Er erwarb 2001

THE GESAMTKUNSTWERK AND THE POWER STATION

In the Energy Field of Wanting to Paint and Being Able to Live

> "Total art asks the question: 'WHAT IS THE POINT OF IT ALL?'
> and answers: *Its goal is to make culture possible…*"
> Bazon Brock

Individuals act as artists when an exemplary communication of creation and work that exacts attention grows out of the unity of their thought, desire, and ability. The audience appreciates the artist, who functions as the governor of his or her own yearning. Brixy is a prototype of joyful desire in the transgressive energy field of life and art: an independent painter in an enclosed Garden of Eden under the towering chimneys of the large power station on the Rhine in Mannheim. The place, the oeuvre, and the person determine one another. An all-encompassing interrelation develops out of this contextual fabric, which brings artistic production and aesthetic experience into close proximity, whereby contemplation and exaltation enter a relationship of direct exchange on both sides.

Born in 1961 to a humble Mannheim family, Brixy developed immense creative powers of compensation from the anachronistic desire for a mythical place surrounded by the tangible beauty of nature, which he created in accordance with his mental image. Through autonomous action, he went on to carve out a successful artist's biography over the course of the last two decades. Ten years after studying at Karlsruhe's art academy, Brixy realized a childhood dream of the future in close proximity to his origins. In 2001, he acquired the old pumping station of Neckerau, which had been robbed of its original function. Over the course of two years he carefully transformed the imposing neo-Gothic industrial monument into an

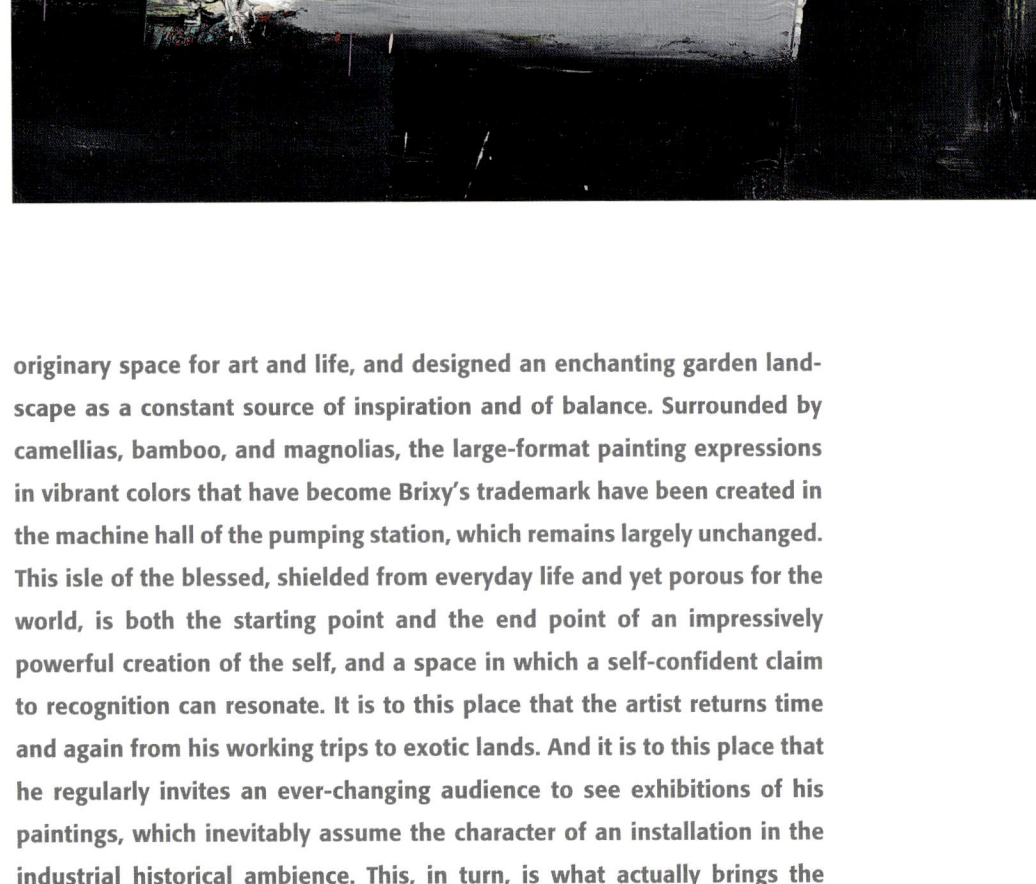

originary space for art and life, and designed an enchanting garden landscape as a constant source of inspiration and of balance. Surrounded by camellias, bamboo, and magnolias, the large-format painting expressions in vibrant colors that have become Brixy's trademark have been created in the machine hall of the pumping station, which remains largely unchanged. This isle of the blessed, shielded from everyday life and yet porous for the world, is both the starting point and the end point of an impressively powerful creation of the self, and a space in which a self-confident claim to recognition can resonate. It is to this place that the artist returns time and again from his working trips to exotic lands. And it is to this place that he regularly invites an ever-changing audience to see exhibitions of his paintings, which inevitably assume the character of an installation in the industrial historical ambience. This, in turn, is what actually brings the event-like nature of the painting to the fore. The place determines the painting. The painting animates the place. Pathos and energy characterize

Discover, 2014
120 × 180 cm

das seiner Funktion beraubte Alte Pumpwerk Neckarau, baute das imposante neogotische Industriedenkmal zwei Jahre lang behutsam zu einem originären Kunst- und Lebensraum um und gestaltete eine zauberhafte Gartenlandschaft als ständigen Quell der Inspiration und des Ausgleichs. Von Kamelien, Bambus und Magnolien umwogt, entstehen seitdem in der atemberaubenden, fast unverändert belassenen Maschinenhalle des Pumpwerks die großformatigen, starkfarbigen Malereiexpressionen, die zum Markenzeichen Brixys geworden sind.

Diese Insel des Seligen, abgeschirmt vom Alltag und dennoch porös für die Welt, ist Ausgangs- wie Zielpunkt eines imponierend kraftvollen Selbstentwurfs, Resonanzraum eines selbstbewussten Anspruchs auf Geltung. Dahin kehrt der Künstler immer wieder von seinen Arbeitsreisen in exotische Länder zurück. Hierher lädt er ein wechselndes Publikum regelmäßig zu Ausstellungen seiner Bilder ein, die im industriehistoristischen Ambiente unweigerlich Installationscharakter annehmen, was die Ereignishaftigkeit der Malerei erst eigentlich zum Vorschein bringt. Der Ort bestimmt die Malerei. Die Malerei beseelt den Ort. Pathos und Energie kennzeichnen beide. Die unnachahmliche Transformationsleistung aber, das eine aus dem anderen hervorgehen zu lassen und beides in der Schwebe zu halten, erbringt der Künstler: Keine Abwässer wälzen sich mehr durch die perfekt geformten unterirdischen Kanäle des Pumpwerks, vielmehr ergießt sich ein alles verschlingender Malstrom wirbelnder Farbmassen und Formfragmente über die Oberflächen überlebensgroßer Leinwände.

Insofern kann die Malerei Brixys als ortspezifisch gelten. Indem sie beispielhaft Szenarien der Entgrenzung – von Zeit und Raum, Natur und Kultur, Ort und Malerei – repräsentiert, ist sie trotz ihres monomedialen Charakters Ausdruck einer Gesamtkunstwerkskonzeption. Brixys Konzept der Durchdringung von Leben und Malen ist von der Obsession bestimmt, ein Bild vom Ganzen und die persönliche Verkörperung des Ganzen zu realisieren. Der Maler lebt ein Exempel ganzheitlicher Existenz vor, geprägt von einem stimulierenden Sensualismus, dessen Unruhe sich auf sein Publikum überträgt. Die Bilder, entstanden im kontrollierten Rausch des Machens, zielen auf eine Aktivierung aller sensorischen Fähigkeiten zur ästhetischen Erfahrung und definieren die ästhetische

both. The inimitable transformative achievement of causing one to grow out of the other and of keeping both up in the air, however, is effected by the artist. No wastewater churns its way through the perfectly formed subterranean canals of the pumping station now. Instead, an all-engulfing maelstrom of swirling masses of color and fragments of form is discharged upon the surfaces of larger-than-life canvases.

In this respect, Brixy's painting can be considered to be specific to the place. By providing exemplary representations of scenarios of the transgression of boundaries – of time and space, of nature and culture, of place and painting – it is an expression of a gesamtkunstwerk conception despite its mono-medial character. Brixy's concept of the penetration of life and painting is governed by an obsession with the realization of a painting of the whole, and a personal embodiment of the whole. The painter's life provides a model for holistic experience, characterized by a stimulating sensualism whose disquietude is transferred to the audience. The paintings, which were created in a controlled frenzy of action, aim to achieve an activation of all sensory capabilities to perceive aesthetic experiences, and define the aesthetic experience itself as a continuing performative act brought about by the indissoluble tension between the represented and the representation, between the viewer and the work of art.

Brixy works in the tradition of artist-entrepreneurs, who always also understood themselves as creators of worlds in keeping with a metaphorical analogy to the God of Creation, which has existed since the Renaissance: the mover and definer of the self. As a painter, Brixy is the lord of the aesthetic manor. He has mastered the apparatuses and the historical codes of the medium. This makes it possible for him to live the bearable lightness of being as an artist. His paintings prove to be windows not on the world, but on other paintings and the paintings of others. They develop meta-orders of the observation of painting and of the history of painting. Like microscopes, they show selected details up close or at a distance; they

Erfahrung selbst als andauernden performativen Akt, hervorgerufen von den unauflösbaren Spannungen zwischen Dargestelltem und Darstellung, Betrachter und Werk.

Brixy agiert in der Tradition des Künstler-Unternehmers seit der Renaissance, der sich in metaphorischer Analogie zum Schöpfergott immer auch als Weltschöpfer verstand: Selbstbeweger und Selbstdefinierer. Als Maler ist Brixy Herr im ästhetischen Haus. Er beherrscht das Apparateprogramm und die historischen Codes des Mediums. Dies ermöglicht ihm die erträgliche Leichtigkeit des Seins als Künstler. Seine Bilder erweisen sich als Fenster nicht auf die Welt, sondern auf andere Bilder und die Bilder Anderer. Sie entwickeln Meta-Ordnungen der Beobachtung von Malerei und Malereigeschichte. Wie Mikroskope rücken sie ausgewählte Ausschnitte in die Nähe oder Ferne, kombinieren Bruchstücke, Malmethoden, Materialien, beobachten physikalische Gesetzmäßigkeiten und mechanische Wirkungen. Schicht um Schicht stapelt Brixy Farbmaterie übereinander, legt sie partiell wieder frei, wischt und kratzt, arbeitet mit Pinseln, Spachteln, Händen, presst Feigenblätter oder Palmwedel in die pastosen Massen, hinterlässt darin mit Kämmen, Rakeln, Fingern physische Spuren.

Diese Malerei setzt den mobilen Blick voraus, der fragmentiert und filtert, reproduziert und kondensiert, der seinen Fokus variiert, immer neue Perspektiven einnimmt und sich in „metastasierender Vervielfältigung" (Christian Janecke) multipliziert. So entstehen Bilder, die wie bewegliche Fenster sind, mit variablen Tiefenschärfen und vielfältigen Verweisen auf die Gleichzeitigkeit des Ungleichzeitigen wie auf die Parallelität von Handschriften und malerischen Konditionierungen. Dabei überwindet der Maler den Gegensatz von abstrakt und figurativ und erschließt sich ein neues Feld der nicht allegorischen, sondern formalen Narration. Brixy liefert seine Beispiele der Dissemination des Visuellen in der Gegenwart aus einem Atelierparadies, das direkt an die fünf aktiven Blöcke eines Energiegroßlieferanten auf Steinkohlebasis grenzt: ein zündendes Sinnbild dafür, dass er mit seiner Malerei der Beobachtung zweiter Ordnung ziemlich präzise im Energiefeld von Gesamtkunstwerk und kultureller Produktion der Gesellschaft operiert.

combine fragments, painting methods, and materials, and they observe physical principles and mechanical effects. Brixy piles layer after layer of paint matter one on top of the other, partially exposes them again, wipes and scratches, works with paintbrushes, scrapers and hands, presses fig leaves and palm fronds into the pastose masses, and leaves physical traces using combs, squeegees, and fingers.

This painting is premised upon the mobile gaze, which is fragmented and filtered, which reproduces and condenses, which varies its focus, occupies always-new perspectives, and multiplies itself in "metastasizing reproduction" (Christian Janecke). This results in paintings that are like movable windows with variable depths of field and a multiplicity of references to the simultaneity of that which is not simultaneous and to the parallel nature of handwritings and painterly conditionings. In this way, the painter surmounts the opposition of the abstract and the figurative, and enters a new field of narration that is not allegorical but formal. Brixy delivers his examples of the dissemination of the visual in the present from a studio-paradise that directly borders the five active blocks of a large-scale energy supplier that works on the basis of stone coal. This is a powerful symbol for the fact that, with his painting of observation of the second order, he operates at the very heart of the energy field of the gesamtkunstwerk and the cultural production of society.

Discover, 2014
je | each 160 × 50 cm

Ich möchte mich selbst
immer wieder **überraschen**
lassen, mich dem **Zauber
der Bildentstehung**
uneingeschränkt hingeben.

I want to allow myself to be
surprised again and again;
I want to abandon myself entirely
to the **magic of pictorial
creation**.

Discover, 2013
180 × 240 cm

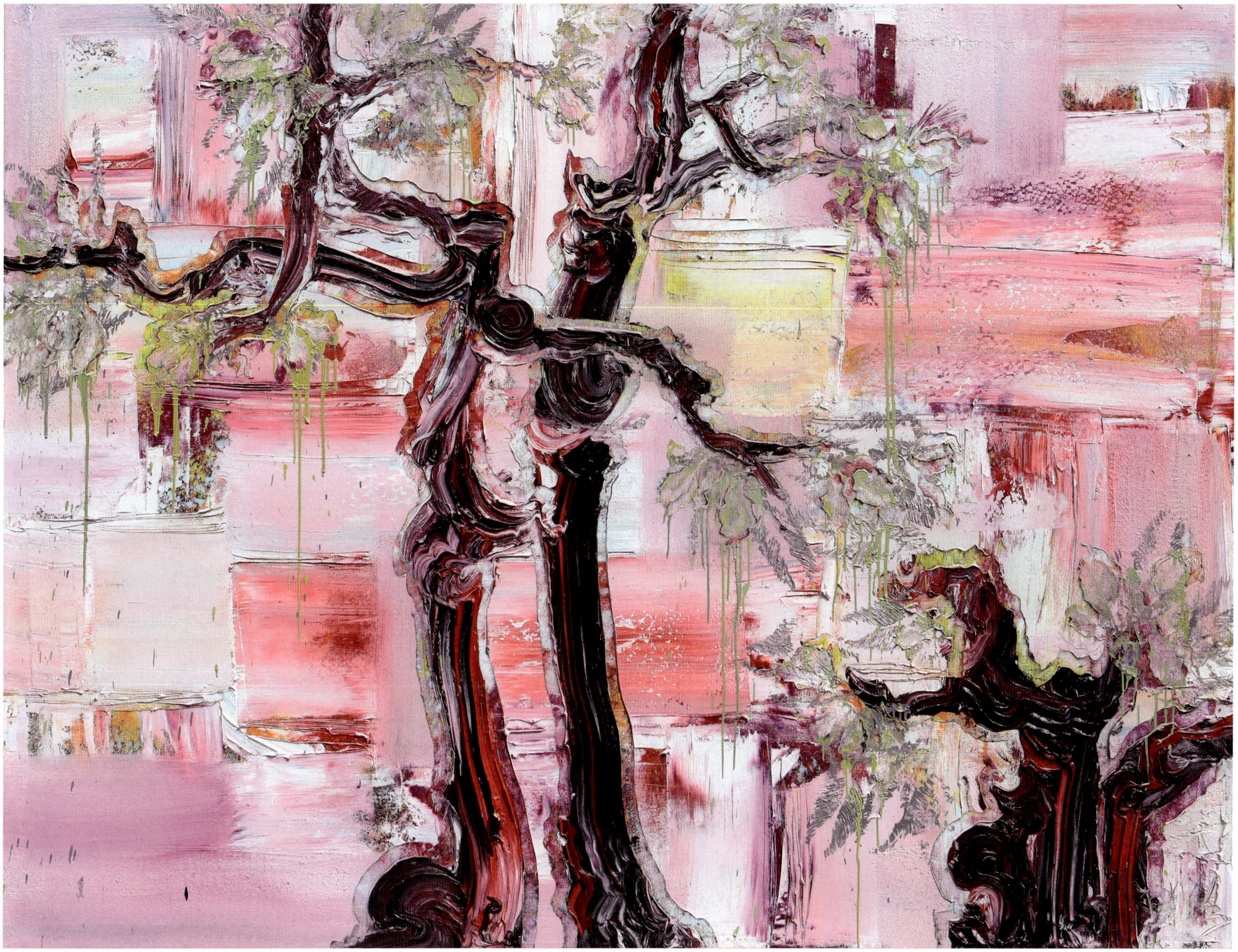

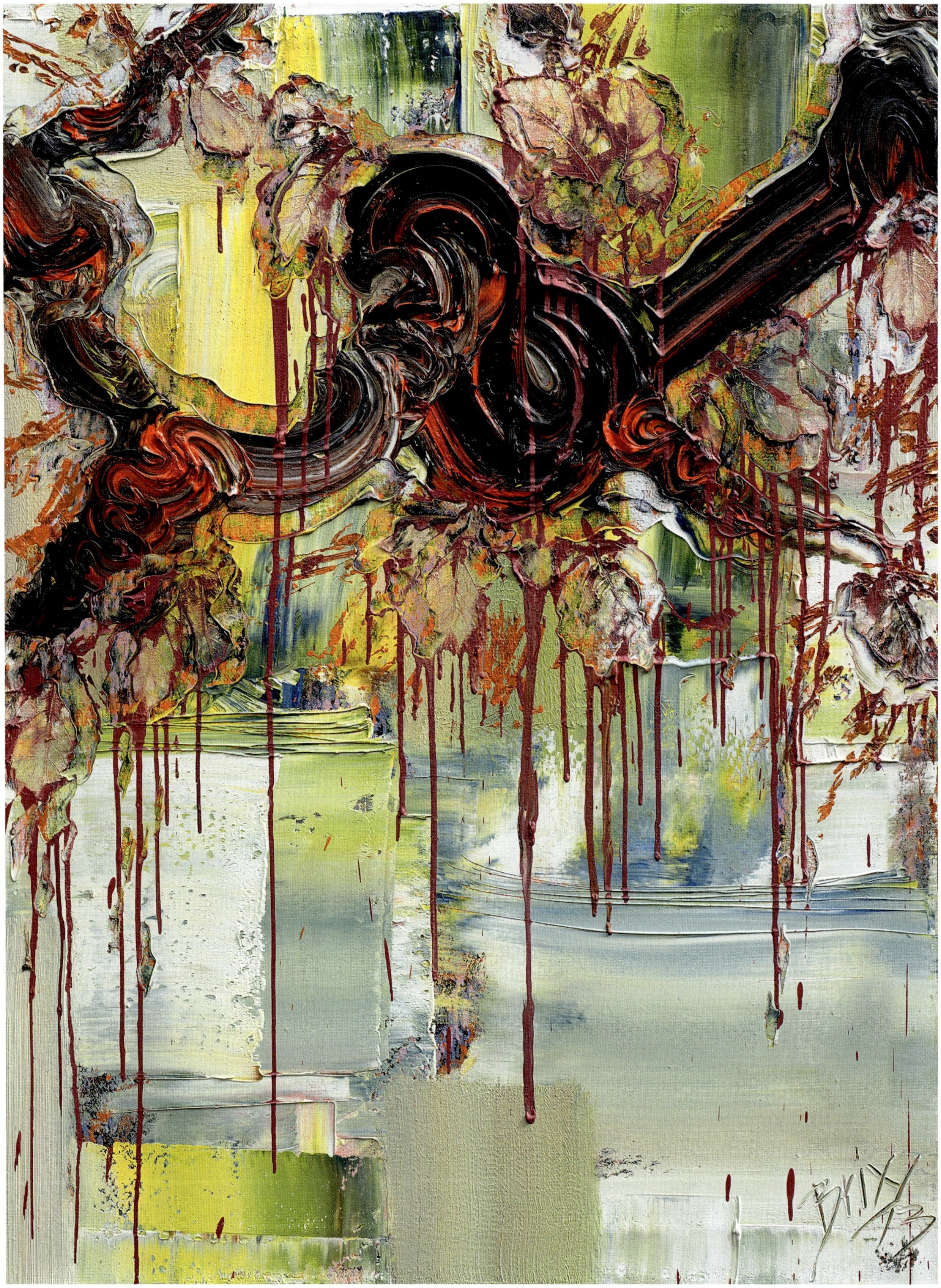
Brix
13

links | left
Discover, 2013
120 × 90 cm

rechts | right
Discover, 2012
120 × 90 cm

Discover, 2012
120 × 240 cm

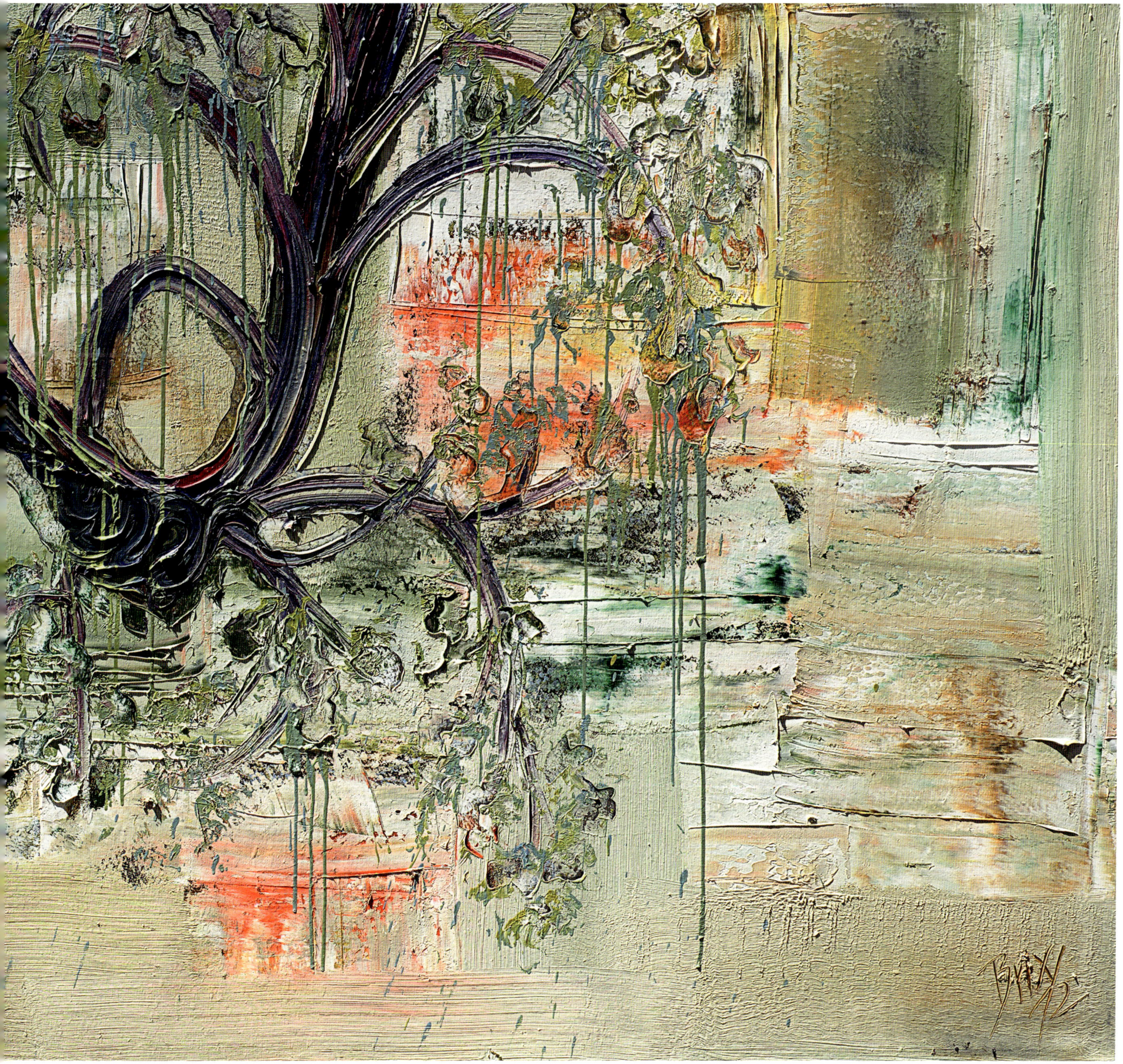

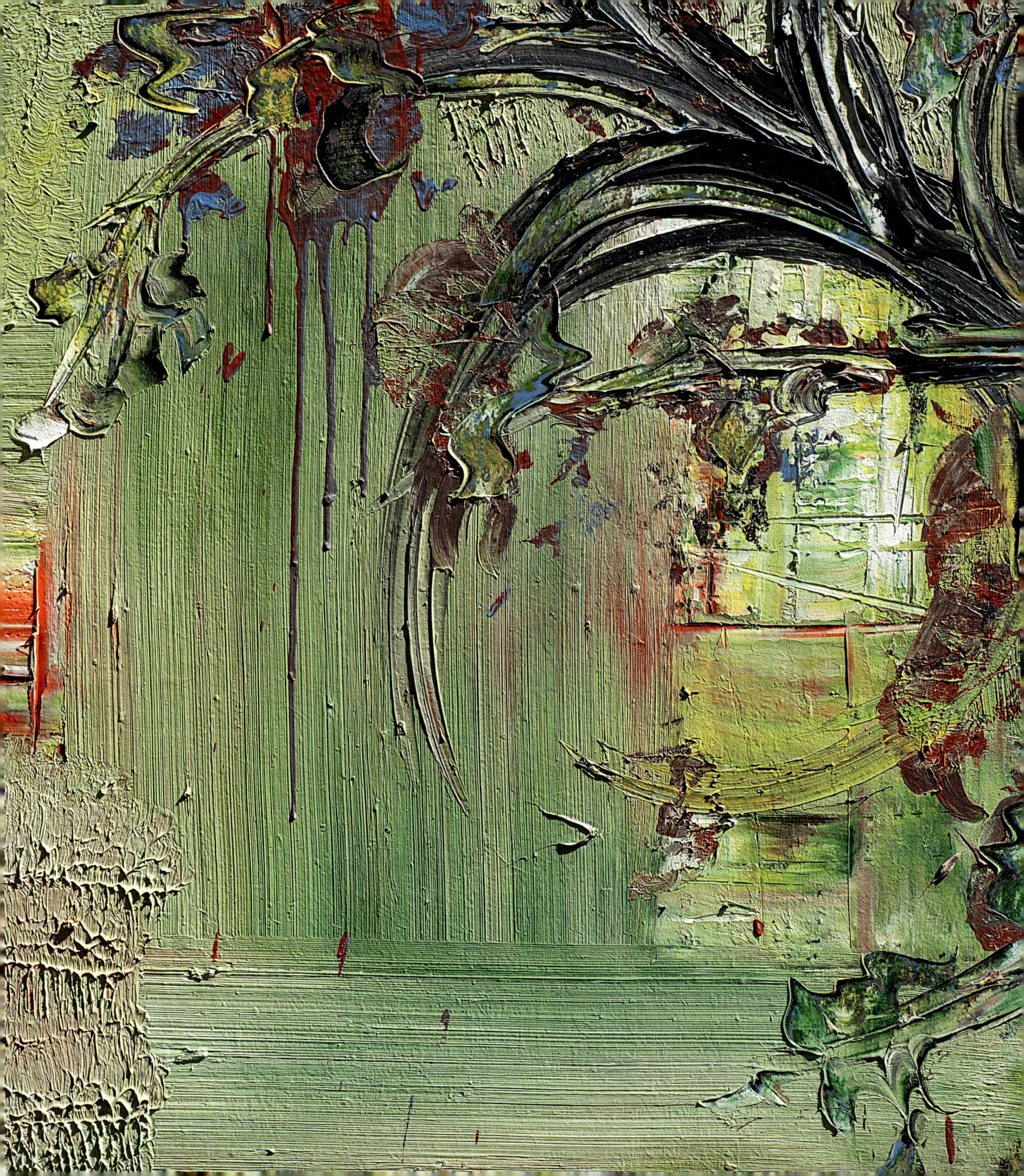

Discover, 2012
120 × 300 cm

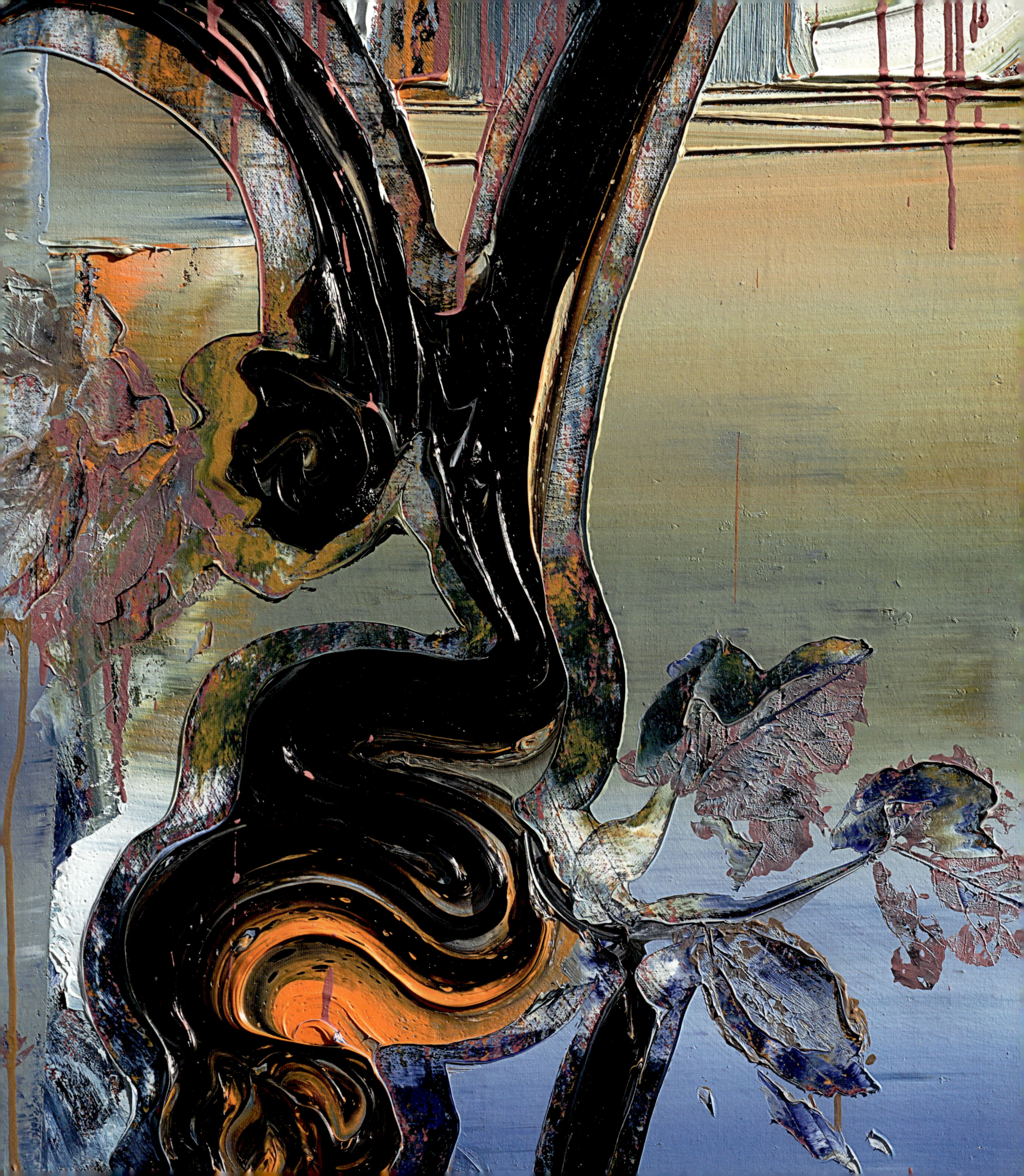

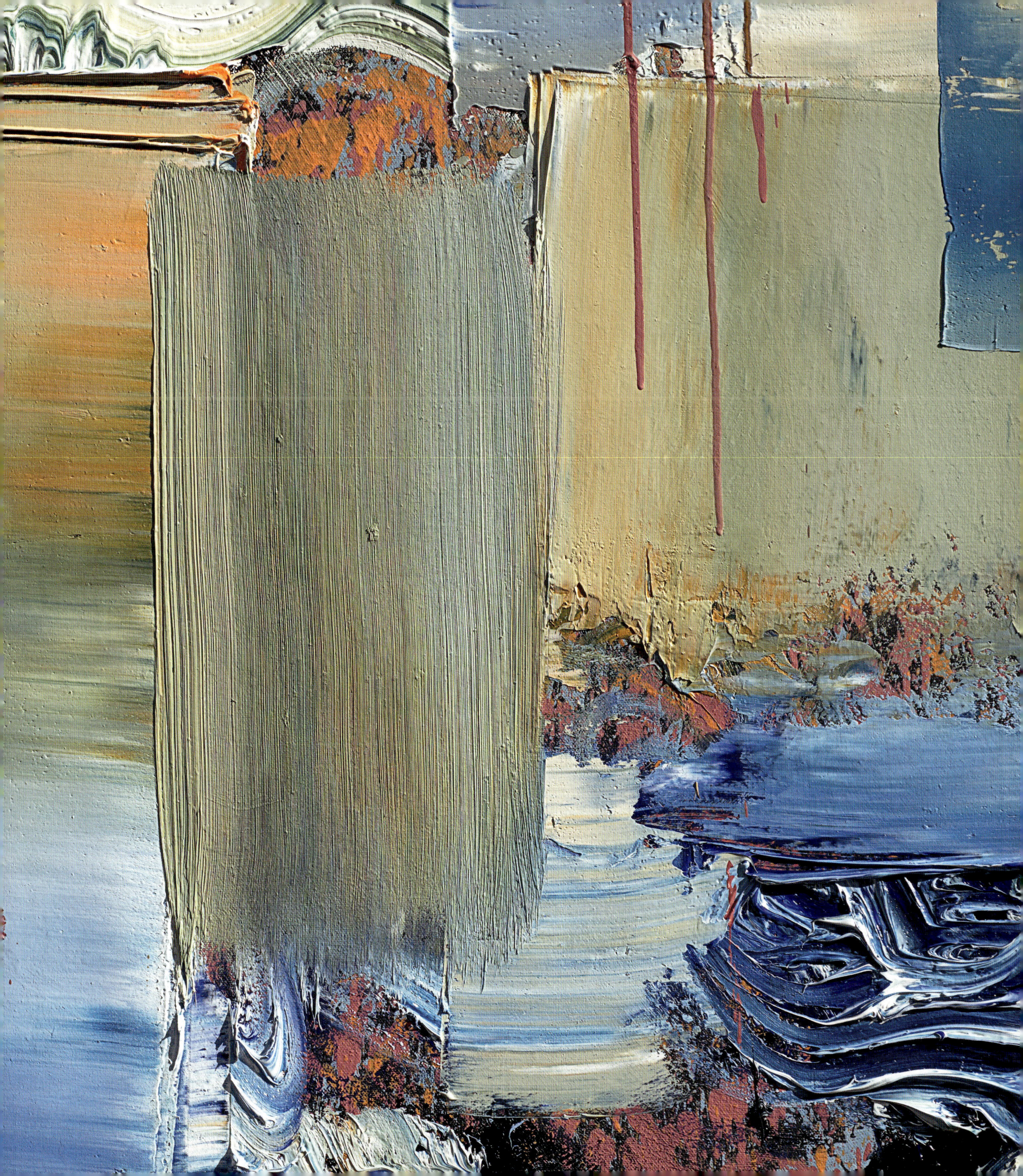

Discover, 2014
120 × 180 cm

vorhergehende Doppelseite |
previous double page
Detail

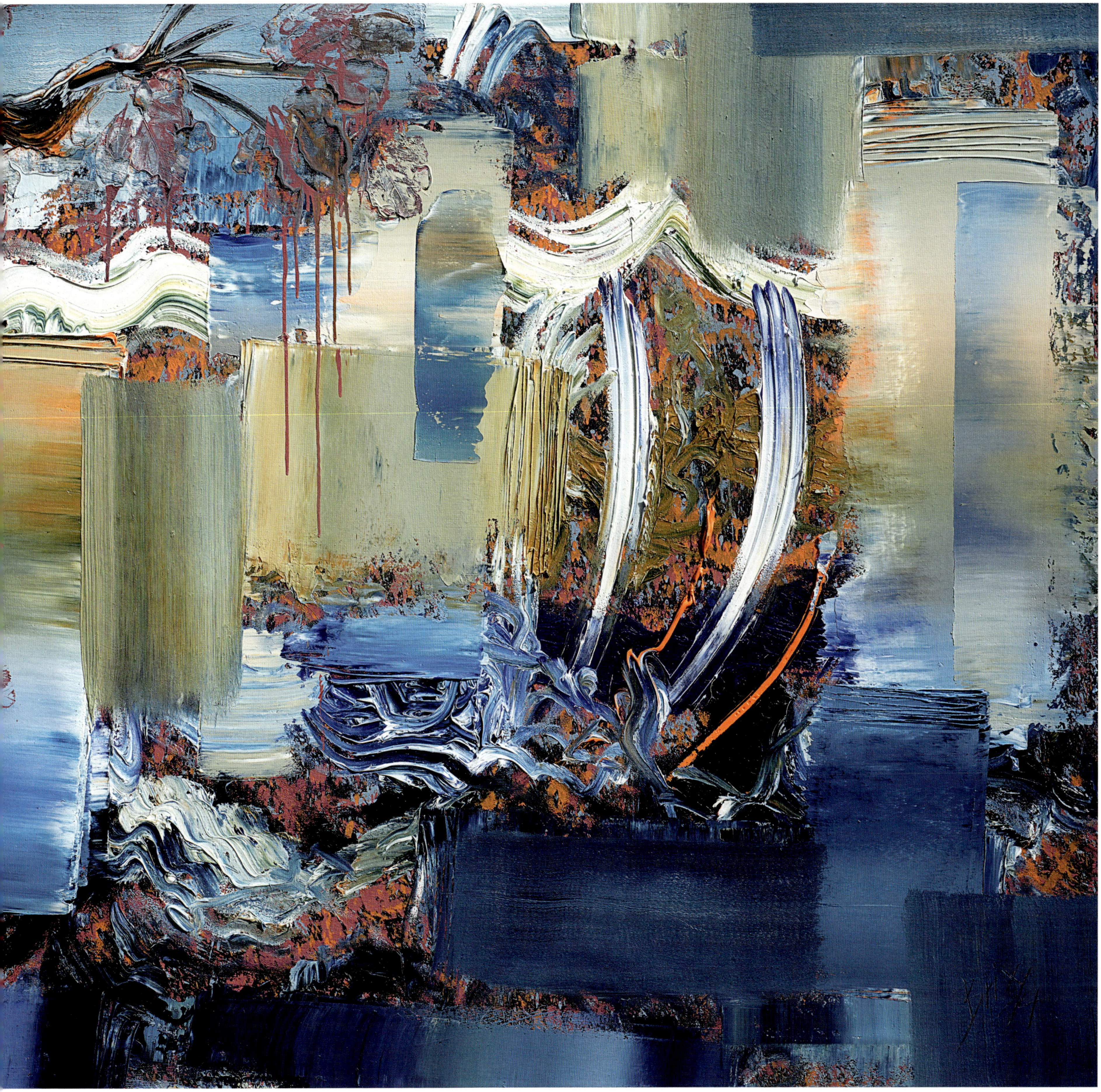

Discover, 2012
180 × 480 cm
(zweiteilig)

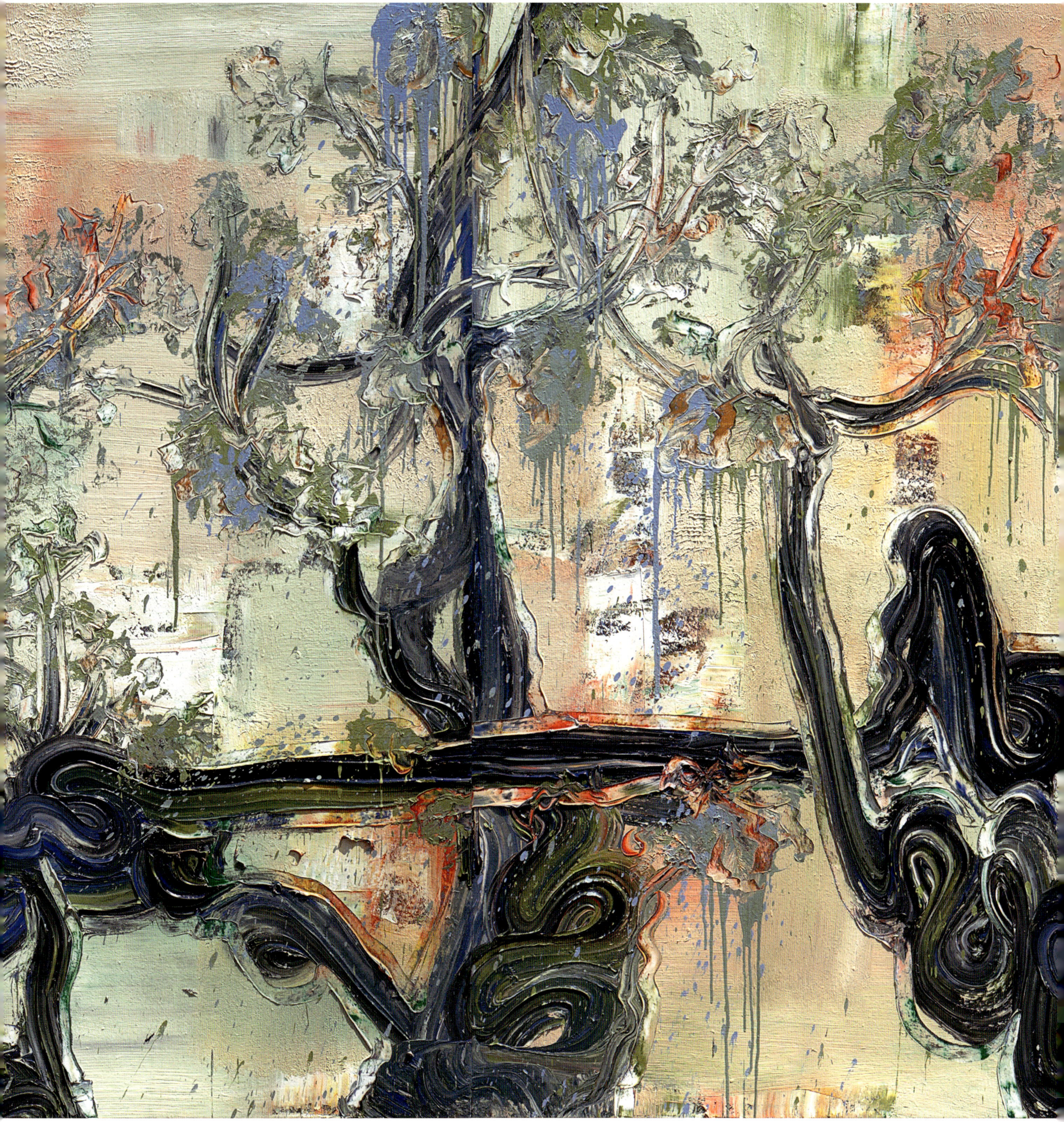

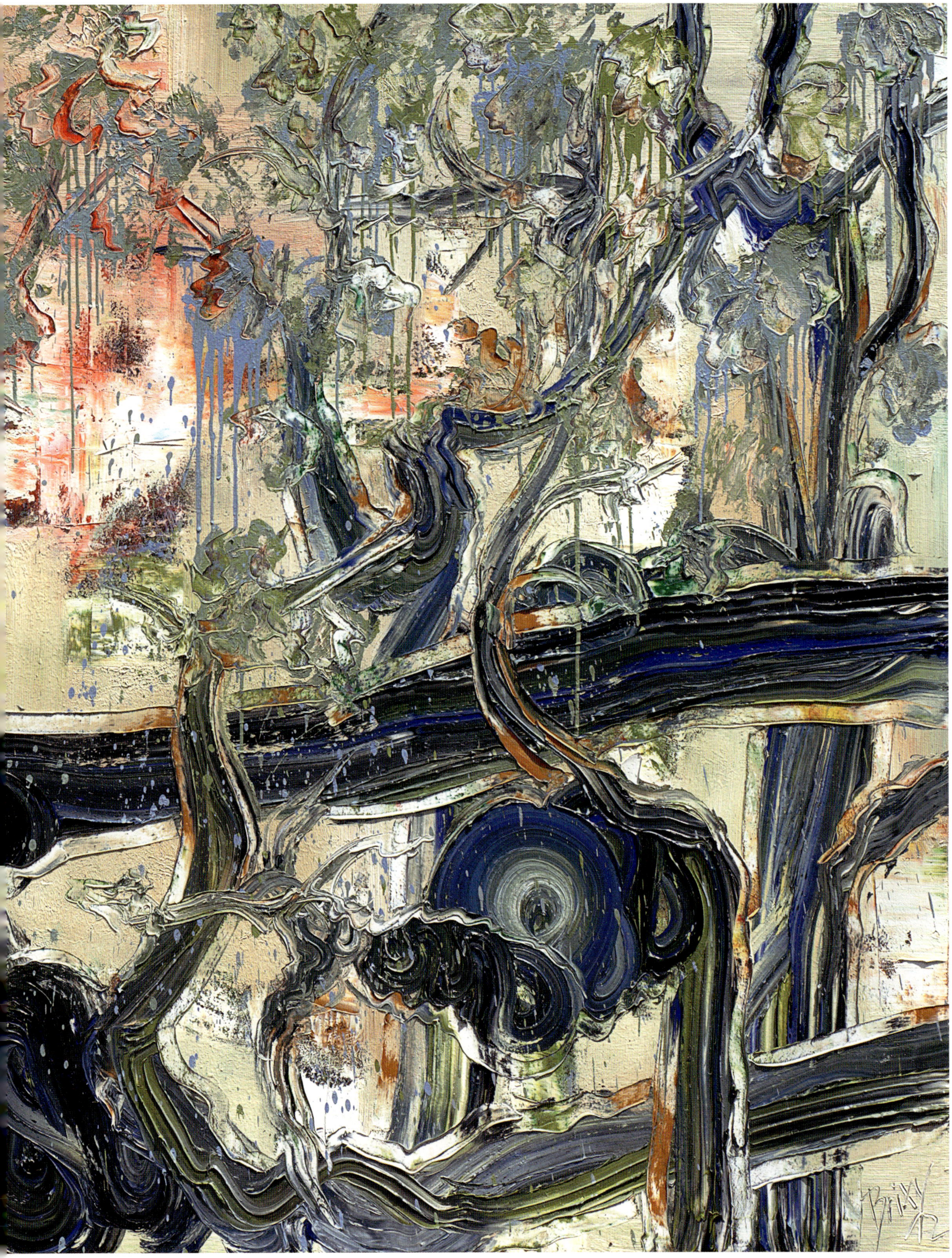

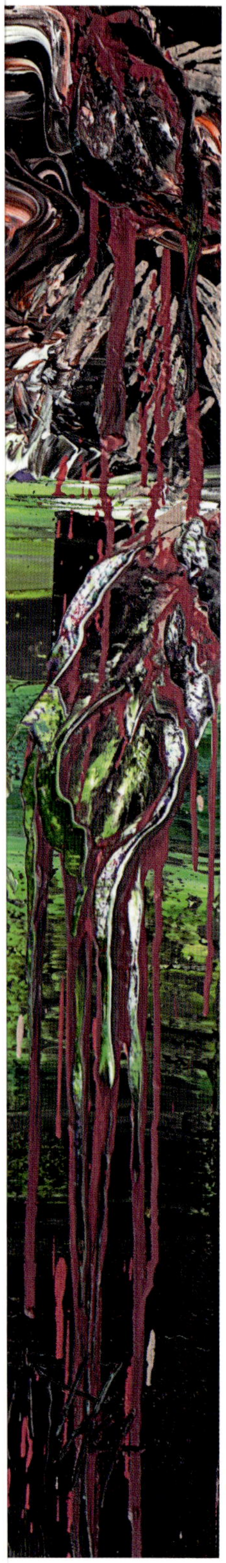

EIN KURZER GEDANKENAUSTAUSCH MIT DIETMAR BRIXY

Melanie Klier

Melanie Klier: „Discover Dich" – bedeutet für jedermann…

Dietmar Brixy: …Leidenschaften nachgehen, Träume verwirklichen. Wenn Du etwas willst, mach es! Beherzt. Mit Mut, Entschlossenheit und Freude.

Was ist an Ihrer Kunst „brixy-typisch"?

Ehrlich, authentisch, nahbar sein. Das will ich in und mit meiner Kunst. Ich folge keinen Trends oder Hyps – und das ist das, was der Kunstbetrachter vielleicht erspürt und nachspüren kann. Ich habe als Maler eine eigene Handschrift entwickelt. Eine expressive, sehr pastose Schichtenmalerei, die bei aller optischen Abstraktion immer der Natur auf der Spur ist. Das war immer so. Das wird bei allen Möglichkeiten meiner künstlerischen „Discovery" bestimmt so bleiben.

Was entdecken Sie persönlich?

Schon in meiner Vergangenheit war ich auf Wanderschaft. Das Leben als Reise, als Wegsuche – ich meine, ich war passionierter Pfadfinder und Gruppenleiter. Ich komme aus bescheidenen Verhältnissen, wir waren zu siebt, fünf Kinder, Mutter und Vater in einer kleinen Wohnung. Den Wunsch, draußen in der Natur zu sein, eins mit ihr zu werden, kennt sicher jeder Mensch. Für mich war es ein Fluidum: In einem Feld liegen, den Wald rauschen zu hören, in den Himmel zu schauen.

Dass ich Künstler werden wollte, wusste ich schon immer. Ich bin ins Unbekannte aufgebrochen. Bin getrampt. Habe das Unvermutete zugelassen. Später bin ich zu Studienreisen unter anderem auf die Seychellen und die Kanaren, nach Bali, Malaysia, Mexiko. War tauchen, auf Berg-

A BRIEF EXCHANGE OF IDEAS WITH DIETMAR BRIXY

Melanie Klier: "Discover yourself" – means to everybody…

Dietmar Brixy: … The pursuit of one's passions, the realization of one's dreams. If you want something, do it! With conviction. With courage, determination, and joy.

What is it about your art that is "typically Brixy"?

Being honest, authentic, approachable. That is what I want in and through my art. I do not follow trends or hypes – and that is perhaps what the viewer of my art can sense and detect. I have developed my own "signature" as a painter. An expressive, very pastose style of painting in layers that is always in pursuit of nature, despite its optical abstraction. That has always been the case. And it will definitely always stay that way, even in the face of all of the possibilities of my artistic "Discovery"!

What do you – personally – discover?

I have always been on a journey, even in my past. Life as a voyage, as a search for paths – I mean that I was an impassioned scout and group leader. I come from a humble background, and there were seven of us – five children, mother and father – in a small flat. The desire to be outside, surrounded by nature, to become one with it, must be familiar to everybody. For me it was an aura: lying in a field, listening to the rustling of the forest, looking up at the sky.

I have always known that I wanted to be an artist. I set out into the unknown. I hitchhiked. Allowed the unexpected to occur. Later, I went on study trips to places including the Seychelles and the Canary Islands, as well as Bali, Malaysia and Mexico.

I went diving, to the summits of mountains, to the jungle. That is the personal colorful world that has become part of me thanks to my voyages of discovery – in search of an artistic essence.

gipfeln, im Urwald. Das ist die persönliche bunte Welt, die ich durch meine Erkundungstouren in mir trage – auf der Suche nach einer künstlerischen Essenz.

Leben und Malerei – Was haben Sie dafür in die Wiege gelegt bekommen?

Zuerst die Liebe zur Natur, in all' ihren artenreichen Formen. Meine Mutter hatte einen grünen Daumen, mit meinem Vater bin ich gerne in den Wald zum Pilzesammeln, Brombeerenpflücken. Und dann habe ich von meinen Eltern bestimmt auch den Sinn fürs Handwerkliche. Meine Mutter war Korbflechterin, mein Vater Maurer.

In meinem Leben und in meiner Kunst geht es um alles, was man mit den Händen schafft. Ich bin kein Kopfmensch. Dinge bewahren, sichern, aufbauen. Pflanzen in die Erde setzen, Leben pflegen. Ein Zuhause schaffen, heimisch sein. Von meiner künstlerischen Herkunft betrachtet, komme ich ursprünglich von der Skulptur und Zeichnung. Nicht zuletzt daher hat meine Malerei enorm viele plastische Momente

Ihre Träume? Deren Verwirklichung?

Ich hatte einen Kindheitstraum: Eine große Flügeltüre, die ich öffnen kann, um in meinen eigenen Paradiesgarten zu gehen. Dieser Traum ist wahr geworden. Nicht zuletzt durch meiner, wenn ich so sagen darf, eigenen Hände Arbeit. Kraft meiner Malerei. Getragen von der Begeisterung der Menschen für meine Kunst und der Treue zu mir.

Ich kann jeden Tag die Pforten öffnen, meine eigene Naturlandschaft als Inspiration genießen, selbst hegen und pflegen. Dies erfüllt mich mit Zufriedenheit, Demut und tiefer Dankbarkeit. Es ist für mich absolut keine Selbstverständlichkeit und ich bin mir bewusst, dass dieses Geschenk, alles was ich hier habe, nur geliehen ist. Ich freue mich unbeschreiblich darüber, dass es geglückt ist. Jeden Tag.

„Discover" – eine malerische Entdeckungsreise?

Als Maler bin ich bemüht, mich weiterzuentwickeln und damit auf einer steten Suche nach immer wieder neuem Umgang mit Farbe, ihrer Materialität und Wirkungsästhetik. Ich begebe mich also tatsächlich auf eine formale und technische Forschungsreise. „Discover" hat sich als Thema und Serie aus einem dschungelartigen, dicht modulierten Bildganzen entwickelt. Spannend hier: Meine

Discover, 2013
21 × 54 cm

Living and painting – which are the relevant attributes that your parents gave to you?

First and foremost, a love of nature in all of its manifold forms. My mother had a green thumb, and I liked going into the forest to collect mushrooms and pick blackberries with my father. And I must have inherited my manual skills from my parents, too. My mother was a basket maker, and my father was a bricklayer.

In my life and in my art, it is all about that which one creates with one's hands. I am not a cerebral person. Keeping things, securing and constructing them. Placing plants into the soil, nurturing life. Creating a home, being homely. Viewed from the point of view of my artistic origins, I actually started with sculpture and drawing. This is a significant reason why my painting has a large number of sculptural elements.

Your dreams? Their realization?

I had a childhood dream: a large double door that I could open in order to step into my own Garden of Eden. This dream has come true. Not least as a result of the fruits of my manual labor, if I may use that expression. Thanks to my painting. It was made possible by people's enthusiasm for my art and their loyalty to me.

Every day I can open the gates and enjoy my own natural landscape as an inspiration; I can take care of it and look after it. This fills me with satisfaction, humility, and deep gratitude. It is by no means a given for me, and I am aware of the fact that this gift – everything that I have here – is merely on loan. I am indescribably happy that it has worked. Every day.

"Discover" – a painterly voyage of discovery?

As a painter, I aim to develop, and am therefore on a constant search for new approaches to paint, its materiality, and the aesthetics of its effects. So it is true to say that I set out on a formal and technical research trip. As a subject and as a series, "Discover" has developed from a jungle-like, densely modulated pictorial whole. What is exciting about it is that my pastose painting gestures, layered in a variety of colors set the stage for paint as an independent surface, which is awarded its own scope of action. Some of the zones of paint have a roughed-up, brushed appearance. Some rise in waves and others fall in creases. Some have rainbow-colored and feather-like structures. And others again are mysteriously diaphanous or thickly opaque, or disappear in the depths of the painting behind dripping areas.

Inside – outside. Opening windows, rooms, doors?
It is a luxury to look out of the studio through generous windows to see nature, or simply to walk out into the garden in order to return indoors filled with inspiration. This interplay of inside and outside animates me, supplies me with energy and strength, and is visibly present in my pictorial world: in the form of vistas, spatial zones, an in-front-of, and a behind. Come to think of it, there is also a relationship to my own art presentation here in the old pumping station of Neckerau. You see, since 2004 I have opened the gates to my artist's house to a broad public, specifically once a year, for a one-month-long exhibition. About 3,500 visitors come on those occasions. But basically the doors are open to art enthusiasts and collectors several times throughout the course of the year. Allowing people "outside" to take part in my art world "in here" also animates me – until I close the gates again for a period of purification and of focusing on that which is inside.

pastosen, mehrfarbig durchsetzten Farbgesten machen die Bühne frei für die Farbe als freie Fläche, der selbst Handlungsspielraum eingeräumt wird. Einige Farbzonen wirken aufgerauht und gebürstet. Manche schlagen Wellen oder werfen Falten. Andere wiederum haben regenbogenfarbene oder gefiederähnliche Strukturen. Wieder andere sind geheimnisvoll durchlässig oder dicht opak oder verschwinden in die Bildtiefe hinter Drippingstellen.

Drinnen – Draußen. Fenster, Räume, Türen öffnen?
Es ist ein Luxus im Atelier durch die großzügigen Fenster nach draußen in die Natur zu blicken oder gleich in den Garten zu gehen und wieder voller Inspiration ins Innere zurückzukehren. Dieses Wechselspiel von Drinnen und Draußen beflügelt mich, lässt mich Energie und Kraft tanken und schlägt sich sichtbar in meiner Bildwelt nieder: In Form von Durchblicken, Raumzonen, einem Davor und Dahinter. Und wenn ich so darüber nachdenke, gibt es auch einen Bezug zu meiner eigenen Kunstpräsentation, hier im Alten Pumpwerk Neckarau. Seit 2004 öffne ich nämlich konkret ein Mal im Jahr für eine einmonatige Ausstellung die Pforten meines Künstlerhauses für ein breites Publikum. Wir zählen dann gut 3.500 Besucher. Im Grunde stehen aber immer wieder übers Jahr die Türen hier für Kunstbegeisterte und Sammler offen. Auch dieses Teilhabenlassen der Menschen draußen an meiner Kunstwelt hier drinnen beflügelt mich – bis ich wieder die Tore schließe für eine Zeit der Reinigung, des Inwendigwerdens.

„Discover" – eine rezeptionsästhetische Expedition?
Man kann in den „Discover"-Werken als Betrachter spannende Effekte entdecken und einiges hineindeuten. Eine Urwaldwildnis, Knorzen-ähnliche Gewächse, Rinden- oder Schlangenhaftes. Durchblicke auf weite, regennasse Horizonte. Auf das stille Dahinfließen von Gewässern. Man fühlt möglicherweise die Frische von Morgenstimmungen oder eine schwüle, tropische Mittagshitze. Das alles sind individuell gesehene Möglichkeiten. Dabei habe ich immer im Focus: Meine Bildwelt soll in ihrer Lesbarkeit für den Betrachter offen bleiben.

Auftragen, Abtragen – Geben, Nehmen. Ein Motto für Malerei… und Leben?
…Sicherlich. Mit den „Discover"-Arbeiten experimentiere ich mit dem Duktus, um die Farbflächen

"Discover" – an expedition into the aesthetics of reception?
As a viewer, one can uncover exciting effects and a wide variety of interpretations in the "Discover" works. A jungle-like wilderness, tree-stump-like growths, elements reminiscent of bark and snakes. There are vistas of wide, rain-wet horizons and of the silent flow of watercourses. One might sense the freshness of an early-morning atmosphere or humid, tropical midday heat. These are all individually viewed possibilities. I always focus on this: my pictorial world should remain open to the viewer in its readability.

Apply, remove – give, take. A motto for painting … and for life?
… Certainly. In the "Discover" works, I experiment with the flow in order to create the areas of paint. It is all about the method of the exposure of paint, about going over it again, peeling it, leaving it where it is, adding to it. A "give and take" with the artistic means that are available to me: fingers, hands, paintbrushes, palette knives, squeegees, and combs. "Give and take" plays a significant role in my everyday life. I attend to a social commitment. For me, it is almost an obligation that one should give back something of what one receives. I remember that well from my childhood. Being given a piece of cake from elsewhere. I have not forgotten that, and have nurtured it.

Drips drop from branches. Streams meander through a pictorial world that whooshes with a powerful force. Everything flows, everything is in flux…
I can allow processes to occur, developments. My artistic requirements of myself are not fixed, not limited by the compulsion to use particular forms, colors or subjects. This nurtures the love of experimentation. I want to allow myself to be surprised again and again; I want to abandon myself entirely to the magic of pictorial creation.

And now things get signed?
The journey there is a time to let things sink in, to observe, and to lean back. But sometimes parallel works can also be created.

zu gestalten. Es dreht sich alles um die Art des Freilegens von Farbe, Darübergehens, Herausschälens, Stehenlassens, Hinzufügens. Ein „Geben und Nehmen" mit den mir zur Verfügung stehenden künstlerischen Mitteln: Fingern, Händen, Pinseln, Malmessern, Spachteln, Kämmen.

In meinem Alltag spielt „Geben und Nehmen" eine gewichtige Rolle. Ich pflege ein soziales Engagement. Für mich ist es fast schon eine Verpflichtung von dem, was man bekommt, etwas zurückzugeben. Ich habe das selbst aus meiner Kindheit in guter Erinnerung. Mal von außerhalb ein Stück Kuchen zu bekommen. Das habe ich nicht vergessen und mir bewahrt.

Es tropft von Ästen. Bäche mäandern durch eine kraftrauschende Bildwelt. Alles fließt, ist im Fluss…

Ich kann Prozesse zulassen, Entwicklungen. Meine künstlerischen Anforderungen an mich sind nicht festgesetzt, nicht begrenzt durch bestimmte Form-, Farb- oder Themenzwänge. Sie pflegt die Experimentierfreude. Ich möchte mich selbst immer wieder überraschen lassen, mich dem Zauber der Bildentstehung uneingeschränkt hingeben.

Jetzt wird signiert?

Der Weg dahin ist eine Zeit des Wirkenlassens, Betrachtens, Zurücklehnens. Manchmal können aber auch parallele Werke entstehen.

Die Weiterentwicklung der Serie „Discover" – die neue, dunkle Bildwelt?

Es gibt ein für mich wegweisendes Gemälde, mein erstes schwarzes „Disvover"-Bild (Abb. S. 133). Es macht den Vorhang auf zu einer Veränderung. Und es ist nicht abzusehen, wo es hingehen wird. Es entstand in einer Zeit des sich anbahnenden Abschiednehmens. Von meiner Mutter.

Die neuen Discover-Werke reflektieren den Tod. Hier werden Bildmuster aufgebrochen, Muster gelöst. Durchsetzt von Hoffnungsschimmern und differenzierten Lichtmomenten. Es ist der malerische Versuch und menschliche Wunsch, das Verkrustete, Ängste, Eingrenzungen ins Diffuse entschwinden zu lassen. Sich in Weites, Freies und Offenes, in Luft zum Atmen wandeln zu lassen. Die Schwere des Lebens zu transformieren in Grenzenloses, Leichtes.

The further development of the "Discover" series – a new, dark pictorial world?

There is a painting that is groundbreaking for me: my first black "Discover" painting (page 133). It pulls back the curtain on change. It is impossible to know where it will lead. It was created during a time of imminent departure. That of my mother.

The new "Discover" paintings reflect death. Pictorial patterns are broken up here, patterns are dismantled. They are interspersed with glimmers of hope and subtle elements of light. It is the painterly attempt and the human desire to let that which has become rigid, fears, and limitations escape into the diffuse. To let oneself turn into the wide open, the free, and the open, into the air that we breathe. To transform the heaviness of life into the boundless, into the light.

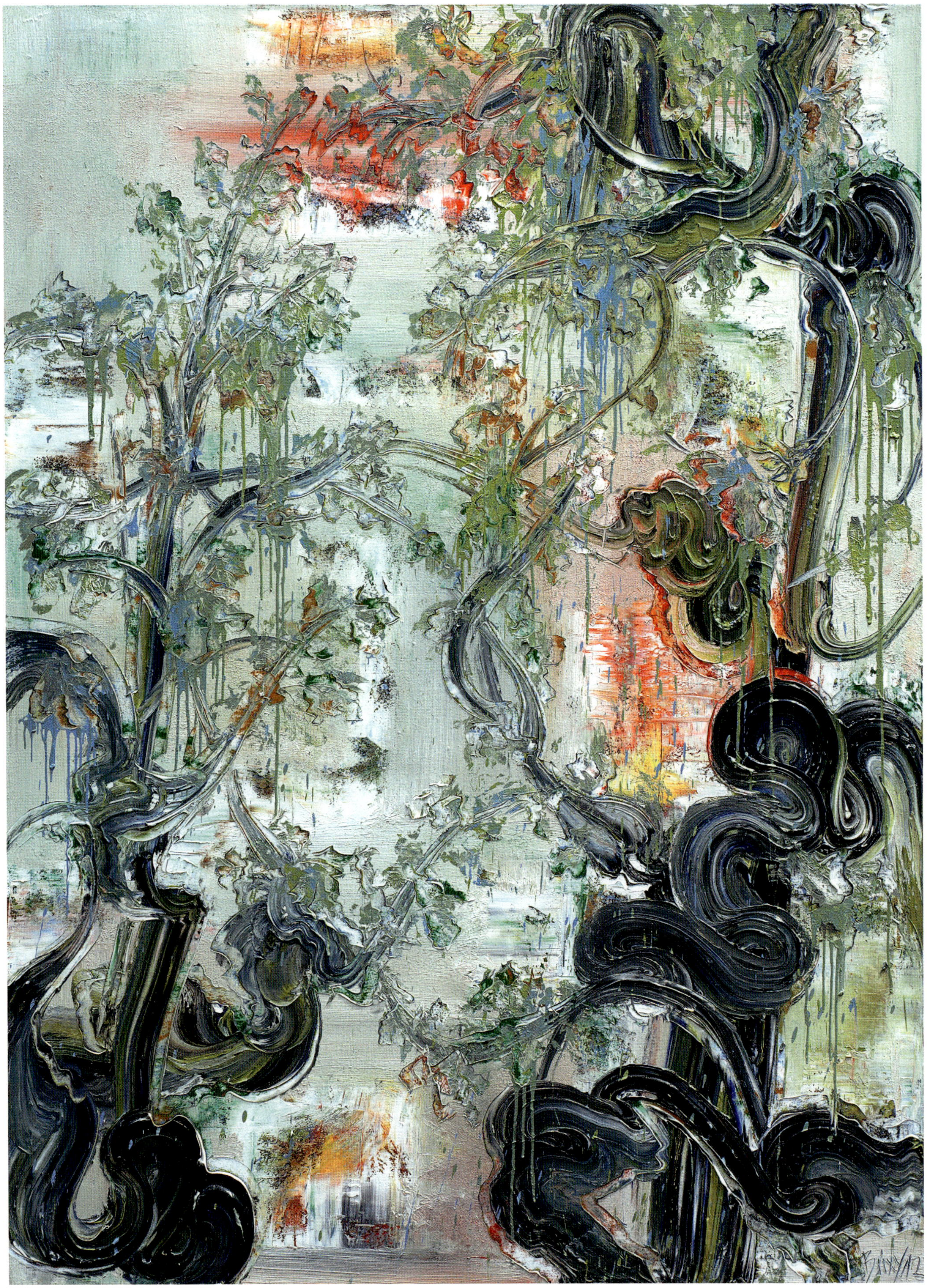

Discover, 2012
240 × 180 cm

Discover, 2012
160 × 210 cm

Discover, 2012
180 × 240 cm

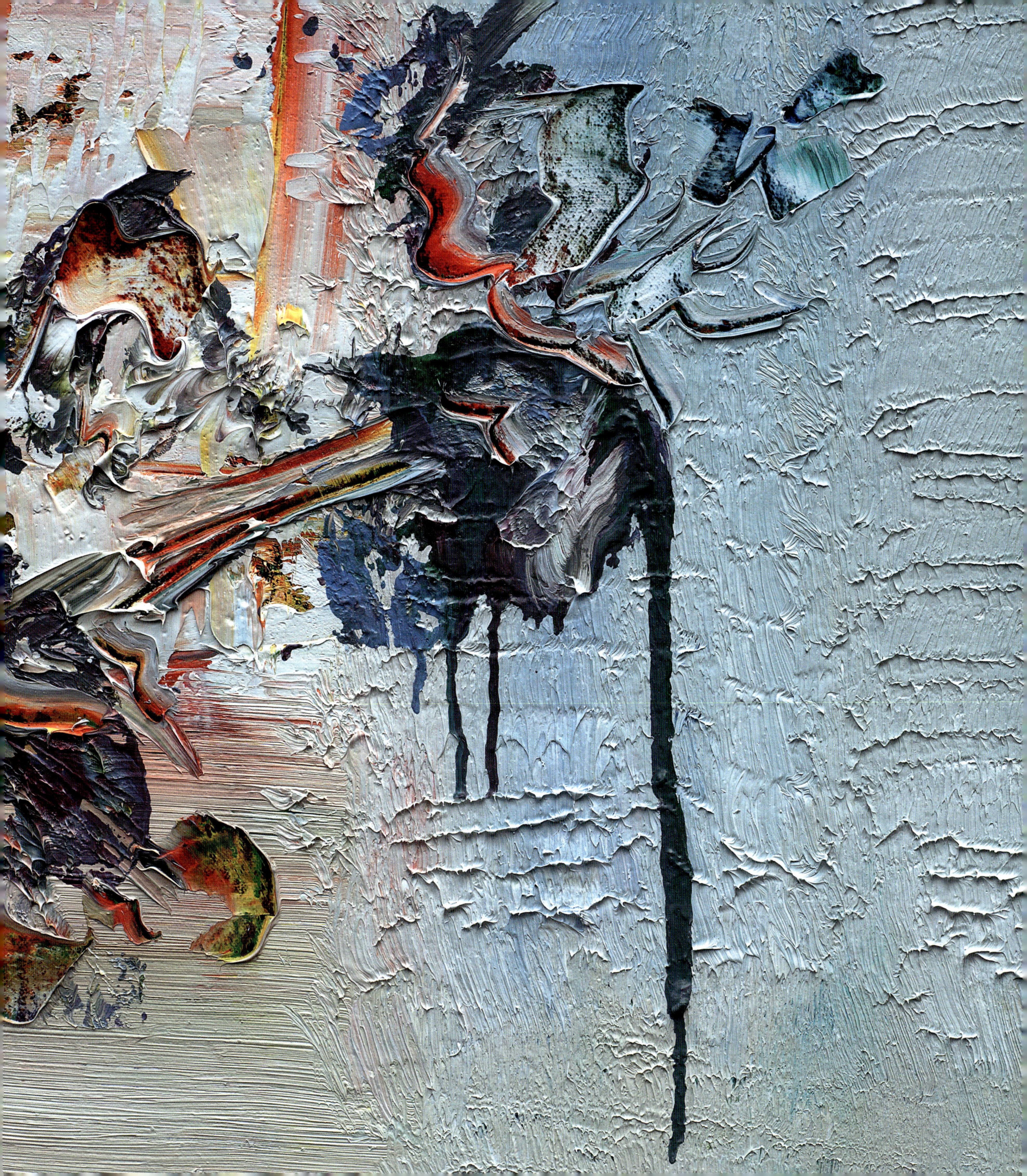

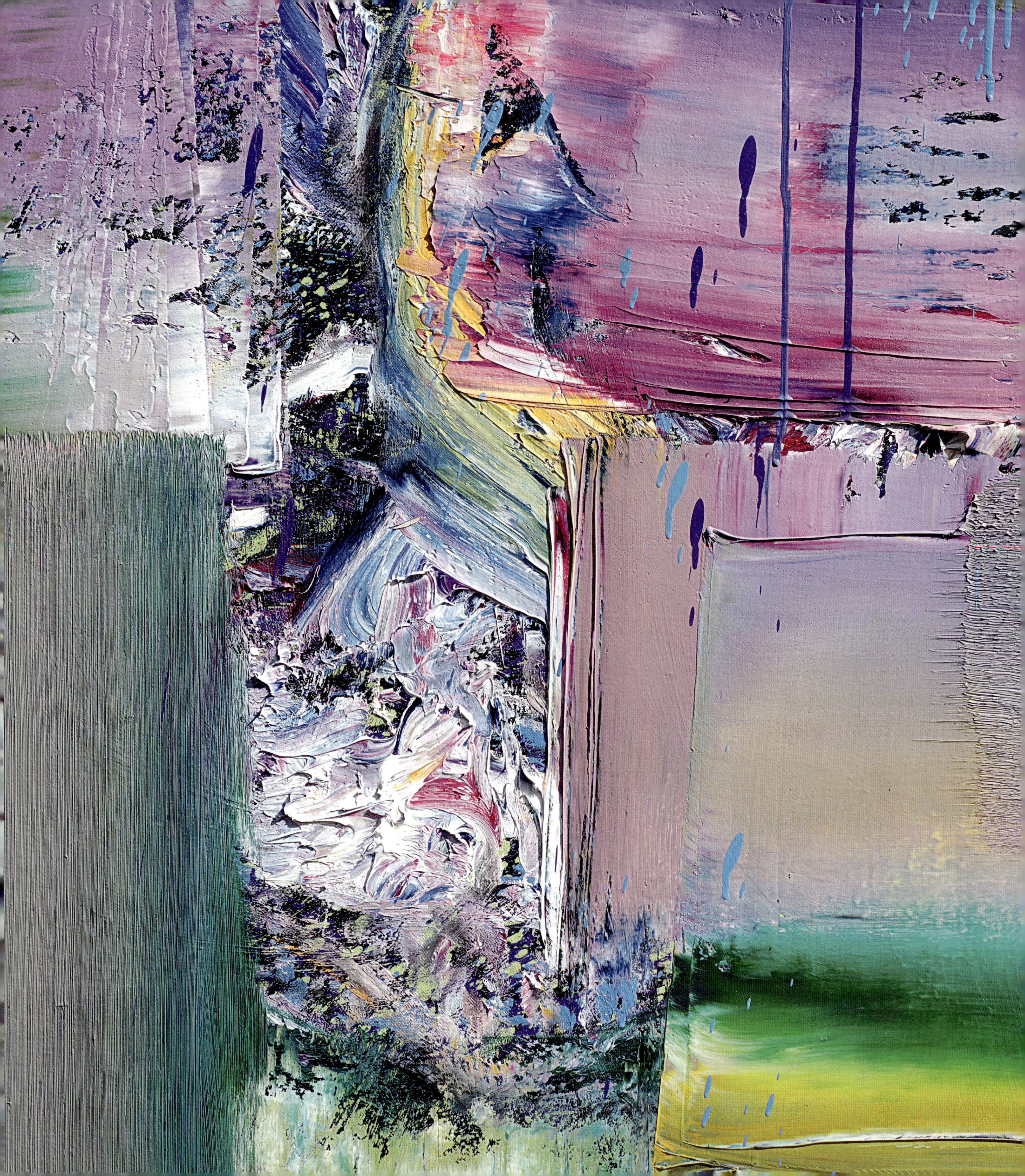

Discover, 2014
180 × 140 cm

Discover, 2012
120 × 300 cm

Meine Bildwelt soll in ihrer Lesbarkeit für den Betrachter offen bleiben.

My pictorial world should remain open to the viewer in its readability.

Discover, 2014
120 × 180 cm

Discover, 2013
60 × 80 cm

Discover, 2012
90 × 120 cm

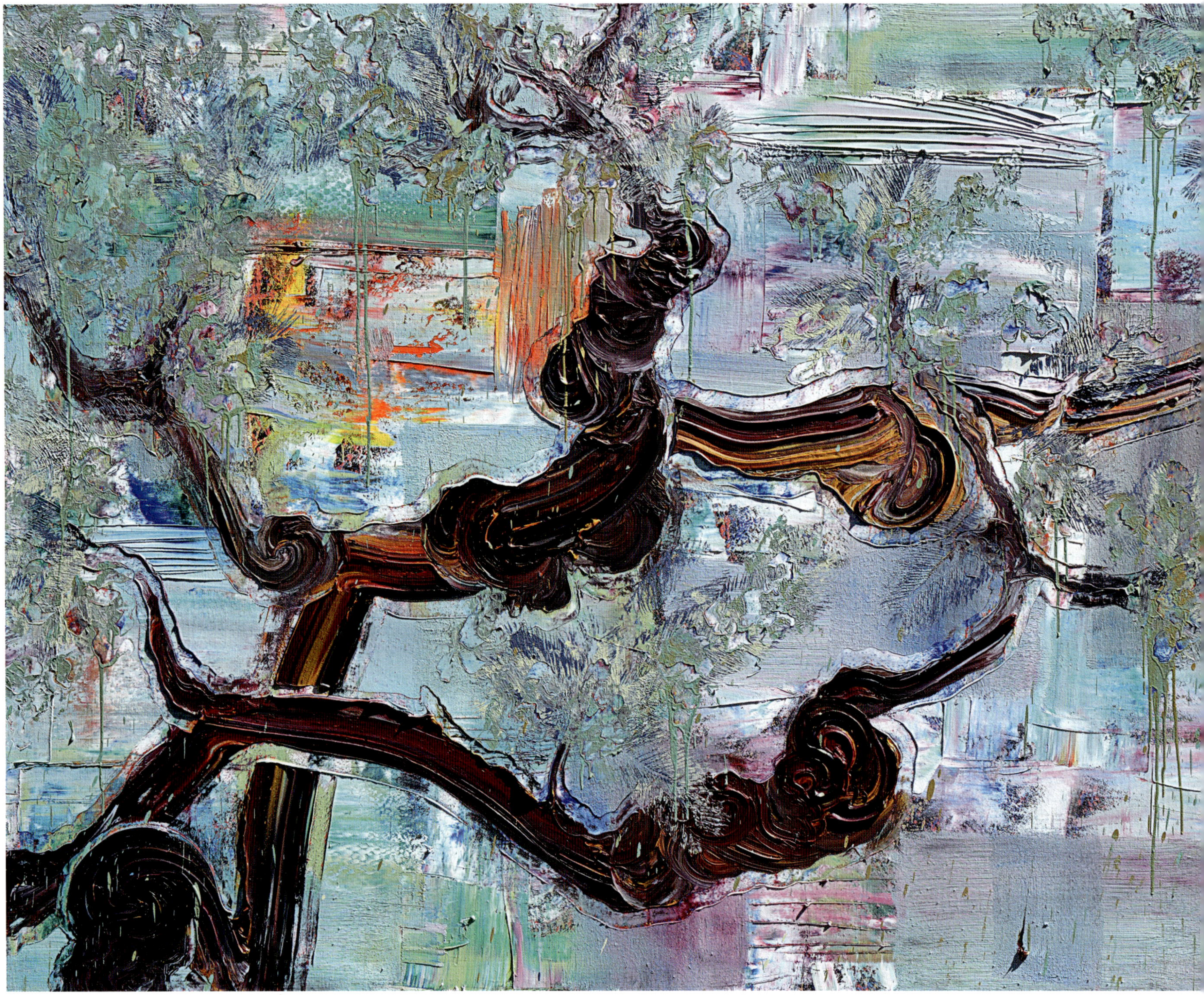

Discover, 2013
160 × 420 cm (zweiteilig)

Discover, 2013
je | each 21 × 54 cm

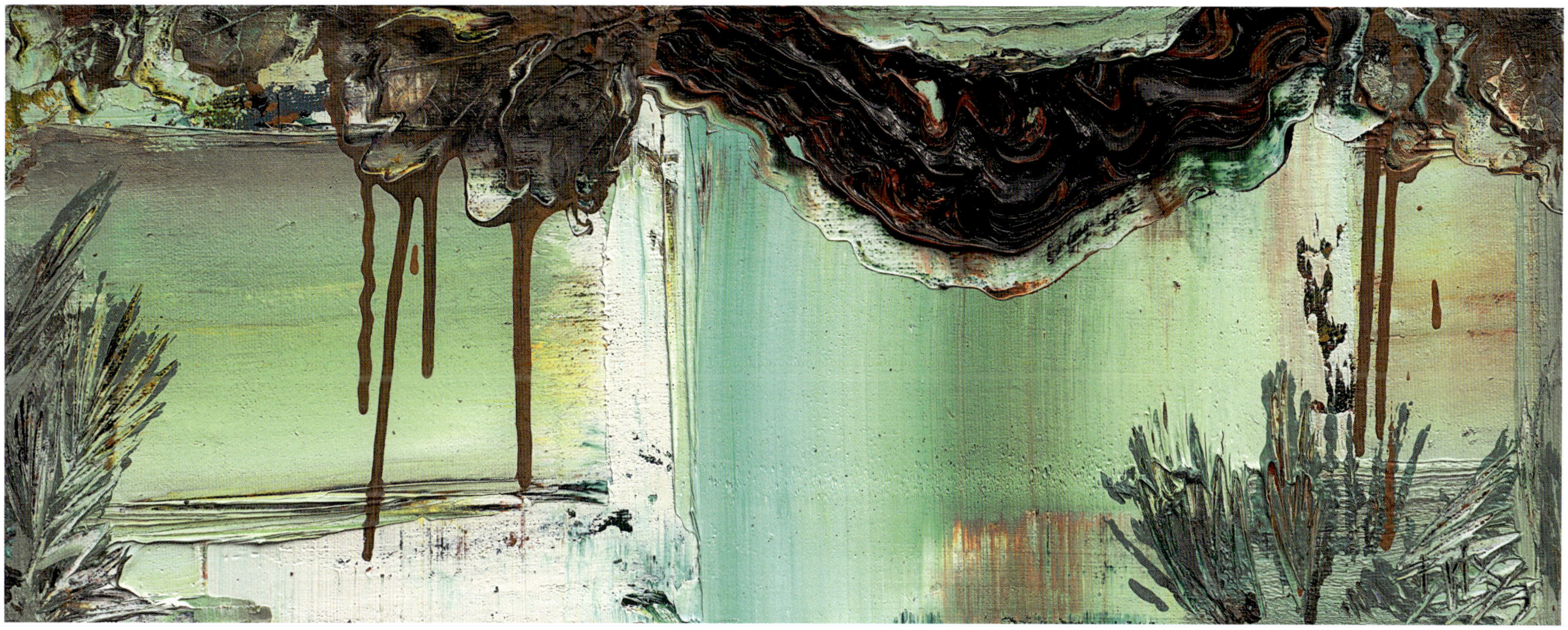

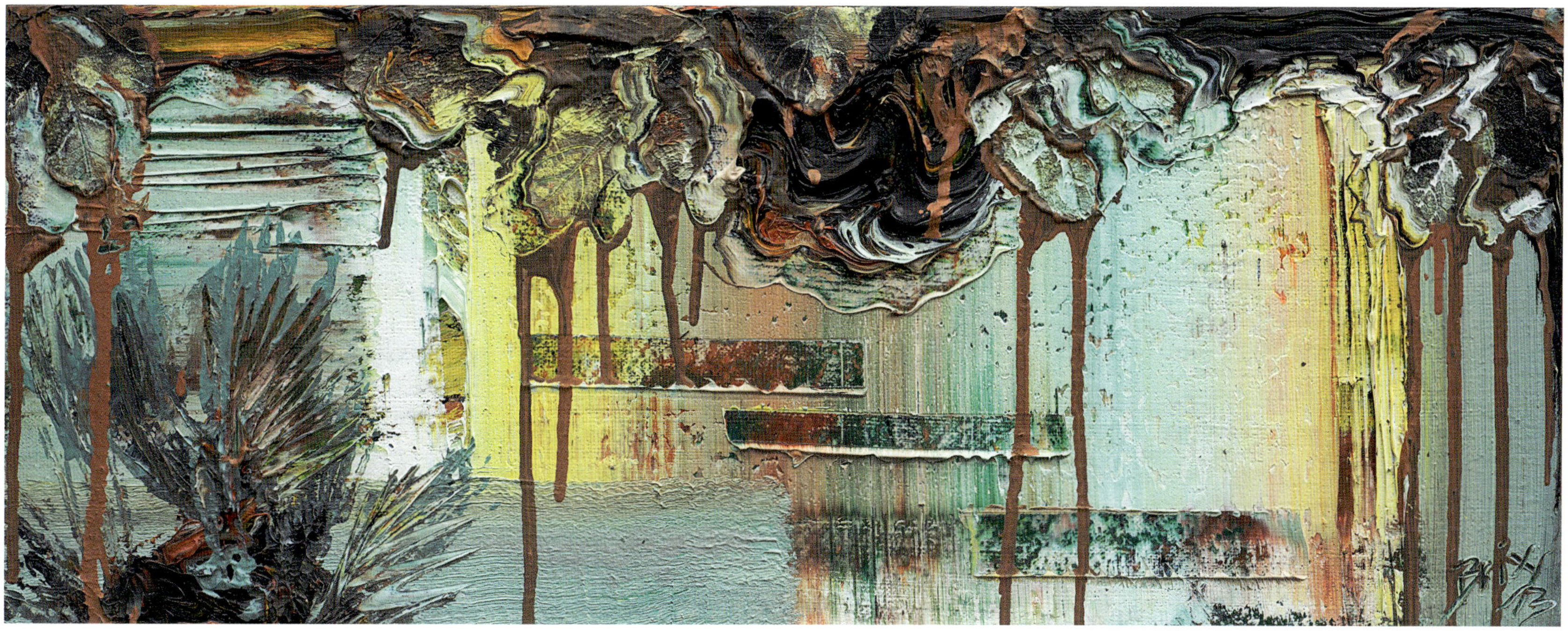

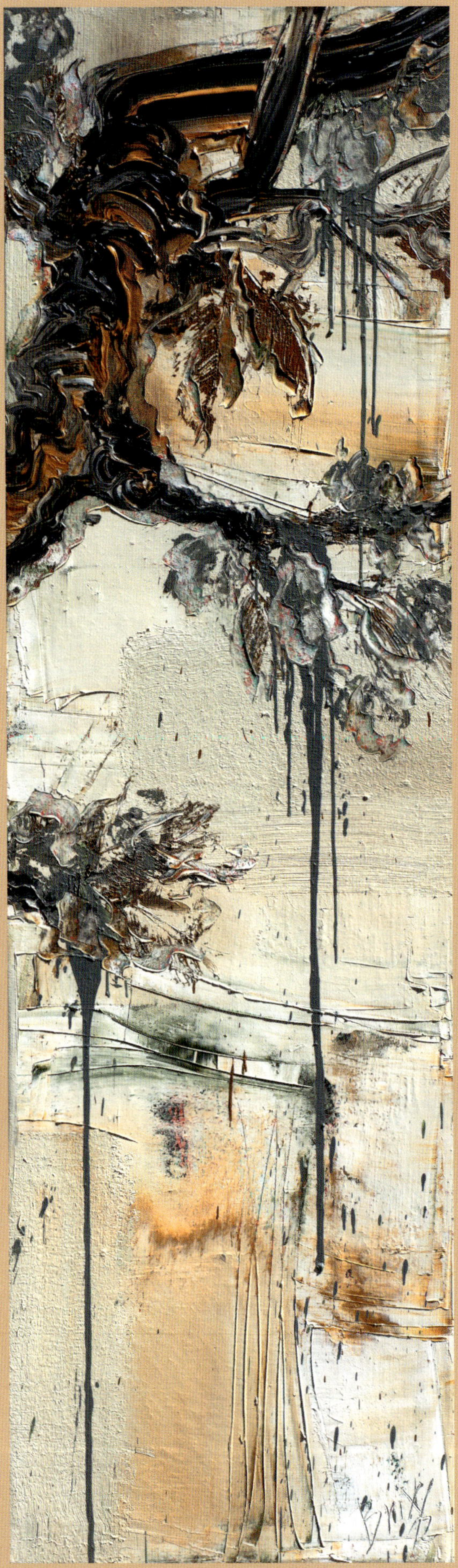

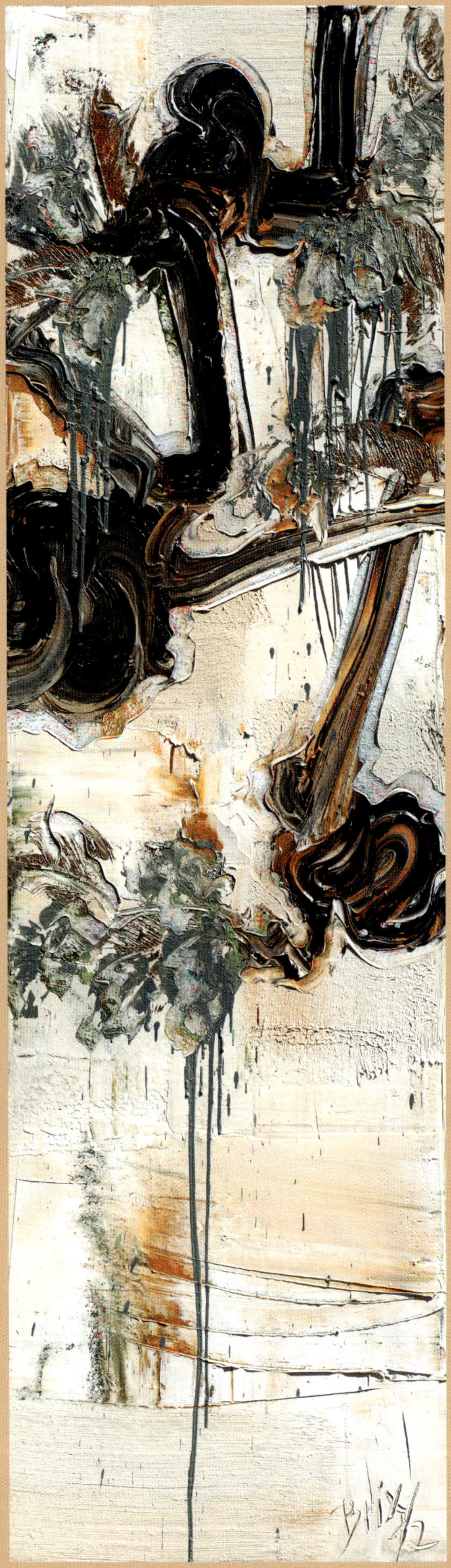

Discover, 2012
je | each 200 × 60 cm

Discover, 2013
160 × 210 cm

oben rechts | above right
Discover, 2012
160 × 210 cm

Mitte | middle
Discover, 2012
120 × 180 cm

unten rechts | below right
Discover, 2012
90 × 120 cm

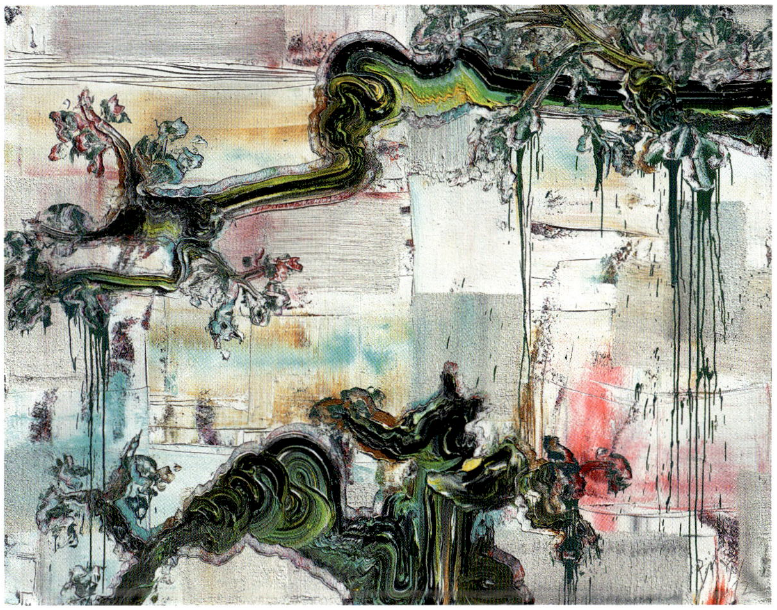

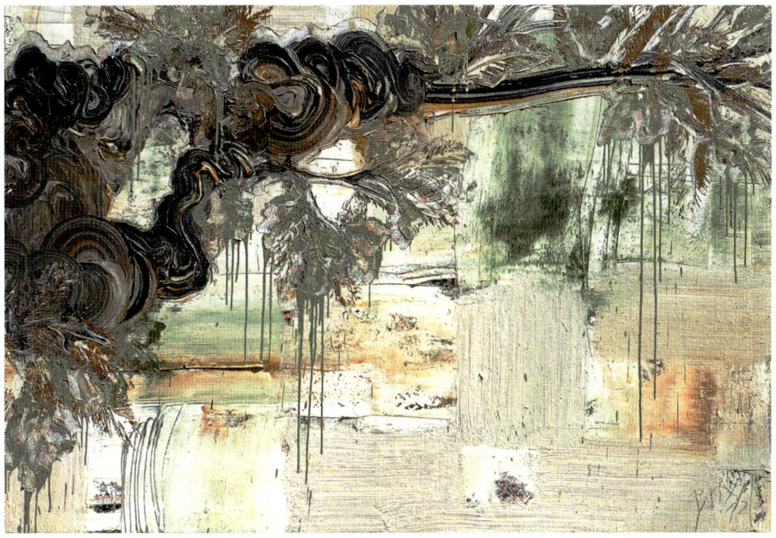

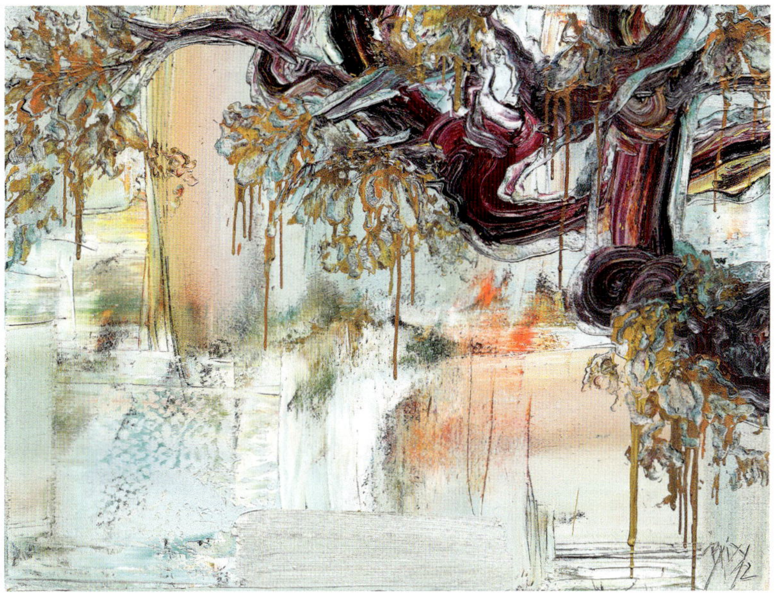

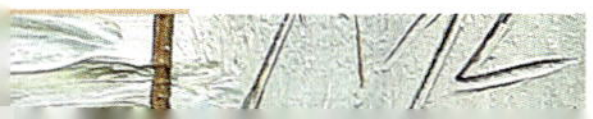

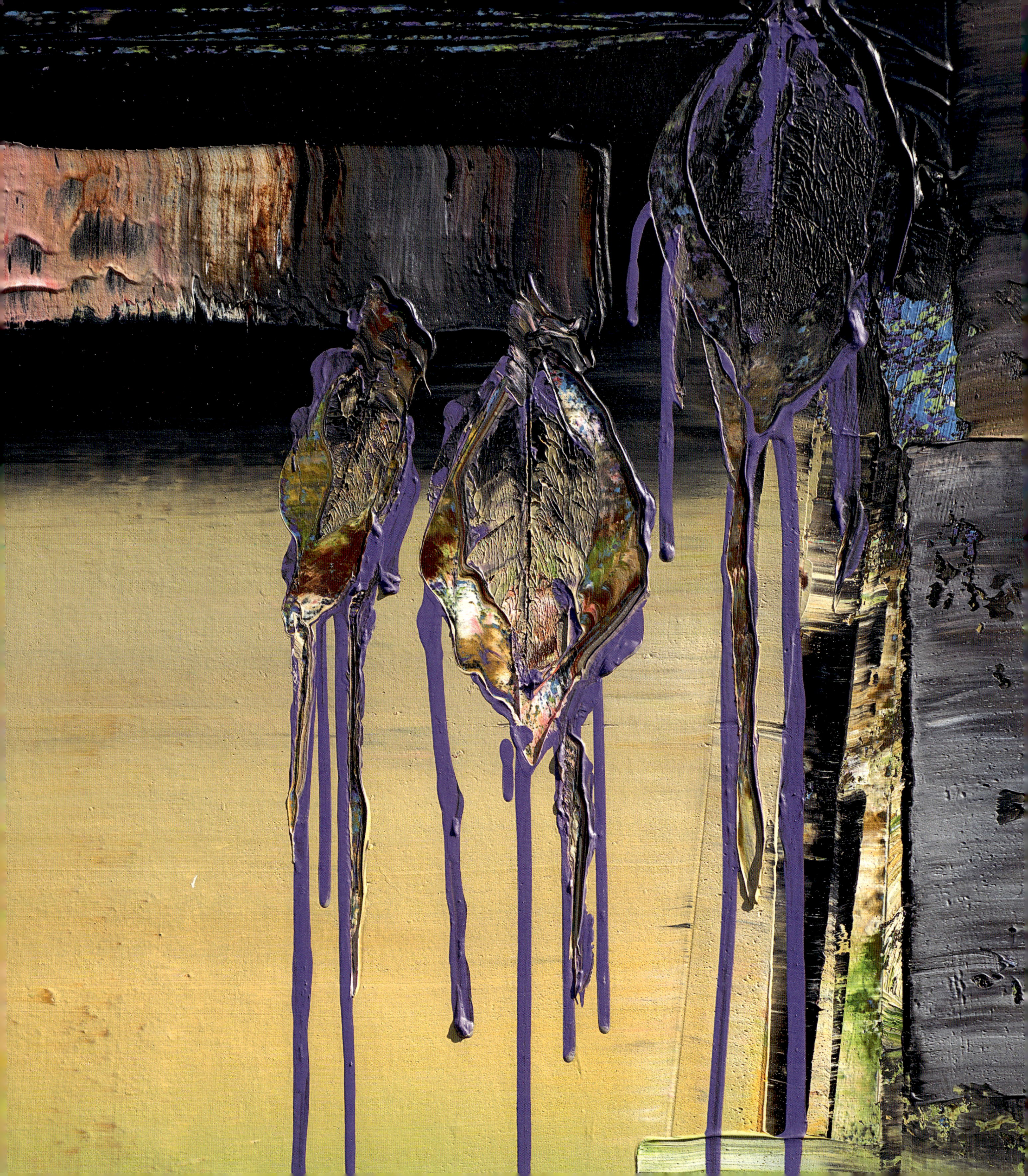

Discover, 2014
120 × 90 cm

Discover, 2014
120 × 90 cm

folgende Doppelseite |
following double page
Detail

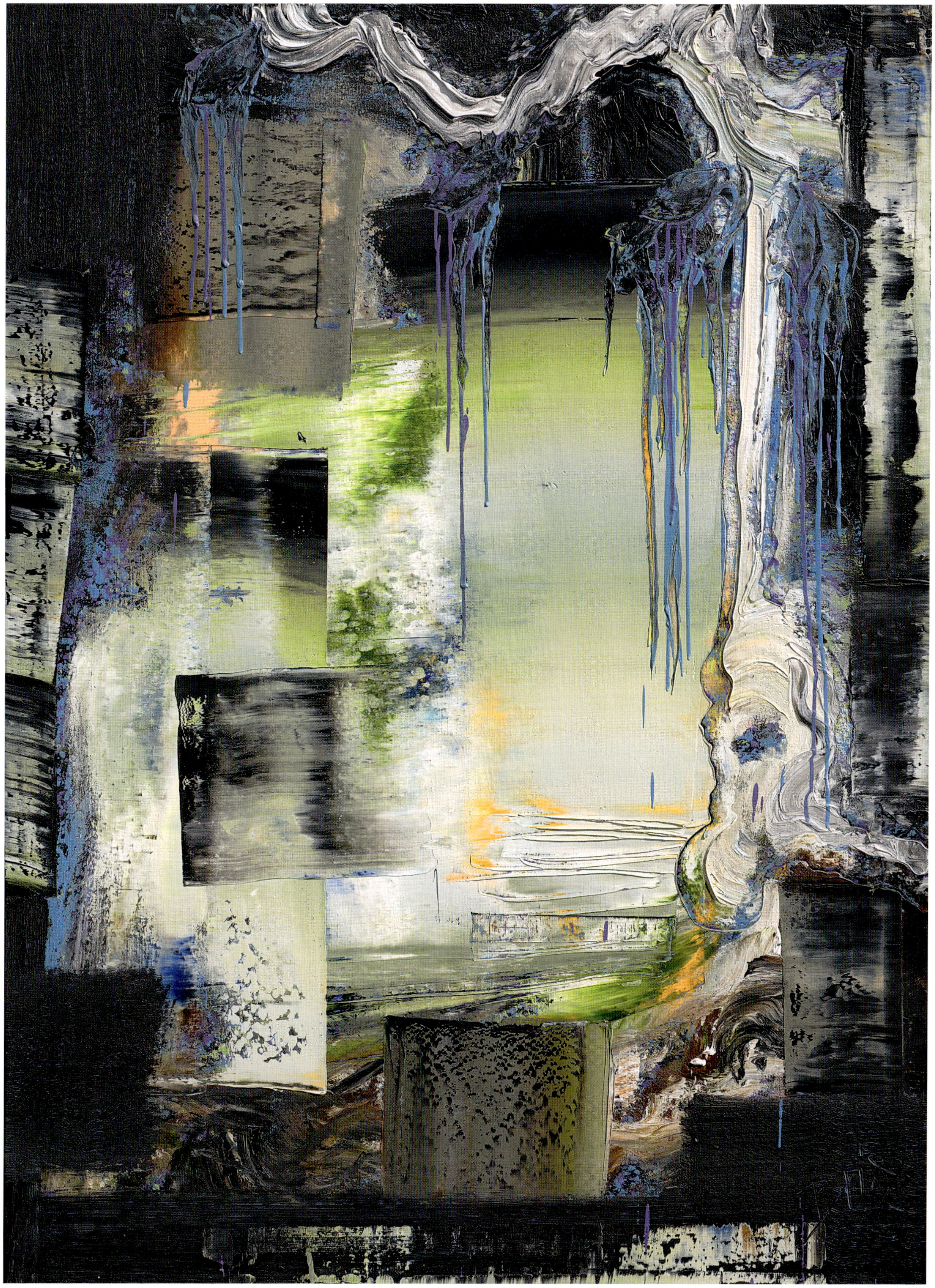

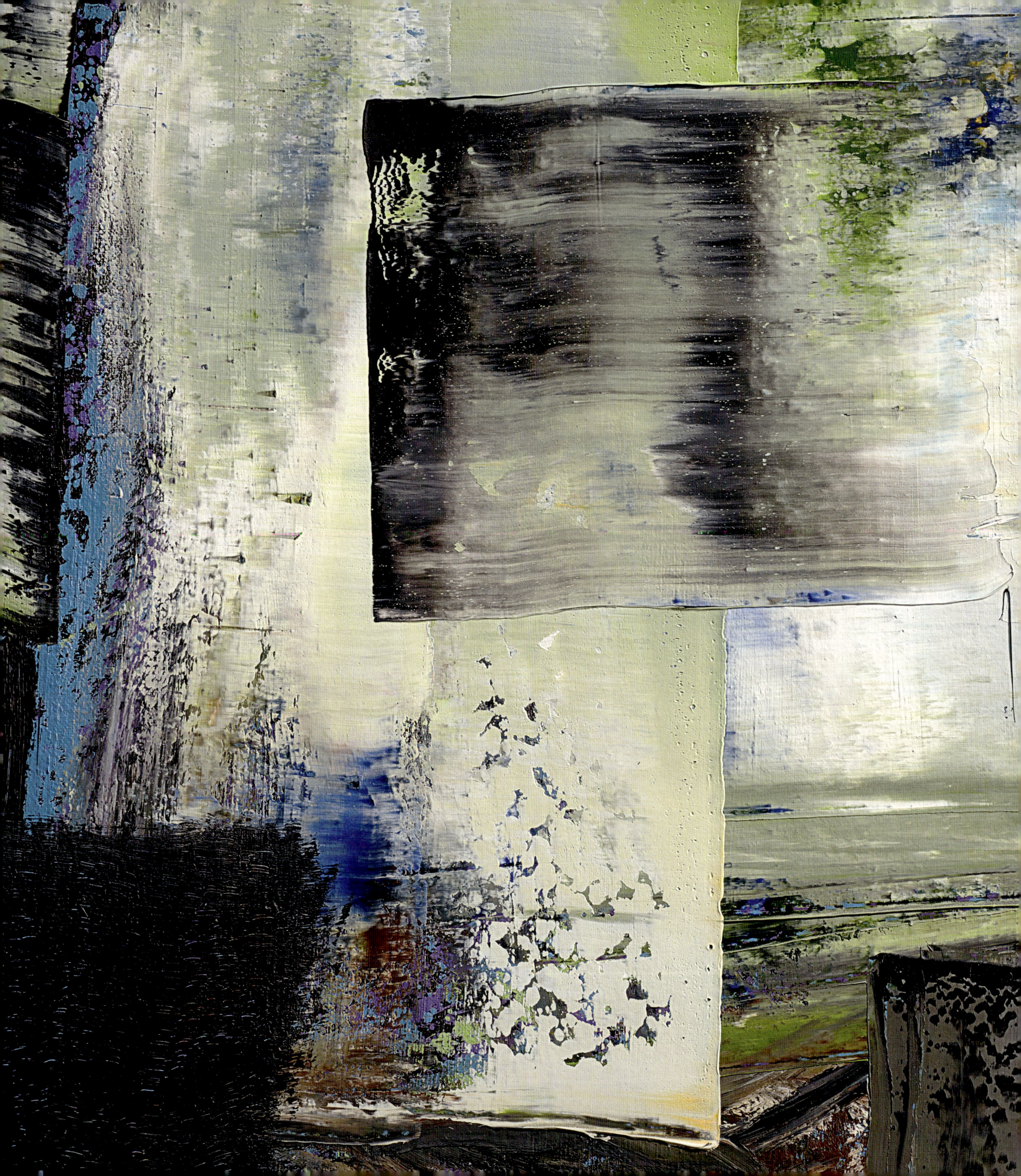

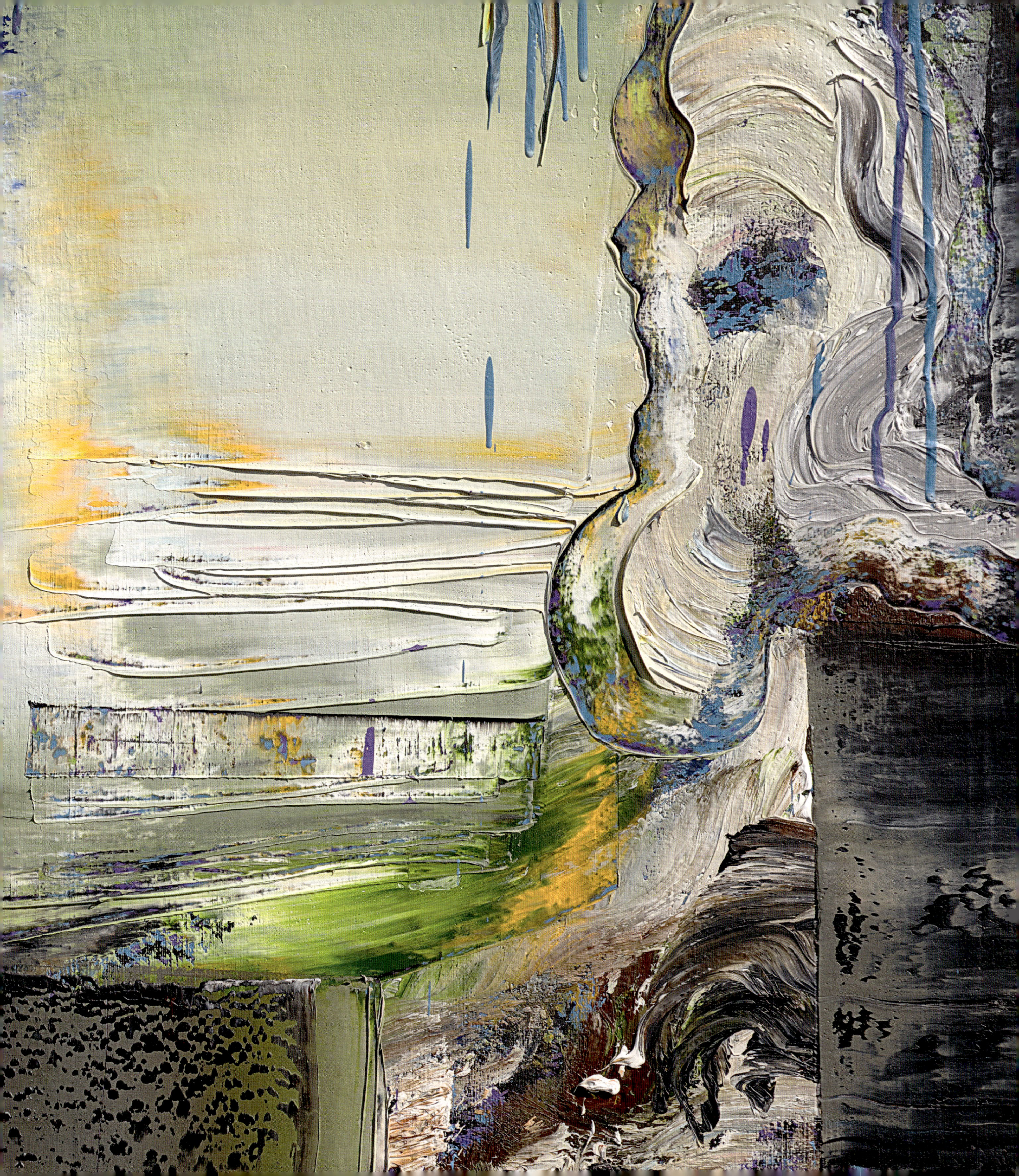

BRIXY AUF ENTDECKUNGSTOUR

Christoph Tannert

Im Alten Pumpwerk von Mannheim-Neckarau hat sich Dietmar Brixy seinen künstlerischen Privatkosmos geschaffen mit der eigenen Person als Zentralgestirn. Kunst und Leben fließen an diesem Ort endgültig zusammen.

Zwischen seinen Bildern und seinem Hausgarten verlaufen unsichtbare Fäden eines dialogischen Wechselspiels. Was seine traumhaft blühende Gartenwelt an frühjahrsästhetischem Mehrwert abstrahlt, animiert ihn, zusätzliche magische Akzente in seinen Bildern zu setzen. Inspiration und Projektion kulminieren in Bildern, die das Gartenerlebnis und das Erleben der Natur des Bildstofflichen miteinander vermischen und den daraus entstehenden Wohlfühlakzent in typisch Brixyscher Psychedelik auf der Leinwand widerspiegeln.

Wenn zuletzt noch Kerzen im Haus angezündet und spezielle Blumen- und Objektarrangements von David Richardson, Brixys Lebenspartner, drapiert werden, wird alles eins. Der Besucher selbst verwandelt sich und wird Teil eines gesamtkunstwerkartigen Ineinanderwirkens. Es ist wie ein großes Om aus Architektur, Licht und Bildern. Dass sich in unmittelbarer Nachbarschaft zum Mannheimer Großkraftwerk (GKM) ein solch' bewegendes Schöner-Wohnen-Feeling einstellen würde, hätte man nicht zu träumen gewagt. Außenstehende werden sich kaum vorstellen können, auf welch' berauschende Weise sich an einem Schönwettertag in Neckarau die Sehnsucht der Europäer nach dem Wahren und Berührenden erfüllt. Deswegen auch laden Brixy und Richardson seit zehn Jahren regelmäßig Gäste zu Vernissagen ein. Und die Kunstbegeisterten wallfahrten heran aus allen Himmelsrichtungen… Brixy versteht seine Kunst als eine hoch repräsentative Angelegenheit, von der er sich viel Resonanz verspricht. Seine Gäste werden bei Atelierbesuchen

Discover, 2012
160 × 100 cm

BRIXY ON A VOYAGE OF DISCOVERY

Dietmar Brixy has created an artistic private cosmos, with himself as the central celestial body, at the old wastewater pumping station of Mannheim-Neckarau. It is here that art and life flow together definitively.

The invisible threads of a dialogic interplay connect his paintings and his garden. He is inspired to incorporate further magical accents into his paintings by the additional benefits of springtime aesthetics exuded by his fantastically blossoming garden world. Inspiration and projection culminate in paintings that combine the garden experience and the experience of the nature of the pictorial fabric, and reflect the resulting pleasurable accents in a psychedelia typical of Brixy.

It all becomes one when candles are lit in the house and special flower and object arrangements by David Richardson, Brixy's life partner, are set up. The visitors themselves are transformed and become part of a gesamtkunstwerk-like multidirectional relationship. It is like a great Om composed of architecture, light, and paintings. Nobody would dare to dream that they might experience such a powerful feeling of the beautiful life in immediate proximity to the Mannheim Großkraftwerk (GKM) power station. Outsiders can hardly imagine the intoxicating manner in which the Europeans' longing for the true and the touching is fulfilled on a gloriously sunny day in Neckarau. This is also why Brixy and Richardson have regularly invited guests to private art viewings over the course of the past ten years. Art enthusiasts set out on a pilgrimage from all four corners of the earth in order to attend … Brixy conceives of his art as a deeply representative matter from which he expects a high degree of resonance. His guests are the recipients of his hospitality, are assisted during their visit to the studio, and find themselves impressed. Brixy reveals himself to be at once cosmopolitan and the guardian of tradition.

betreut, bewirtet, beeindruckt. Brixy zeigt sich weltoffen und zugleich als Bewahrer der Tradition.

Der Hinweis auf ein Prinzip des „Fließens" mag eine vage Beschreibung dessen sein, was in den Bildern Brixys vor sich geht. In seiner seit 2012 auf gut 300 Werke angewachsenen Serie „Discover", in der es Kleinstformate von 18 × 24 bis zu wandfüllenden Rahmen von 180 × 480 cm gibt, eröffnen sich diverse Erzählbögen, in denen das Fließen Form, Kontur und Eigensinn findet. Unzweifelhaft steht das Fließen in einer meditativen, repetitiven Beziehung zu einer religiösen Wahrheit für unsere Zeit, bei der der Weg das Ziel ist. Je weiter sich die Serie fortentwickelte, desto radikaler machte der östliche Zeitbegriff sich geltend, und umso unwichtiger wurden genauere Werktitel oder Archivierungsnummern. Brixy verzichtet auf konkrete Benennungen und datiert höchstens mit einer Jahreszahl. Alles ist im Fluss. Jedes Bild wird in ein rein ästhetisches Dasein entlassen, in dem es im malerischen Entwicklungsgang das wird, was es ist. So webt er unverdrossen am Saum der Ewigkeit. Berührungspunkte mit zentralen Ideen der Postmoderne sind gegeben. Die Welt als asiatisch angehauchtes Rankenwerk und Vorstellung!

„Discover" als bisher noch unabgeschlossene Serie markiert eine Etappe auf einem langen Weg, dessen Ausgangspunkt von einem Konglomerat an erprobten Bildmöglichkeiten gebildet wird und nicht bloß auf die Zukunft gerichtet ist, sondern vor allem Brixys künstlerische Gegenwart reflektiert. Sein Werk ist permanentes Suchen, ostentativ schöpferisch und variantenreich, eine Verwandlung der eigenen Existenz in Farbströme, eine intensive Poetisierung von nicht immer frohen, aber anhaltend lebenszugewandten Erfahrungen.

One might refer to the principle of the "flow" as a vague description of what goes on in Brixy's paintings. A variety of narrative arcs in which the flow finds form, contour, and self-will unfold in his "Discover" series, which has grown to encompass approximately 300 works since 2012 and consists of small 18 × 24-centimeter formats, as well as wall-covering frames measuring 180 × 480 cm. There can be no doubt that there is a meditative, repetitive relationship between the flow and a religious truth for our times, according to which the journey is the destination. As the series continuously developed, the Eastern concept of time manifested itself increasingly radically, and specific painting titles and archive numbers became increasingly insignificant. Brixy eschews concrete designations and does not date the paintings more accurately than with the year of execution. Everything is in flux. Every painting is released into a purely aesthetic existence in which it becomes what it is through a painterly development process. In this way, he assiduously weaves away at the seam of eternity. There are points of contact with ideas central to postmodernism. The world as Asian-inspired scrollwork and vision!

As a series in progress, "Discover" constitutes a milestone on the long path that begins with a conglomerate of tried-and-tested pictorial possibilities and does not focus solely on the future but instead primarily reflects Brixy's artistic present. His oeuvre is a permanent quest, ostentatiously creative and richly varied, a transformation of his own existence into currents of color, an intense transformation into poetry of experiences that are not always cheerful, but continuously life affirming.

The speeds and intensities of "Discover" are derived from the "Eden" series that preceded it. Reinhard Spieler calls it a "laboratory of paradise" (*Paradies-Labor*).[1] Where "Eden" thrives from the jungle-like multiplication and interweaving of media, "Discover" presents itself as more pared down and less dominated by a sense of painterly satiation. There is a reduction in the relief-like compressions, and surfaces have created new

Geschwindigkeiten und Intensitäten von „Discover" leiten sich ab aus der vorausgehenden Serie „Eden". Reinhard Spieler nennt sie ein „Paradies-Labor".[1] Lebte „Eden" jedoch aus der dschungelhaften Vervielfachung und Verflechtung der Mittel, zeigt sich „Discover" entschlackter und wird weniger von einem malerischen Völlegefühl dominiert. Die reliefartigen Komprimierungen haben abgenommen, Flächen schufen sich neue Interaktionsfelder. Die Welten von „Eden" und „Discover" bilden einen inhaltlichen und sinnlichen Verbund. Das den Tastsinn Herausfordernde bestimmt ihre Oberflächenkonstitution. Wobei – „Discover" hat mehr Flow als „Eden".

„To Discover" bietet die Möglichkeit: (alles Bildwesentliche) zu entdecken, aufzufinden, vorzufinden. Durch den Künstler und durch das Publikum.

Zwei bis drei Phasen lassen sich, so meine ich, realisieren. Anfangs wurde die Komposition von Gegenstandsanordnungen in einem Davor und Dahinter bestimmt. Die Reaktion auf das Naturvorbild erfolgte im Sinne einer Realitätserkundung in den Formen der Natur selbst. Im Zuge stärkeren Abstrahierens wechselte Brixy hernach von der Naturerkundung zur Erkundung der Natur der Malerei. Brixy initiierte einen Klärungsvorgang, der bis heute anhält. Spielte anfangs die Abbildung von Gesehenem eine größere Rolle, so steuerte Brixy mehr und mehr hin zu einer Aussage über Empfindungen des Getragenseins durch Natur und Malerei. Brixy definierte sich nun als Reisender in den poetischen wie realen Welten. Gleichzeitig intensivierte der Künstler seinen Dialog zwischen traditioneller asiatischer und moderner europäischer Kunst.

Krankheit und Tod der Mutter Ende des Jahres 2013 änderten Inhalte, gleichwohl nicht das Wesen der Malerei von Dietmar Brixy. Etwa im August 2013 kehrte Dunkelheit ein. Schwärze. Andererseits auch eine größere Farbräumlichkeit. Der pastos zugespachtelte Bildgrund gab plötzlich nach und Fenster in ein Irgendwo taten sich auf. Noch nie hatte der Künstler die Eigengesetzlichkeit der Farbe solcherart respektiert. Ein verlockend großes Leuchten elektrisierte die Bilder. Mag sein, dass da eine transzendentale Erwartung mitschwang.

Momentan schickt uns Brixy auf eigentümlich entgrenzte Weise an die Grenzen der Wahrnehmung. Er staffelt Ebenen und ankert im Dazwischen. Nachdem er sich durch diverse Entwicklungs-

fields of interaction for themselves. The worlds of "Eden" and of "Discover" form a relationship of content and of sensuality. Their surface constitution is shaped by that which challenges the sense of touch. And yet – "Discover" has more flow than "Eden" does.

"To discover" provides the opportunity: to find, to reveal, to uncover (all that is essential to the painting). By the artist and by the viewers.

It seems to me that two to three phases can be realised. To begin with the composition was determined by arrangements of objects as "in front of" and "behind." The reaction to the model provided by nature took place in terms of an investigation of reality in the forms of nature itself. In the course of increasing abstraction, Brixy then shifted from the exploration of nature to the exploration of the nature of painting. Brixy initiated a clarification process that continues to this day. Whereas the depiction of that which is seen played a more important role at the beginning, Brixy veered closer and closer to a statement about senses of being held by nature and by painting. From this point onwards, Brixy defined himself as a traveler in the worlds of both poetry and reality. The artist simultaneously intensified his dialogue between traditional Asian and modern European art.

The illness and death of his mother in late 2013 changed the content, though not the nature, of Dietmar Brixy's painting. Darkness descended around August 2013. Blackness. And yet this was accompanied by a greater degree of the spatiality of color. The pictorial ground pastosely applied with a putty knife suddenly gave way, and windows opened up onto undefined places. Never before had the artist respected the inherent laws of paint in this way. A seductively powerful glow ran through the paintings like a current. It is possible that a transcendental expectation played a part.

At present, Brixy takes us to the fringes of perception in a manner shaped by a singular blurring of boundaries. He staggers levels and drops anchors in the intermediate spaces. After he has painted his way through various

stufen hindurchgemalt hat, vom Naturbild über die Abstraktion zum Rundbild als Augenbild zur luminalen Fokussierung, glüht Farbenergie die Bilder auf. Brixy hat Fragestellungen reifen lassen und Engführungen ausgelotet, um zu einer Conclusio zu gelangen, die mit allem Bisherigen connected ist, durch ihre kompositorischen Mischungsverhältnisse im selben Augenblick dabei darüber hinausweist.

Und Brixy „discovered" sich und sein malerisches Agieren zunehmend selbst. Man könnte fast sagen – zwischen „Eden" und „Discover" blitzt eine binäre Trennung auf, die das Verhältnis zwischen einer äußeren und einer inneren Identität neu justiert. Das Innere wird allerdings nicht über das Äußere gestellt. Beides ist in Porosität miteinander verbunden. Die Malhäute von „Eden" und „Discover" atmen.

Das Bildklima, die rasche, aber doch ausbalancierte Art des elementaren Kontrastaufbaus hält ein Basis-Pathos bereit, wie wir es u.a. auch von Gerhard Richter, Fritz Winter, Kuno Gonschior her kennen – freilich, und das ist das Angenehme, ohne das mitschwingende Gerieren der Bedeutsamkeit.

Hauptmittel seiner Kunst, die Art wie die Vergegenwärtigung von Plastizität verdichtet wird, ist bei Brixy nicht gerade Genügsamkeit. Er ist er ein ruheloser Arbeiter. Melanie Klier nennt ihn einen „disziplinierten Pflichtethiker"[2]. Brixy schafft und formt mit einem überbordenden Pensum des Sichselbsternstnehmens. Diszipliniert fährt er in seinem Zauberberg groß auf, sogar im kleinen Format. Jeder Bildbau ist komplex. Für jedes Bild hat der Vollblutmaler ein Rezept, das eine Reihe von aromatischen Details aufweist, die dem Ganzen Kreativität und Aktualität verleihen. Mal ist es das Prozesshafte, das im Vordergrund steht, mal das haptische Moment der Oberfläche, mal dreht sich ein Ansatz um das Denkbare, dass das Bild davon befreit, nur Objekt oder Ware zu sein. Brixy bietet uns ständig neue Ansätze an, damit wir auf lebendige Weise mit seinen Bildern kommunizieren können. Manchmal scheint es, ein Herausforderungssüchtiger mache Kopfstand auf des Messers Schneide.

Brixys Bilder sind von zupackender Gegenwärtigkeit. Jedes seiner Bilder ist ein organisches Faktum.

levels of development, from the nature painting via the abstraction to the circular painting as an eye image for luminal focussing, the paintings begin to glow with coloristic energy. Brixy has allowed questions to mature and has explored rapprochements in order to reach a conclusion that is connected to all that has gone before, while simultaneously pointing far beyond through the compositional ratio.

And Brixy increasingly "discovers" himself and his painterly action. One might even say that a binary separation flashes up between "Eden" and "Discover," resulting in a readjustment of the relationship between an external and an internal identity. And yet, the internal is not given precedence over the external. Both elements are connected to one another in a porous relationship. The painterly skins of "Eden" and "Discover" breathe.

The pictorial climate, the rapid and yet balanced form of elementary contrast construction, provides a basic pathos with which we are familiar from the works of Gerhard Richter, Fritz Winter, Kuno Gonschior, et al. Of course it is not, and this is what is pleasing about it, characterised by the accompanying presence of significance.

The main medium of Brixy's art, the manner in which the realization of plasticity is intensified, cannot be said to be frugality. He is a restless worker. Melanie Klier describes him as a "disciplined proponent of duty ethics."[2] Brixy creates and forms with an unlimited capacity for taking himself seriously. He takes a definitive stand in a disciplined manner in his Magic Mountain, even on a small scale. Every pictorial composition is complex. The full-blooded painter has a recipe for every painting, featuring a series of aromatic details that imbue the whole with creativity and topicality. At times, the focus is on the processual, at other times on the haptic aspect of the surface, and sometimes the approach revolves around the thinkable, which liberates the painting from being a mere object or commodity. Brixy constantly offers us new approaches so that we can communicate with his paintings in an animated manner. Sometimes it

Sie erzählen von nichts anderem als vom Fluss künstlerischer Energie. Immer geht es um ganz archaische Dinge, die jeden angehen, jeden Betrachter affizieren. Jedes Bild ist ein Mikrokosmos, in dem alles künstlerische Tun exemplarisch, nie schematisch vorgeführt wird.

Brixy trägt pro Bild zwischen sieben und neun Ölfarbschichten auf. Als Erstes wird mit Schwarz grundiert. Dann begibt sich der Künstler in eine Phase des Action Painting, in der die Pinsel tanzen und die Leinwand mit zufälligen Farbspuren übersät wird. Im nächsten Schritt werden diverse farbige Markierungen mit der Hand vorgenommen. Dass Brixy Bildhauerei studiert hat, sieht man sofort. Er verschiebt Volumina über die Leinwand. Sein Malen ist ein Kraftakt. Dieser Leinwandbezwinger arbeitet mit dem Pinsel, mit dem Spachtel, mit der Hand. Er greift die Farbe direkt aus dem Eimer, aus der Tube, mischt sie mit der Hand, wischt und gräbt Linienverläufe, lässt Lava gurgeln und Kühlwasser. Das ist nicht Entertainment, sondern Existentialismus. Brixy rührt und reliefiert und beweist uns, wie sich eine klassische malerische Basis mit traditionellen Elementen in unterschiedlicher Form modernisieren lässt.

Im Weiteren kommt es zuweilen dazu, dass diverse Blattformen, z. B. Ginko, Feige, Zitronenbaum und Nadelpalme (Cycas revoluta), in die Farbe eingedrückt werden. Brixy dynamisiert anschließend das Bild durch Farbdripping und diverse Praktiken, die einen Vermischungseffekt nach sich ziehen. Diese Arbeitsmethodik bietet ihm Flexibilität und sichert ihm den Umgang mit den belebenden Elementen des Zufalls.

Brixy schlemmt heftig Farbe ins Keilrahmengeviert. Er kehrt sein Innerstes nach außen. Wülste und insulare Gebilde lassen den Blick beim Abtasten der Leinwand stolpern. Die Dinge überschlagen sich. Spontan wird Brixy handgreiflich, er schliert, er umkreist knetend und prüfend das Malstoff-

Discover, 2013
90 × 120 cm

seems as though a challenge-addict is doing a headstand on the knife's edge.

Brixy's paintings are of a gripping actuality. Each of his paintings is an organic factum. They speak of nothing but of the flow of artistic energy. It is always about thoroughly archaic things that are relevant to everybody, that affect every viewer. Every painting is a microcosm in which all artistic actions are presented in an exemplary, but never in a schematic, way.

Brixy applies between seven and nine layers of oil paint per painting. As a first step, black is used for priming. The artist then enters an Action Painting phase in which the paintbrushes dance and the canvas is strewn with coincidental paint traces. In the next stage, various colored markings are executed by hand. The viewer will immediately recognize that Brixy studied sculpture. He shifts volumes over the canvas. His painting is an act of considerable strength. This conqueror of canvases works with the paintbrush, the putty knife and the hand. He grasps the paint directly from the bucket, from the tube, mixes it by hand, wipes and digs lines, causes lava to gurgle and cooling water. This is not entertainment but existentialism. Brixy stirs and creates reliefs and shows us how a classical painterly basis with traditional elements can be modernized in different forms.

In what follows, various leaf forms, including the leaves of the gingko, fig, lemon tree, and needle palm (Cycas revoluta), are sometimes pressed into the paint. Brixy finally introduces dynamism through paint dripping and a variety of practices that entail a mixing effect. This method of working provides him with flexibility and ensures that he will be exposed to the enlivening elements of coincidence.

Brixy slams plenty of paint onto the stretcher-frame square. He externalizes his innermost being. Bulges and insular formations cause the gaze to trip up as it feels its way across the canvas. One thing vies for space with another. Brixy spontaneously uses his hands, he streaks and circles around the painterly substance with a kneading hand and an examining eye, and

liche und treibt mit der Malerpranke die Bildwerdung voran. Das Bild kennt dann nur noch ein Ziel: seine materielle Diversität zur Anschauung zu bringen. Umschweifiges Weltanschauen lässt die Farbe strudeln. Die entstehenden bildnerischen Existenzzonen entziehen sich der Konformität. Ob die Farbe Grenzfluss zwischen Faktizitäten oder feuchter illustrativer Nebel ist, wird von unserer Imagination entschieden. Brixy zählt nicht zu den eingleisigen, linearen Konzeptoren. Vielmehr gibt er sich in seinem enorm fleißigen und forschenden Ansatz als experimenteller Geist zu erkennen. Die inneren Beweggründe seiner Kunst sind zirkulär strukturiert. Damit ist gemeint: Malerische Tatsachensetzungen, Wiederholungen, Echos, Sättigungen, Korrekturen, Neulandgewinnungen bringen Bewegung in sein Denken und Schauen. So wie der Künstler sich in jedem Bild selbst überrascht, können auch die Betrachter sich diesen Bildern ohne Wenn und Aber und aus diversen Richtungen nähern – in einer unmittelbaren emotionalen wie intellektuellen Auseinandersetzung. Im selben Sinne sieht sich Brixy bei jeder neuen Arbeit vor die Aufgabe gestellt, seine Ausgangsposition erneut zu überdenken.

Jedes seiner Bilder ist frei, weil es aus seiner inneren sowie auch äußerlich offenen und prozessualen Beweglichkeit heraus lebt. Es wirkt ganz stark aus der Farbe und weniger aus einer Aura bzw. einer Heiligkeit, ein Kleinod zu sein. Brixys Bilder bringen uns vielmehr aus der Fassung, weil sie selbst als permanente Grenzüberschreitungen angelegt sind, die kein Substrat fixieren wollen, sondern zeigen, wie notwendig es im Leben ist, sich auch einmal aus der Einheit zu entbinden.

1 Reinhard Spieler, *Brixy im Paradies-Labor*, S. 144
2 Melanie Klier, im Rahmen eines Ateliergesprächs beim Künstler am 22.04.2014

spurs on the pictorial creation with his painter's hand. The painting has just one goal then: the realization of its material diversity. A wide-angle view of the world causes the paint to whirl. The sculptural zones of existence created in this way elude conformity. Our imagination determines whether the paint is a border river between facticities or a damp illustrative fog. Brixy is not a single-track, linear conceptualist. Instead, he reveals himself to have an experimental spirit in his tremendously assiduous and inquisitive approach. The inner motives of his art are structured in a circular manner. This means that painterly statements of fact, repetitions, echoes, satiations, corrections and the reclamation of new land introduce movement into his thinking and his gaze. Just as the painter surprises himself in every painting, the viewer can approach these paintings from a variety of directions without ifs or buts – in an immediately emotional and intellectual encounter. In the same way Brixy, sees himself confronted with the challenge of rethinking his starting position in each and every new painting.

Each one of his paintings is free because it lives from its flexibility, which is internally and externally open and processual. Its power derives almost entirely from the paint, and not so much from its aura or the sanctity of being a treasure. Instead, Brixy's paintings have such a profound effect on us because they are themselves set up as permanent transgressions that do not aim to fix a substrate, but to show how important it is in life to occasionally disengage from uniformity.

1 Reinhard Spieler, *Brixy's Laboratory of Paradise*, p. 144
2 Melanie Klier, during a conversation at the artist's studio on 22.04.2014

Discover, 2013
100 × 80 cm

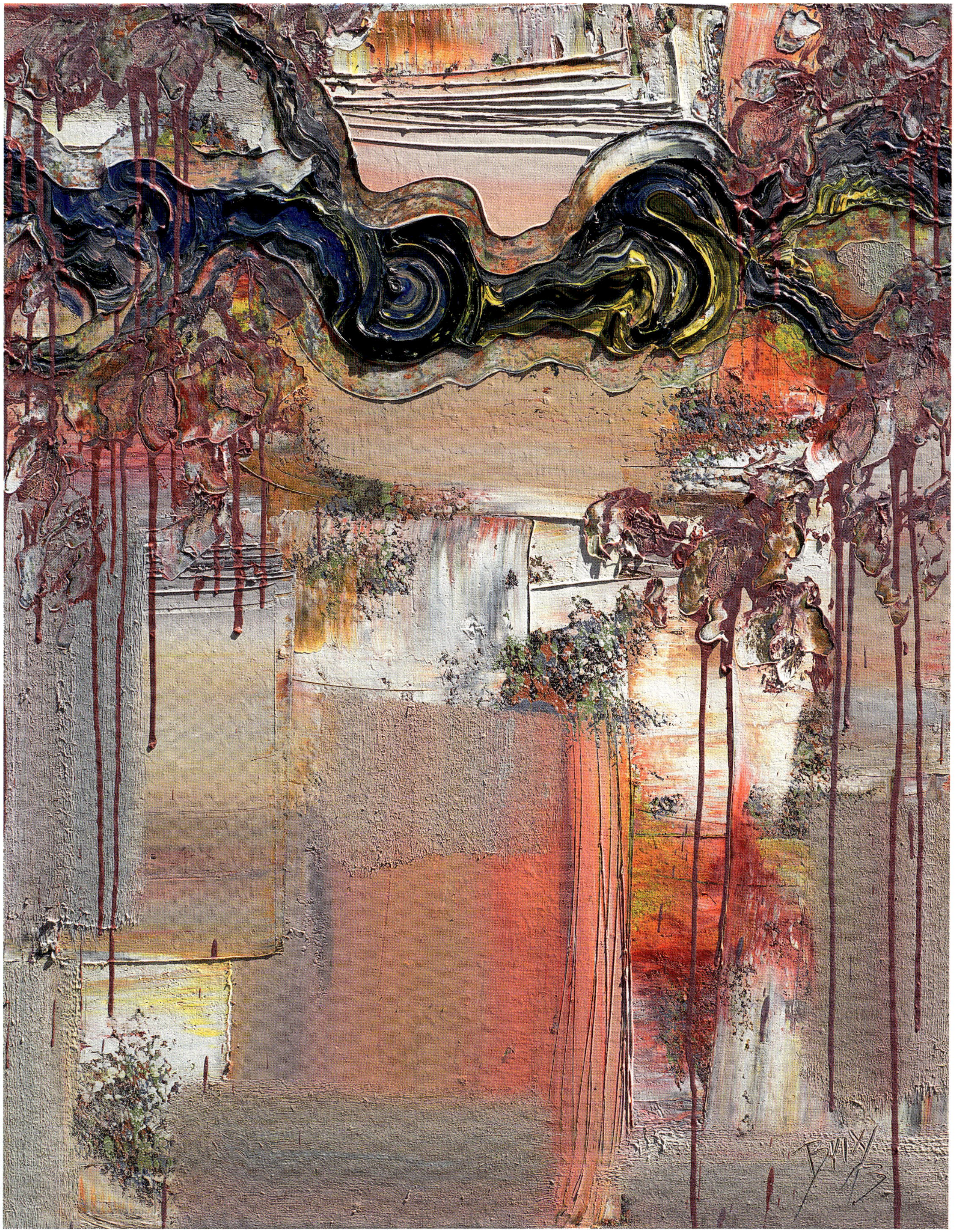

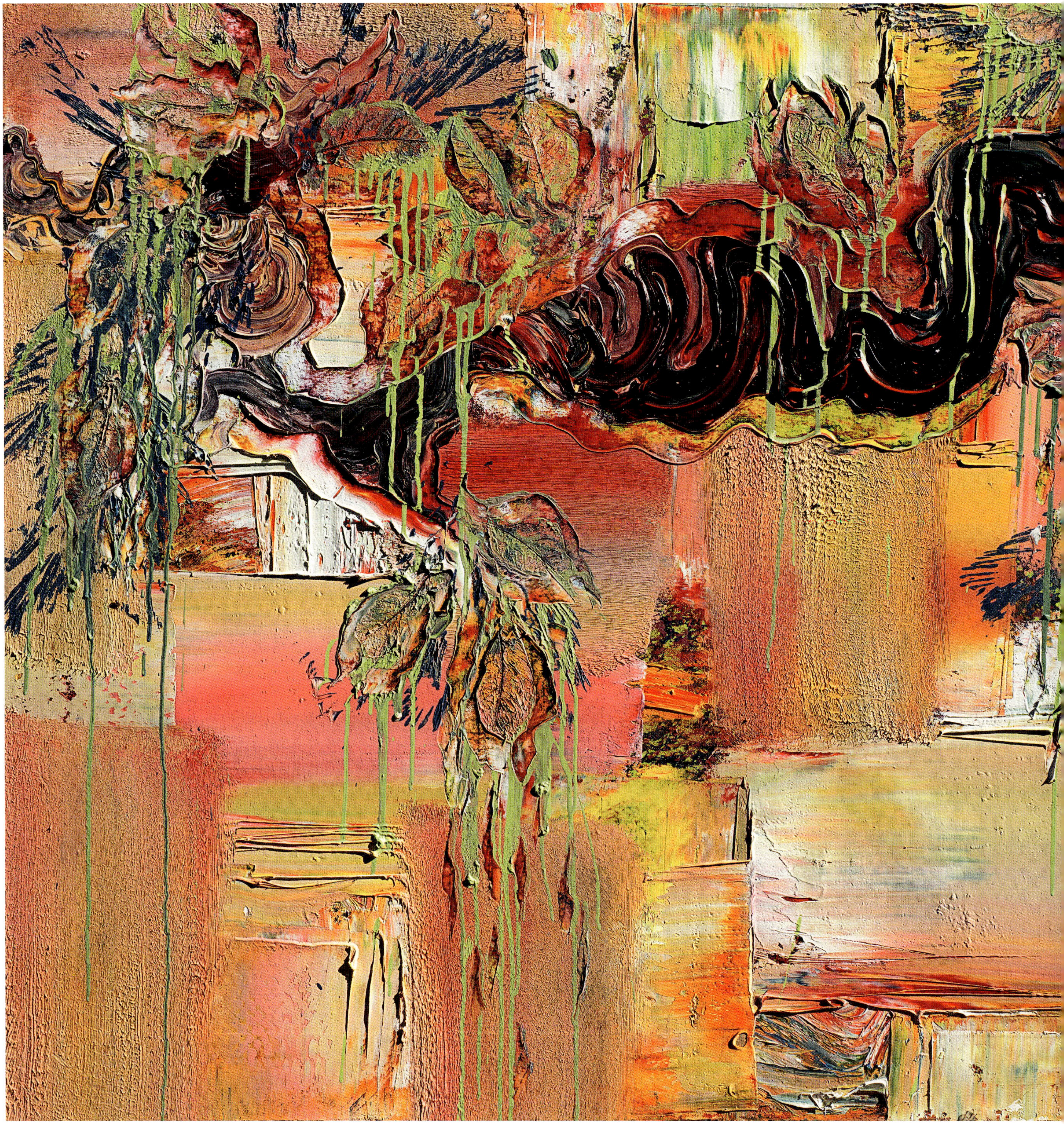

Discover, 2014
90 × 120 cm

Discover, 2014
100 × 140 cm

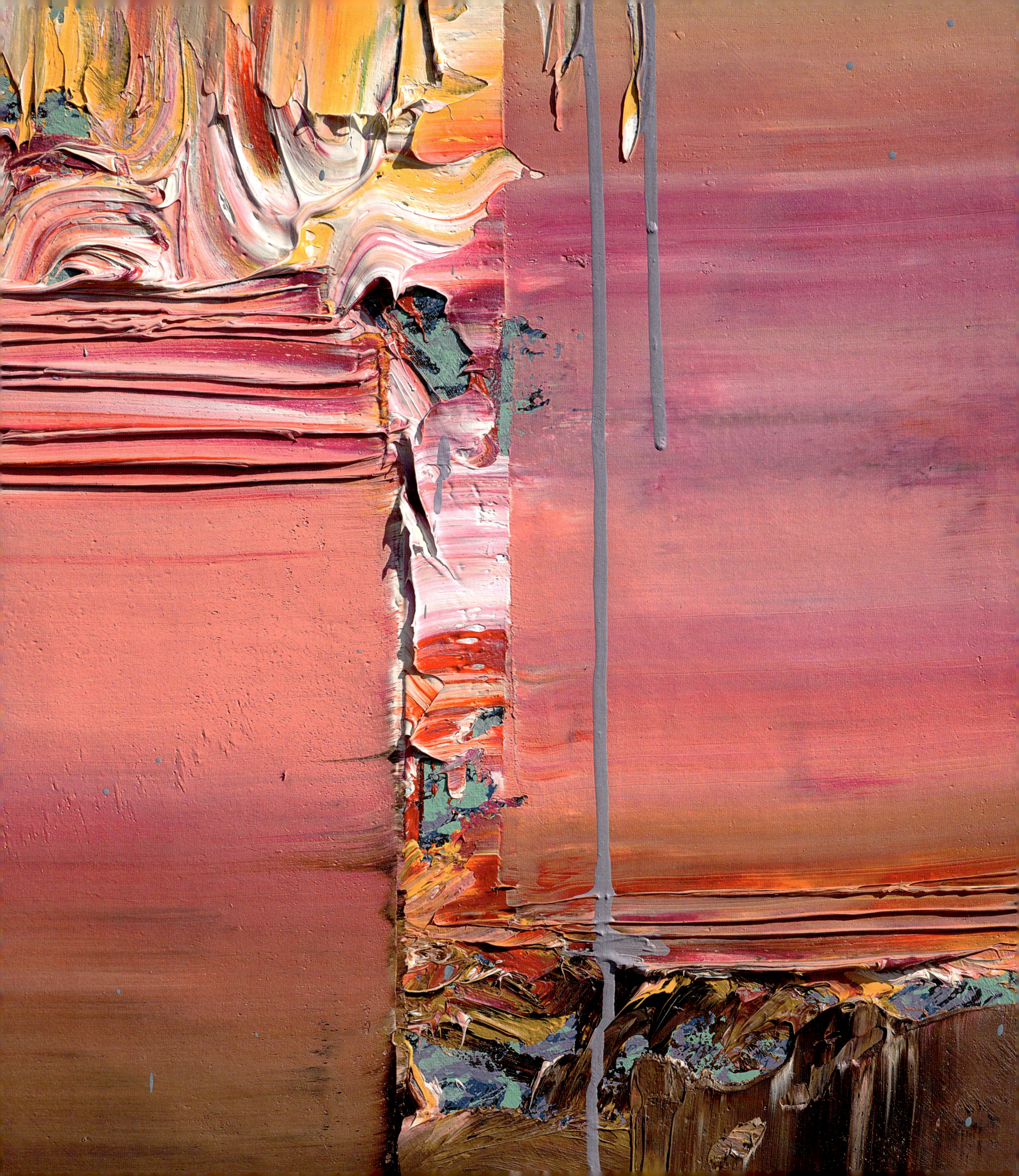

Discover, 2013
50 × 40 cm

Ehrlich, authentisch, nahbar sein.
Das will ich in und mit meiner Kunst.

Being honest, authentic, approachable.
That is what I want in and through my art.

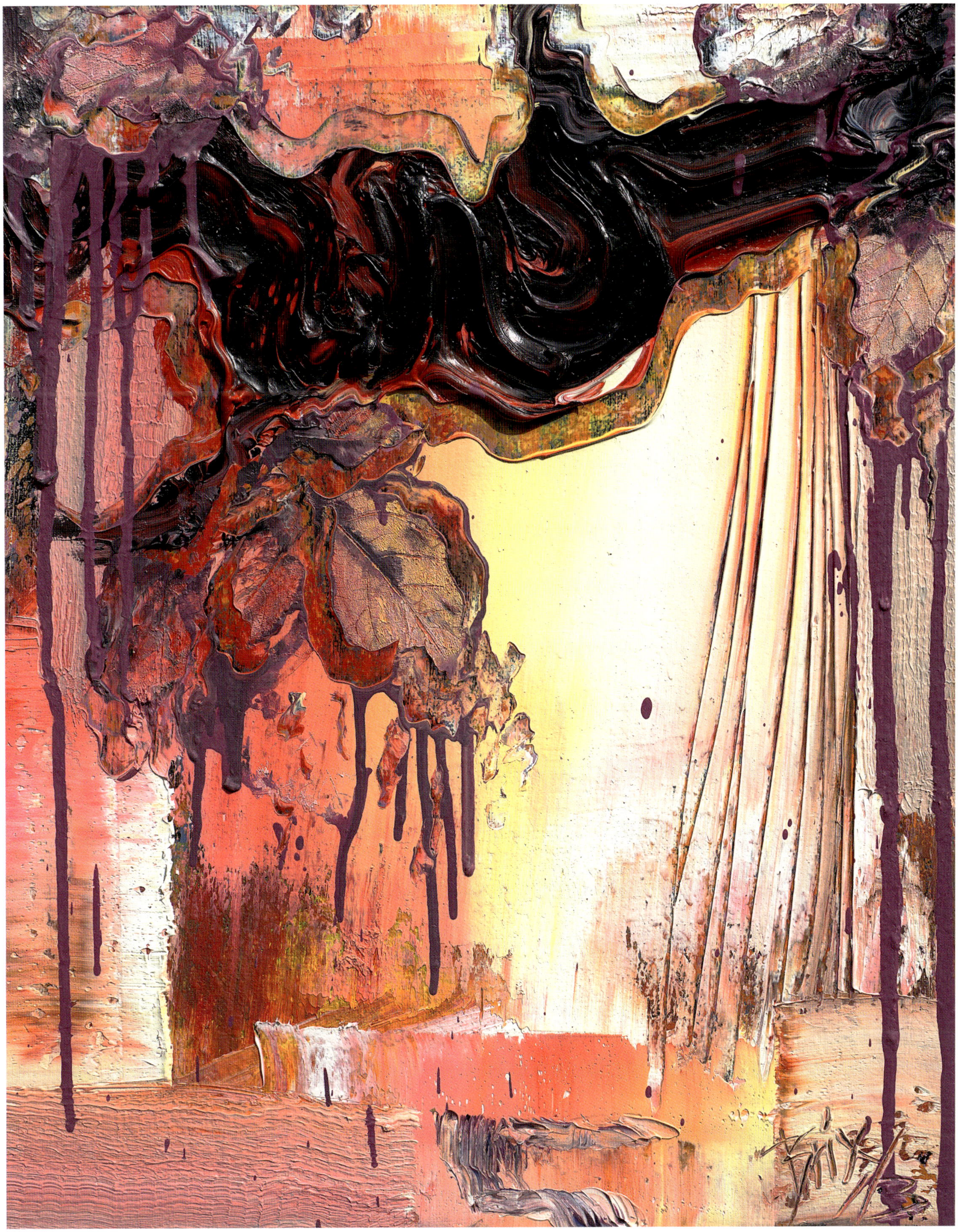

Discover, 2012
130 × 240 cm

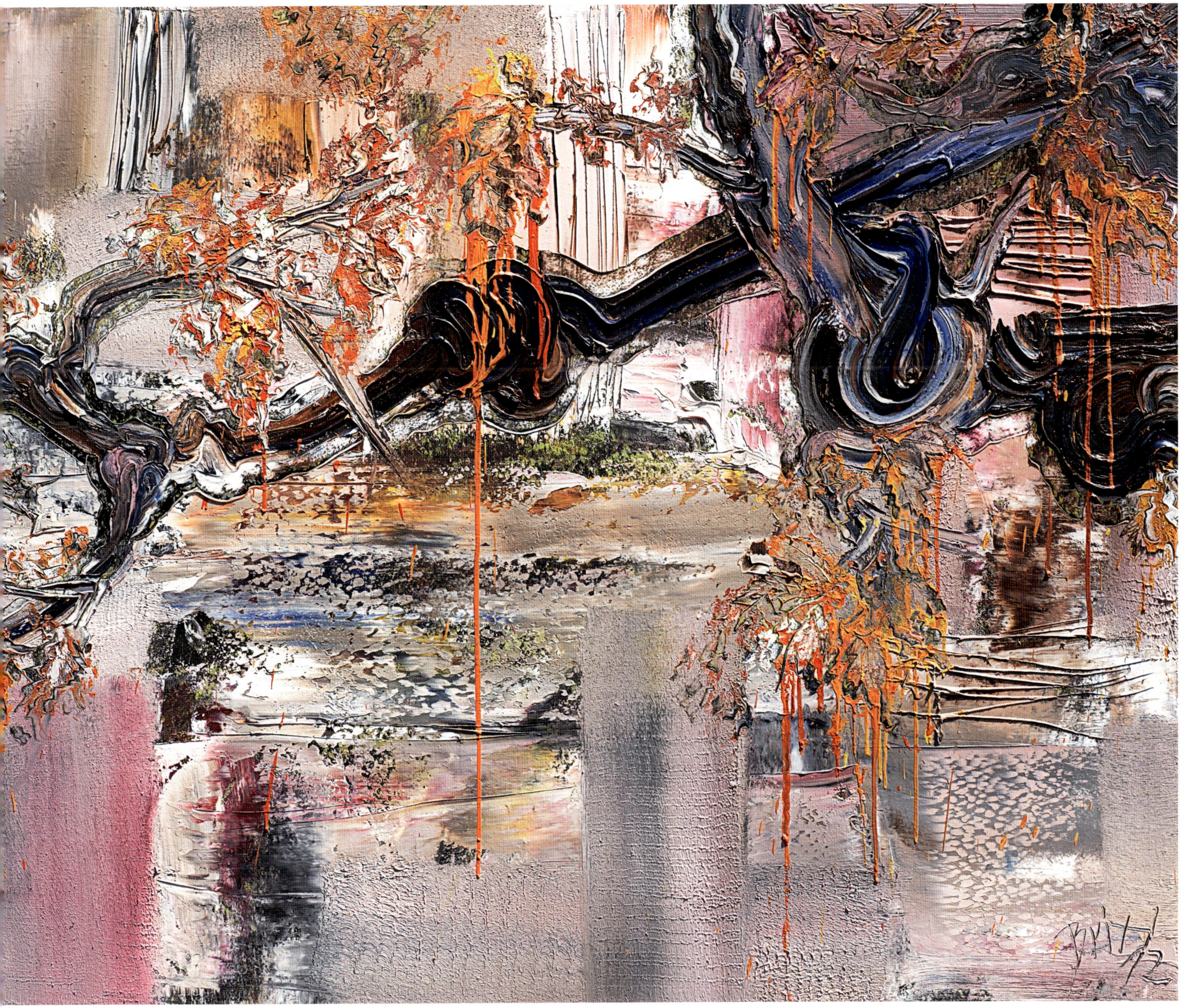

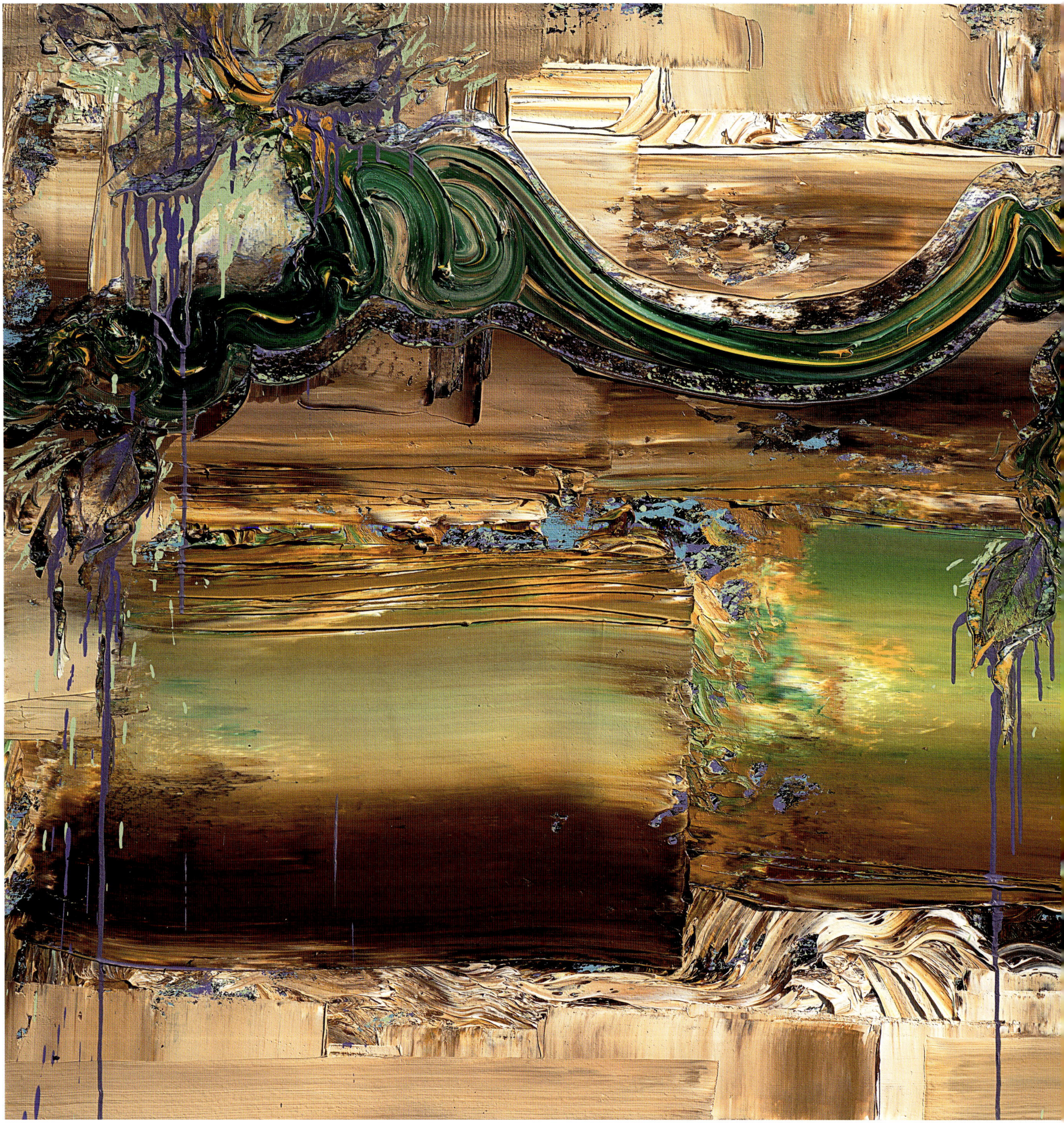

Discover, 2014
100 × 140 cm

Meine Mutter war Korbflechterin,
mein Vater Maurer.

**My mother was a basket maker,
and my father was a bricklayer.**

Discover, 2012
100 × 200 cm

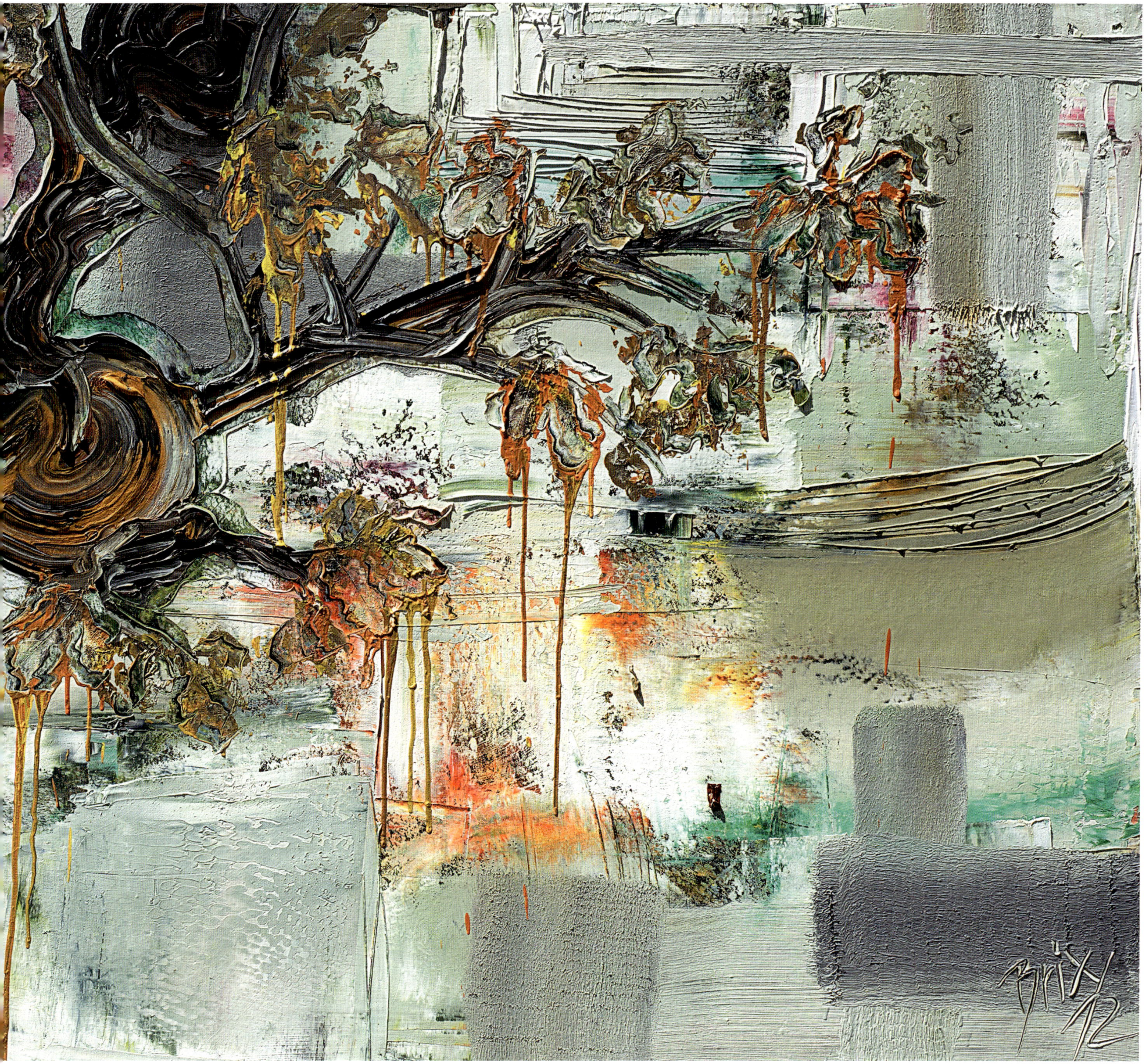

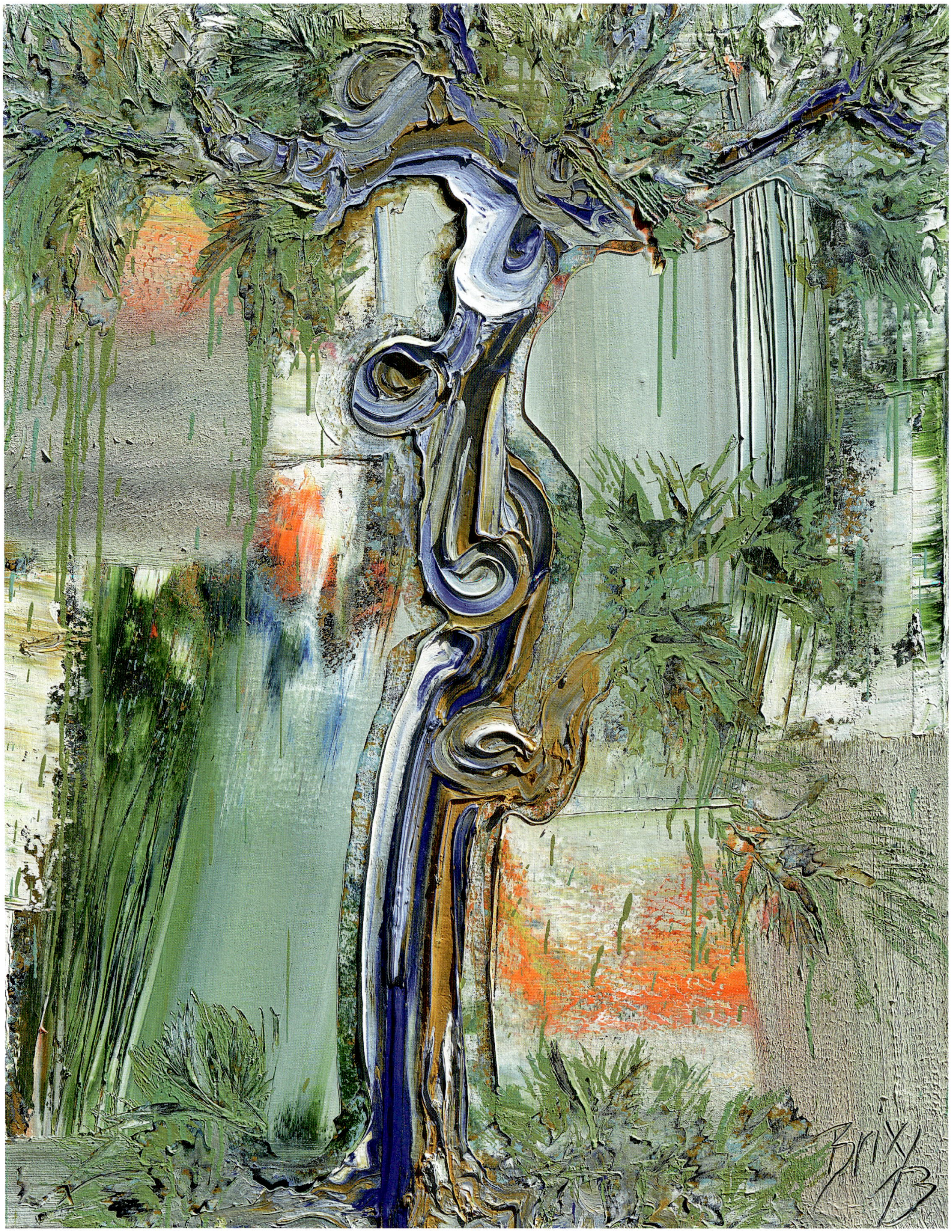

links | left
Discover, 2013
100 × 80 cm

rechts | right
Discover, 2012
180 × 140 cm

Discover, 2014
120 × 180 cm

Discover, 2014
je | each 100 × 160 cm

… **Leidenschaften** nachgehen, **Träume** verwirklichen. Wenn Du etwas willst, mach es!

… **The pursuit of one's passions, the realisation of one's dreams.** If you want something, do it!

Discover (Detail), 2014
90 × 200 cm

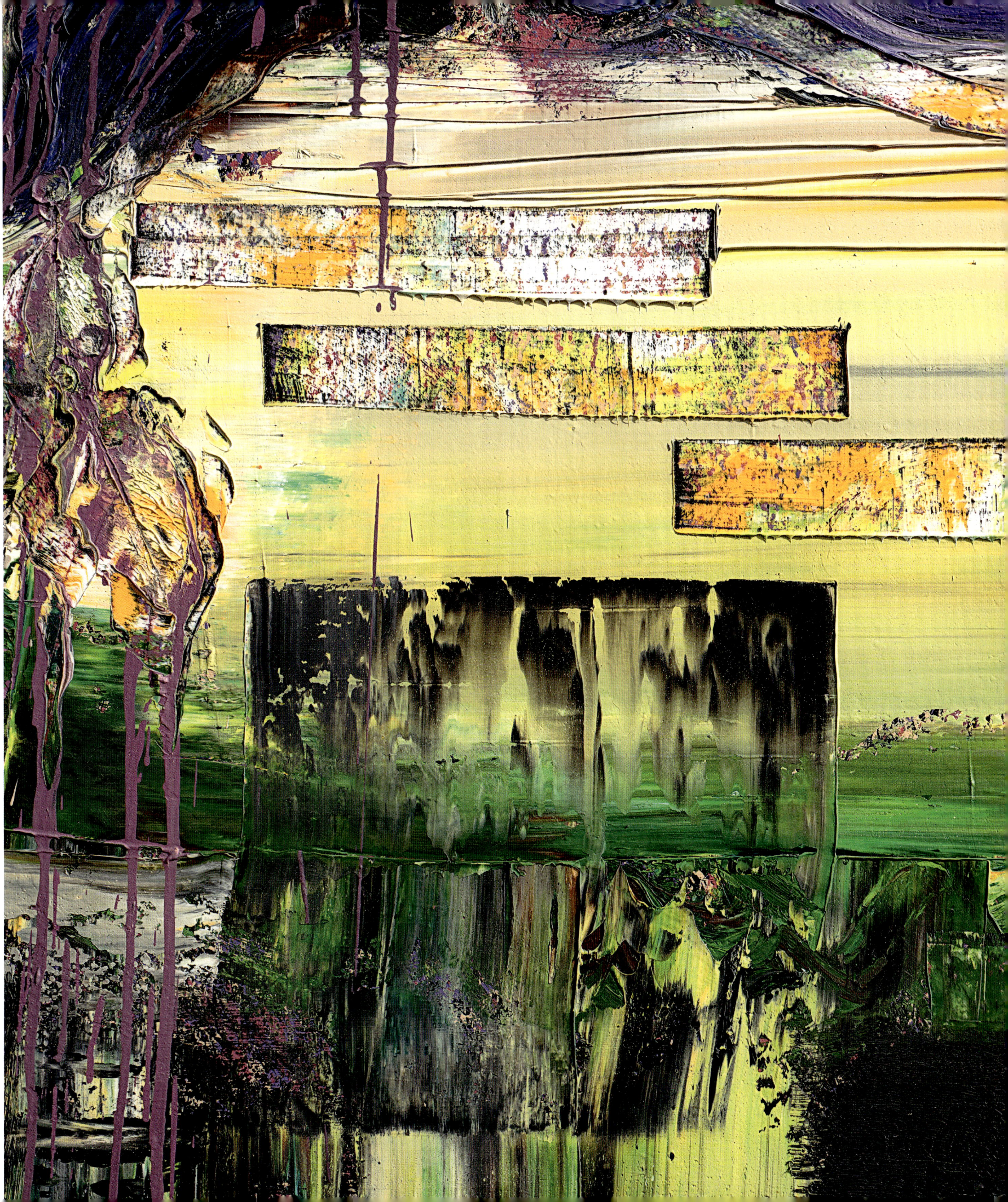

Discover, 2014
90 × 200 cm

Die Schwere des Lebens zu transformieren
in Grenzenloses, Leichtes.

**To transform the heaviness of life
into the boundless, into the light.**

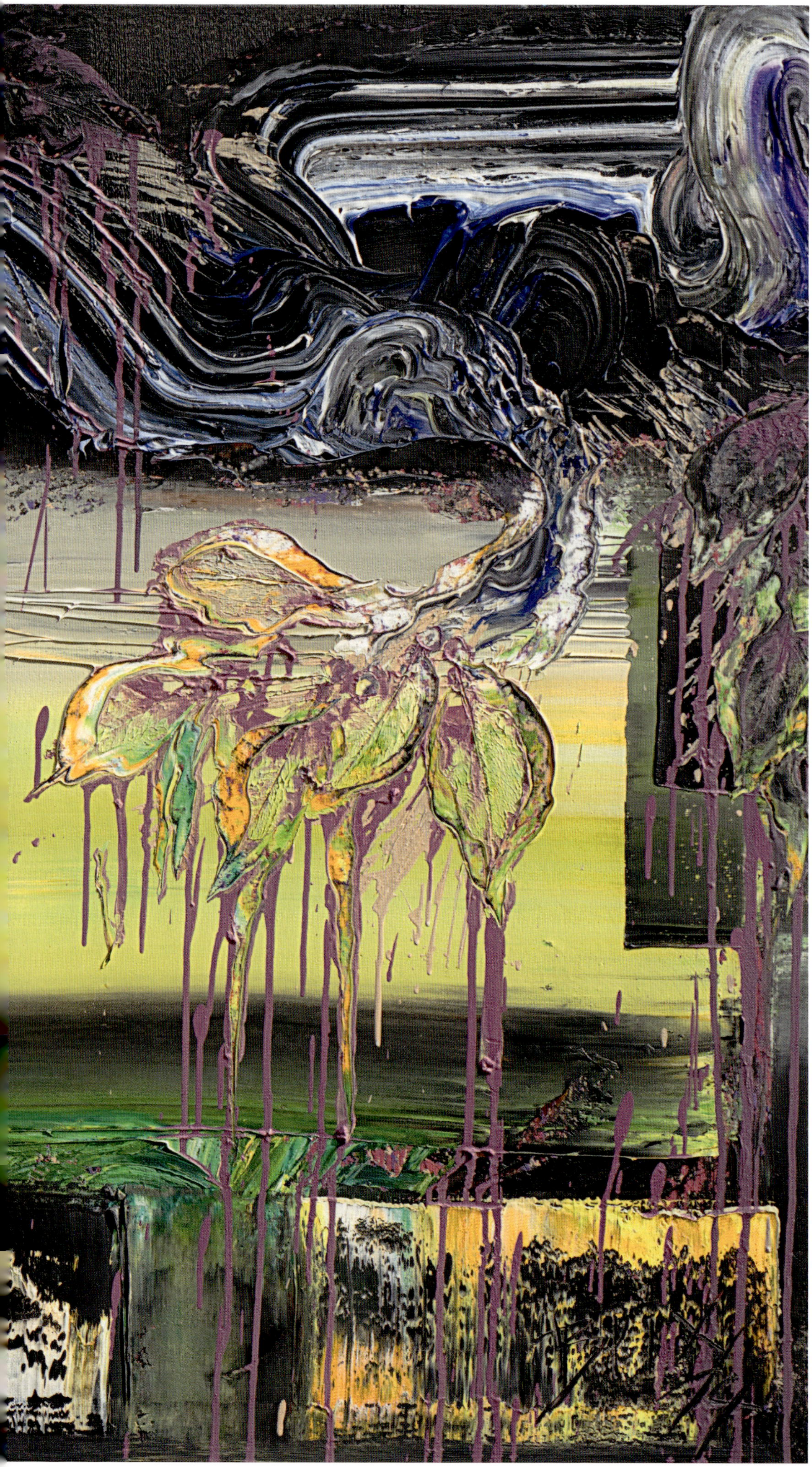

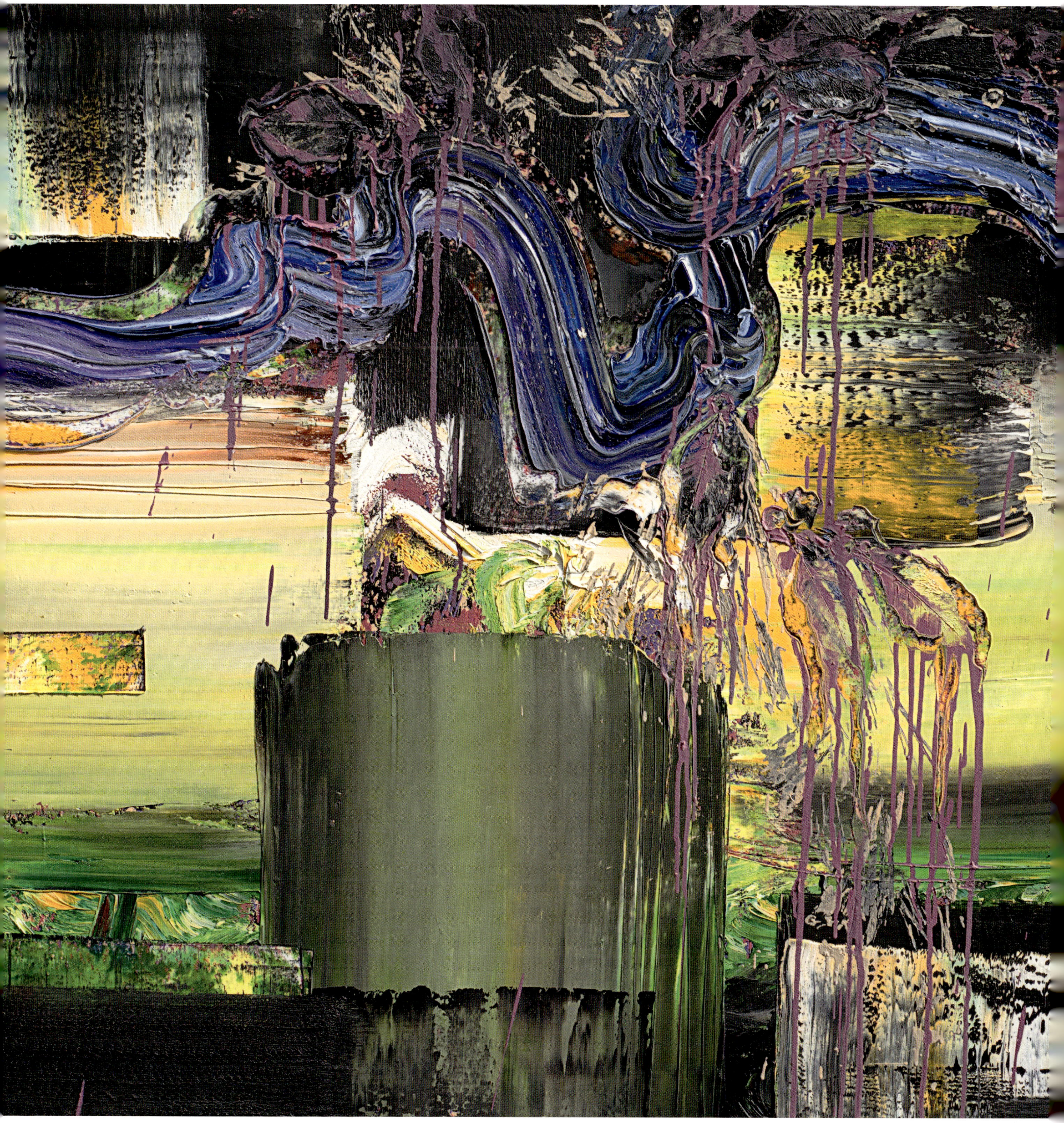

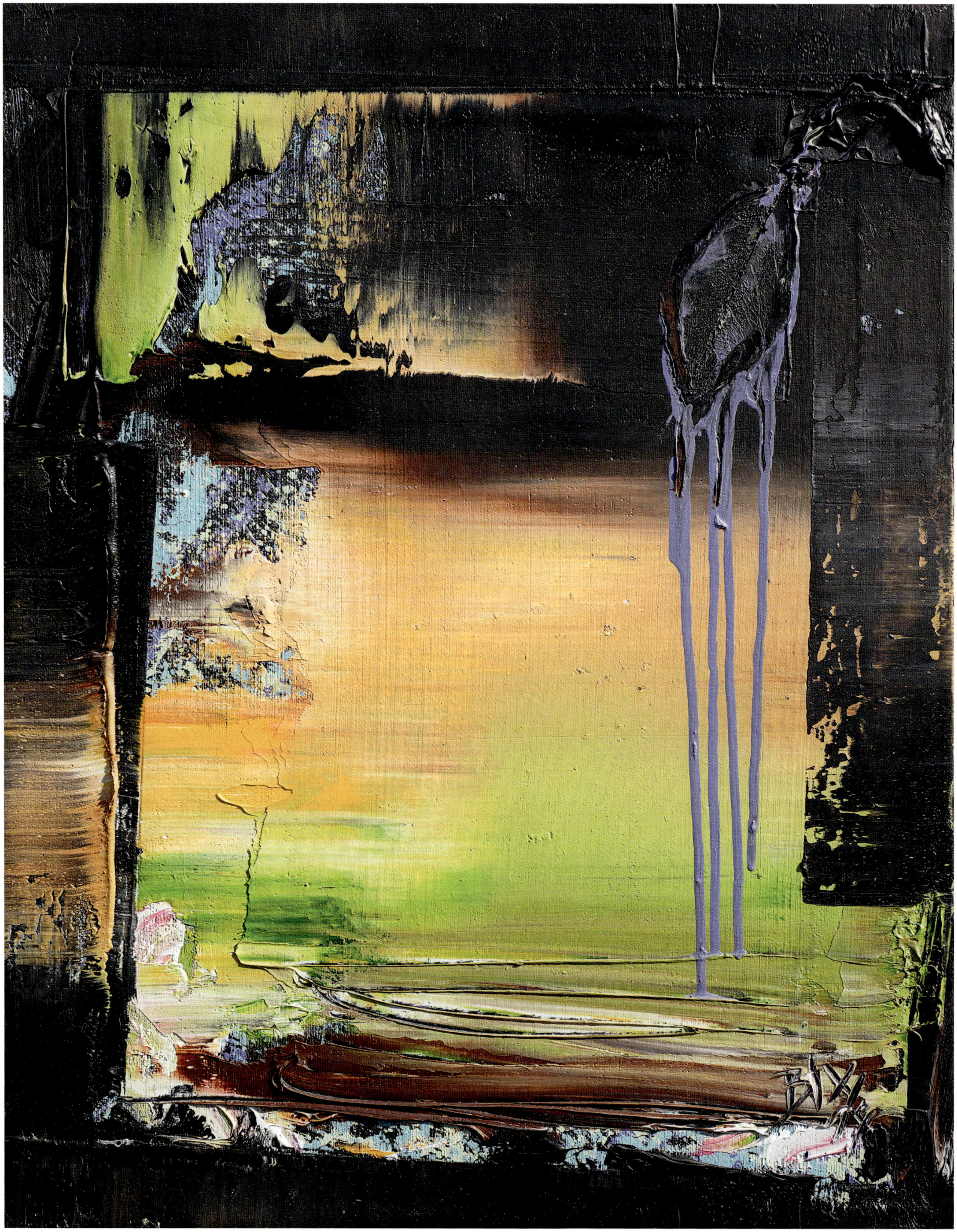

Discover, 2014
50 × 40 cm

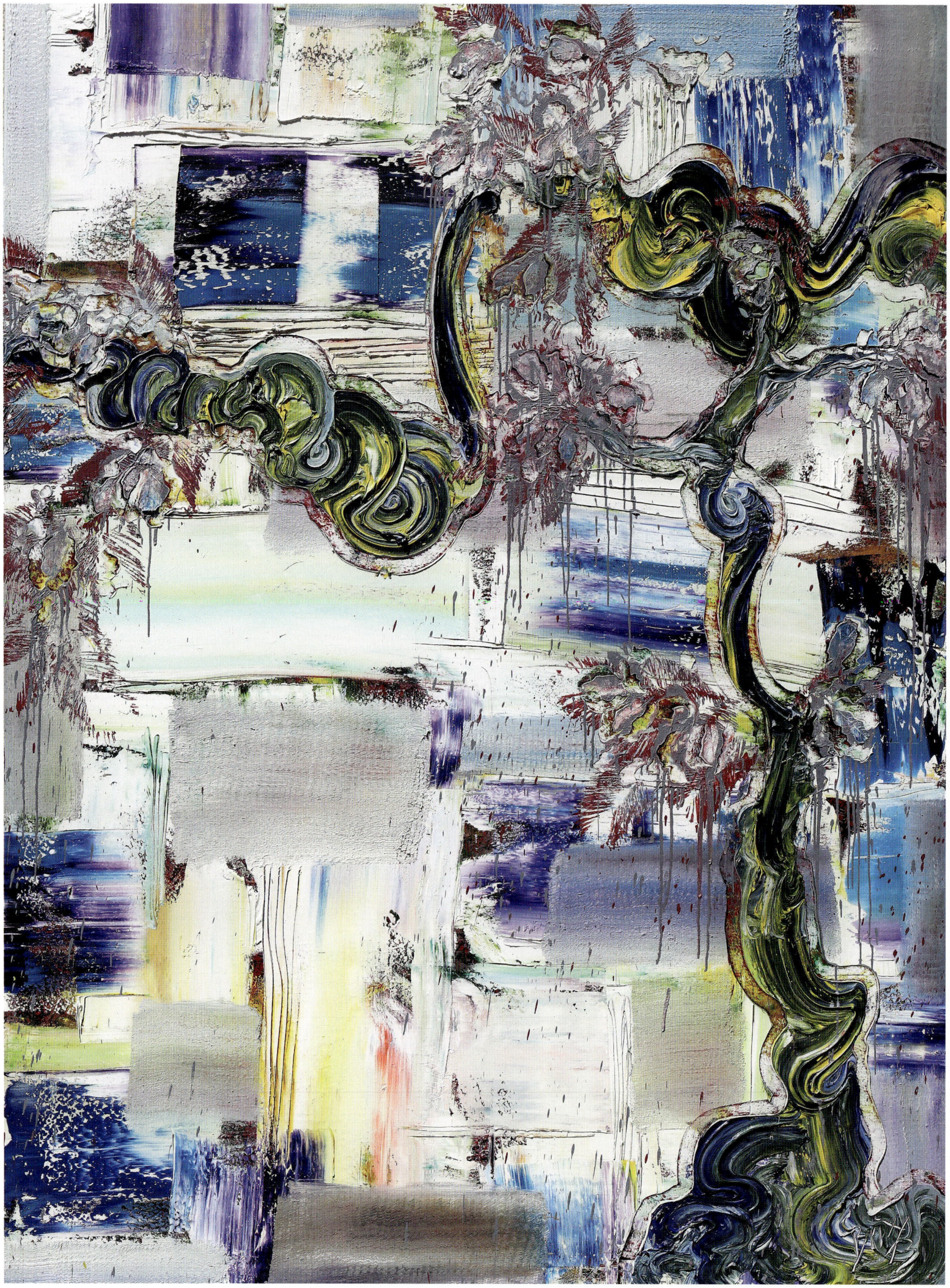

Discover, 2013
240 × 180 cm

Discover, 2012
140 × 180 cm

Discover, 2013
120 × 90 cm

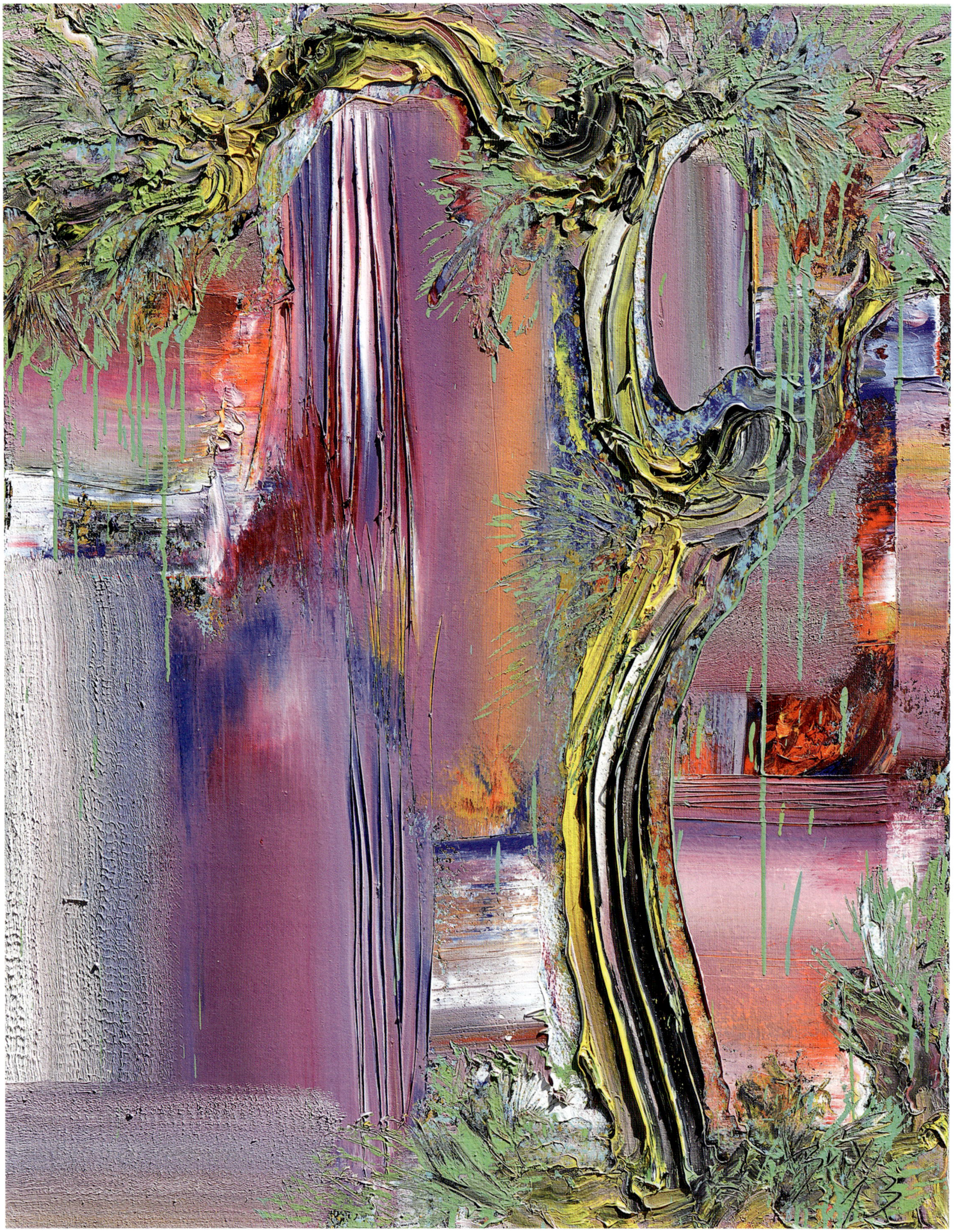

links | left
Discover, 2013
100 × 80 cm

rechts | right
Discover, 2012
180 × 120 cm

Discover, 2013
50 × 60 cm

Discover, 2013
50 × 60 cm

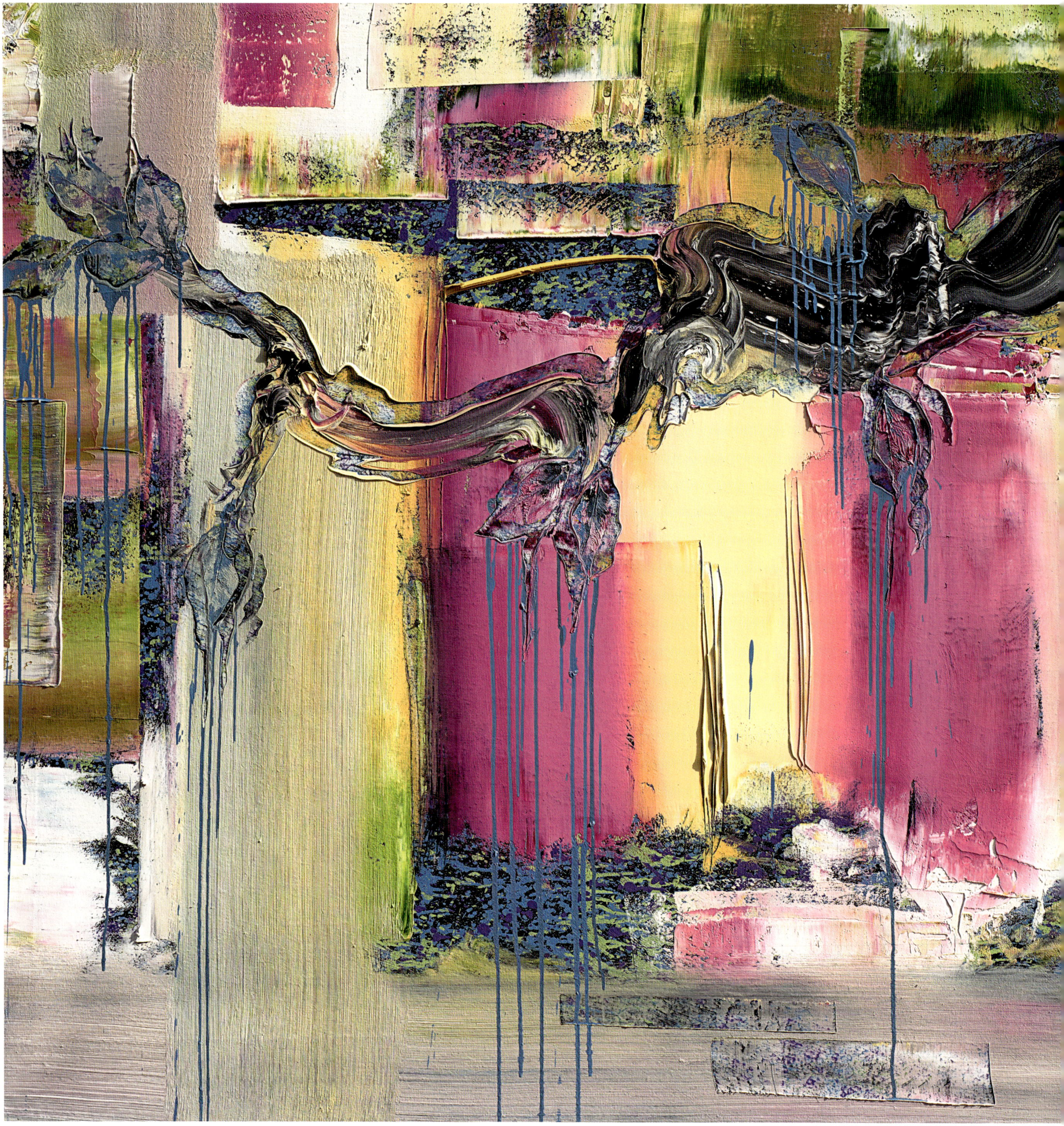

Discover, 2014
120 × 180 cm

Discover, 2014
100 × 140 cm

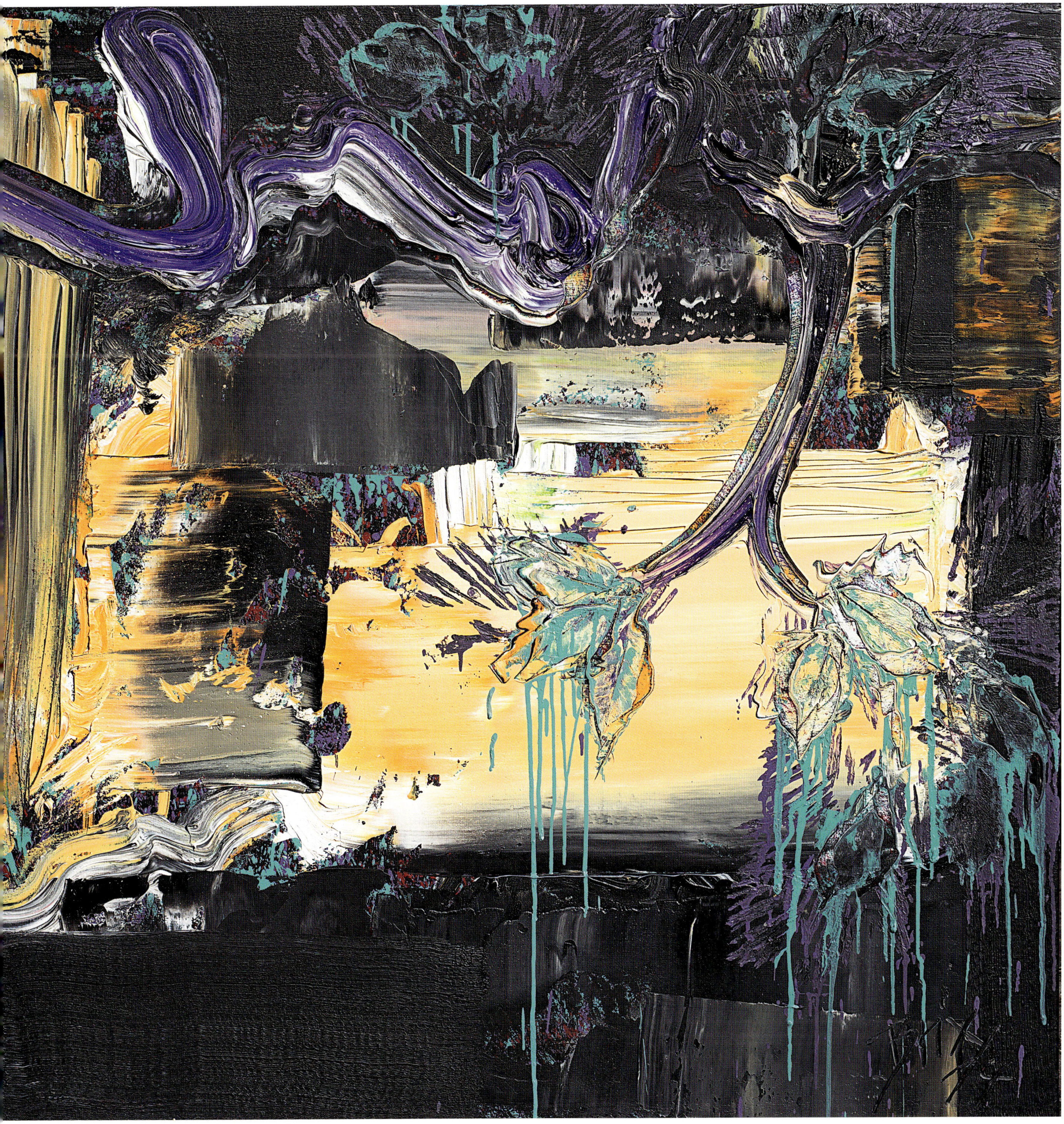

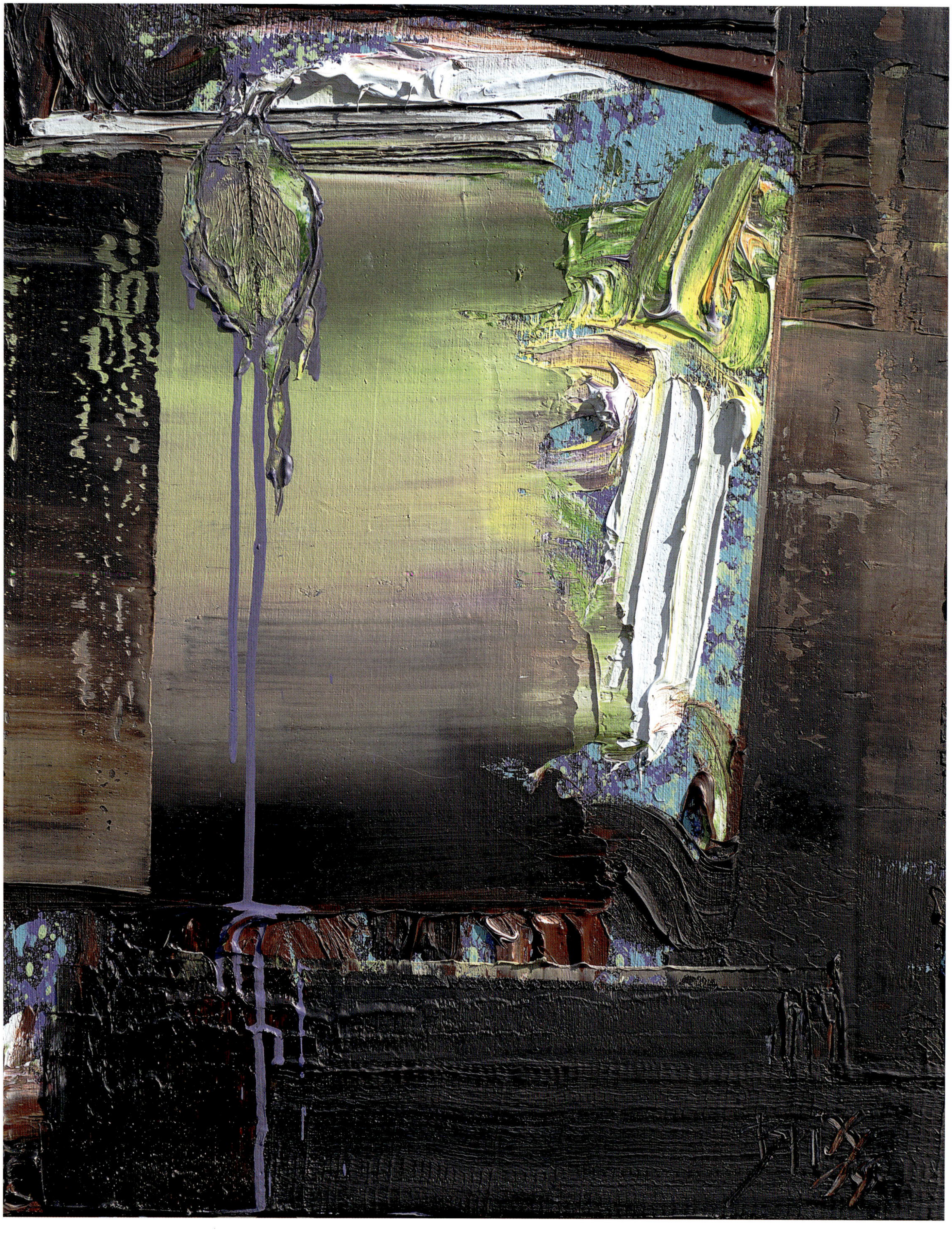

links | left
Discover, 2014
50 × 40 cm

rechts | right
Discover, 2014
120 × 90 cm

Discover, 2014
50 × 40 cm

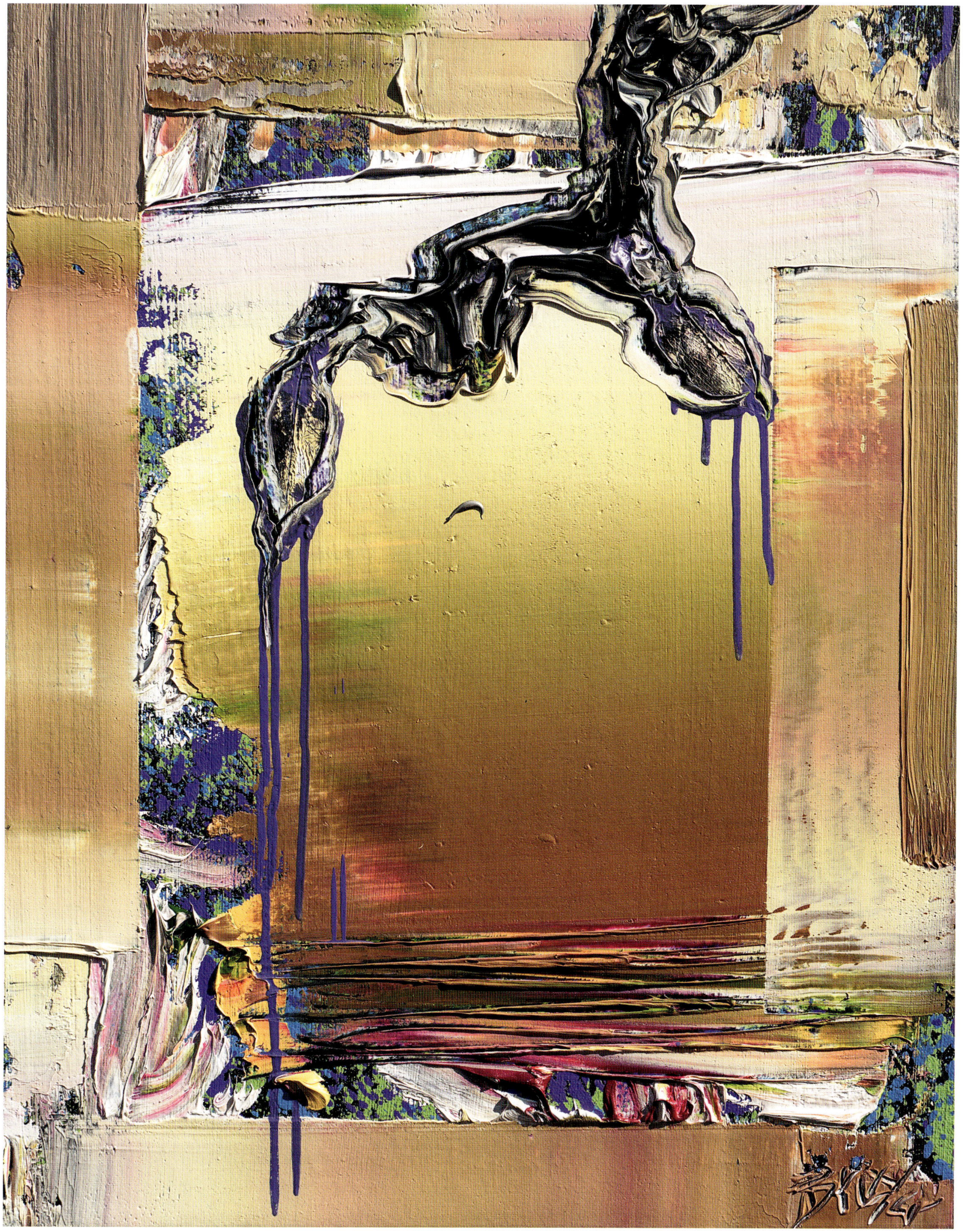

oben | above
Discover, 2012
100 × 200 cm

rechts | right
Discover, 2012
90 × 120 cm

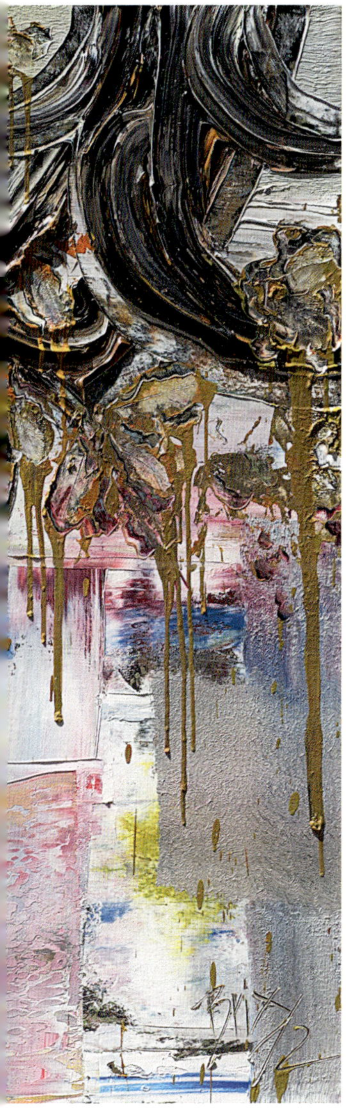

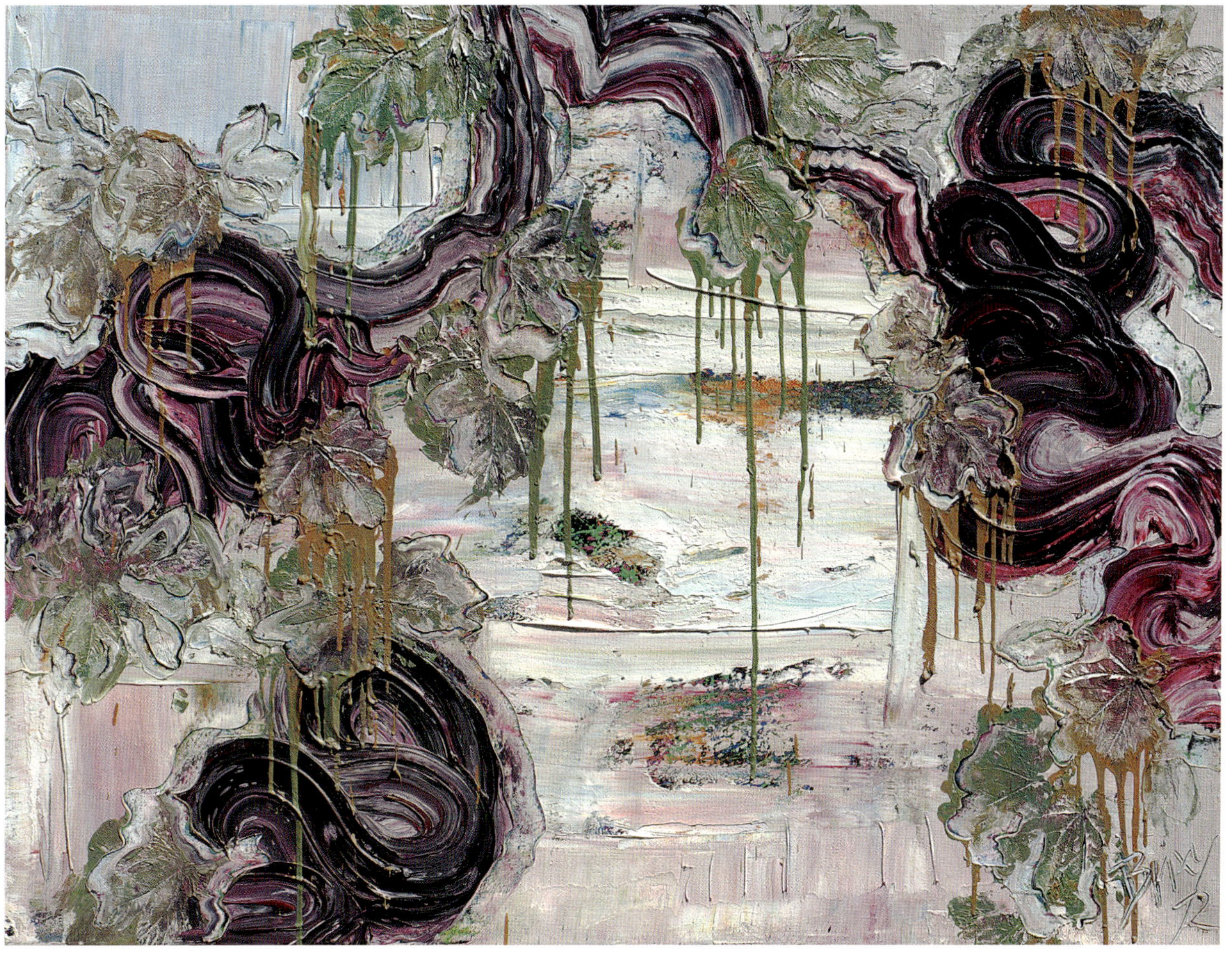

Discover, 2014
80 × 100 cm

Discover, 2014
je | each 160 × 50 cm

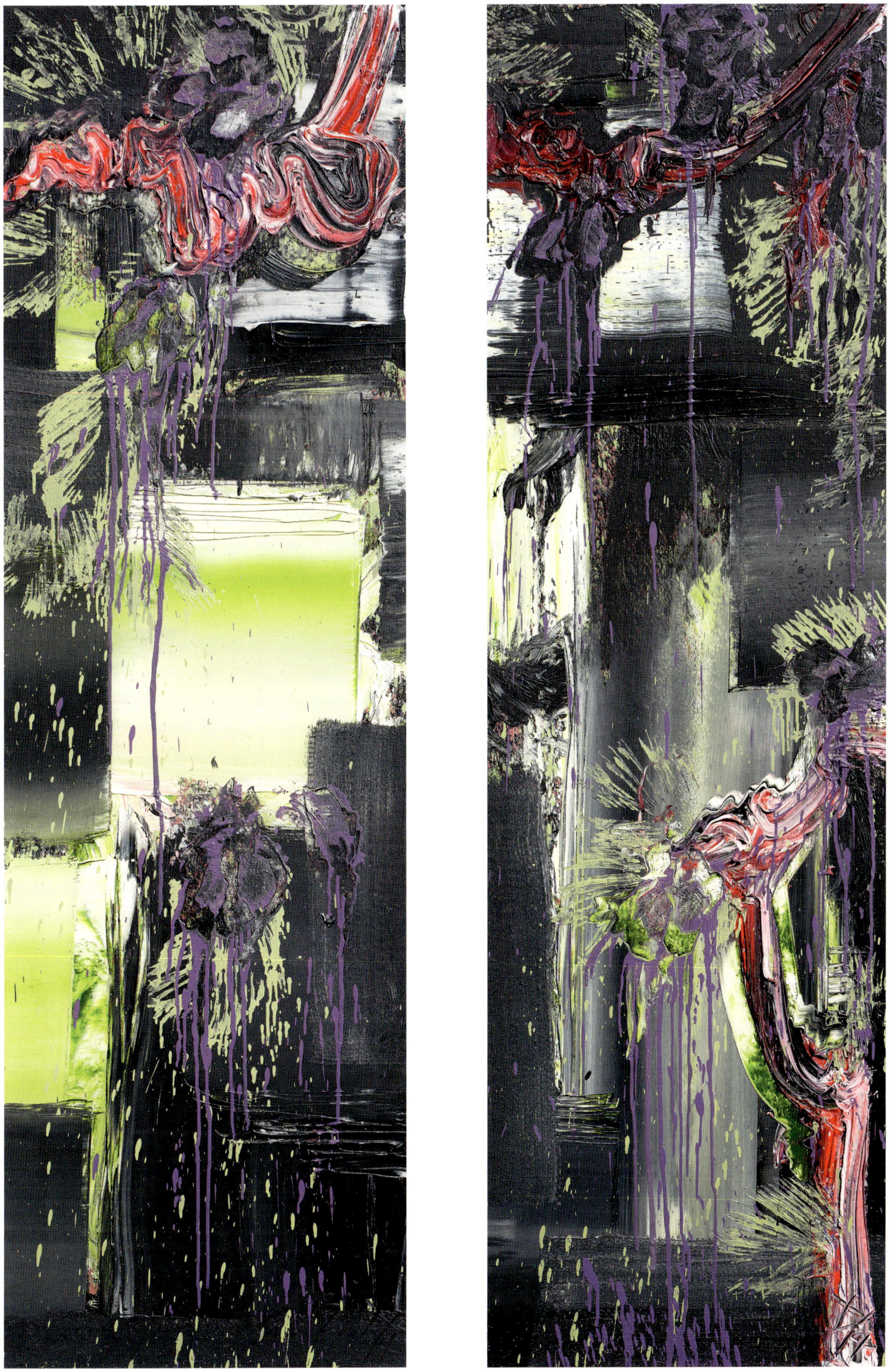

Discover, 2014
140 × 100 cm

Discover – Tryptichon, 2013
je | each 180 × 60 cm

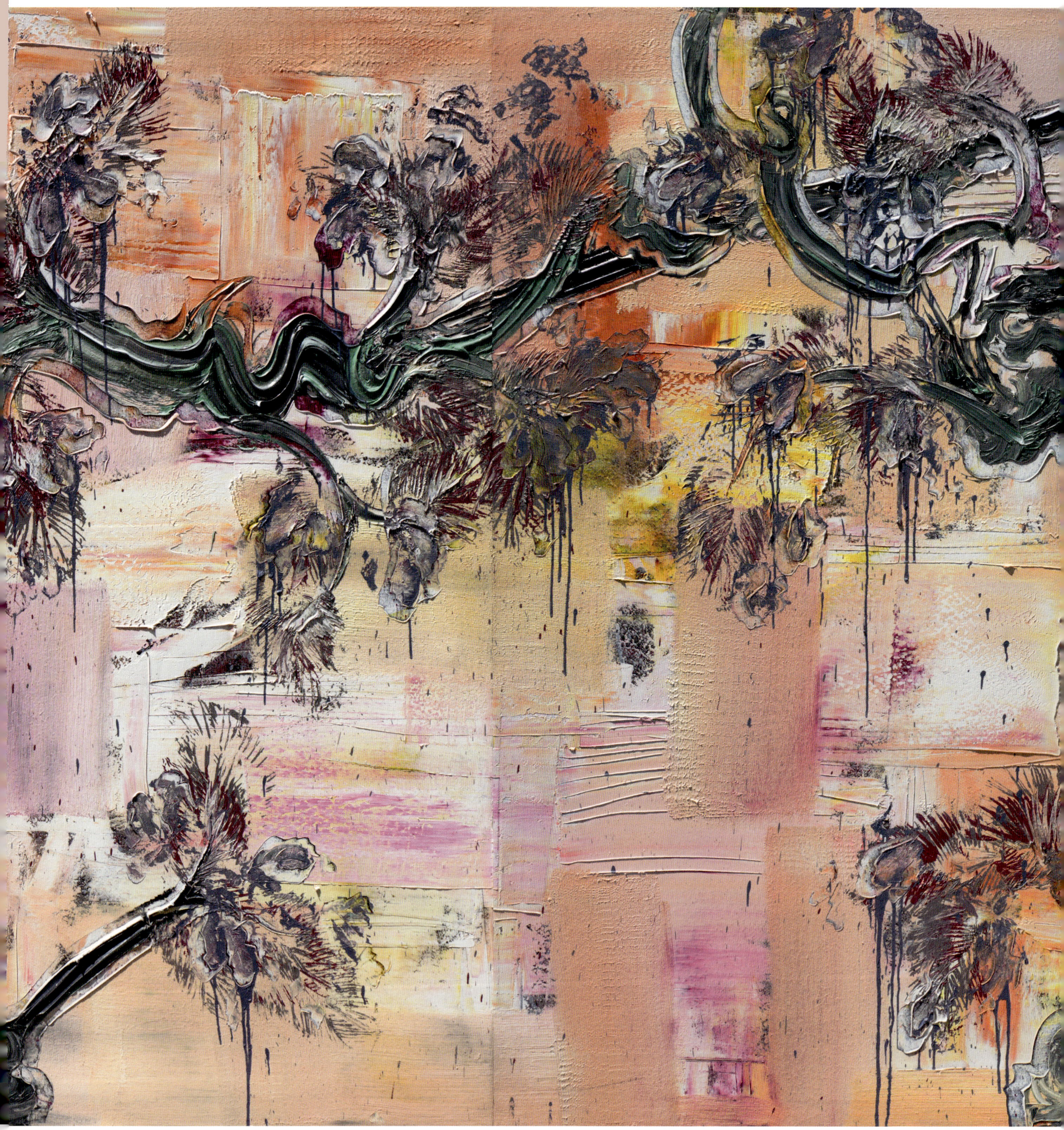

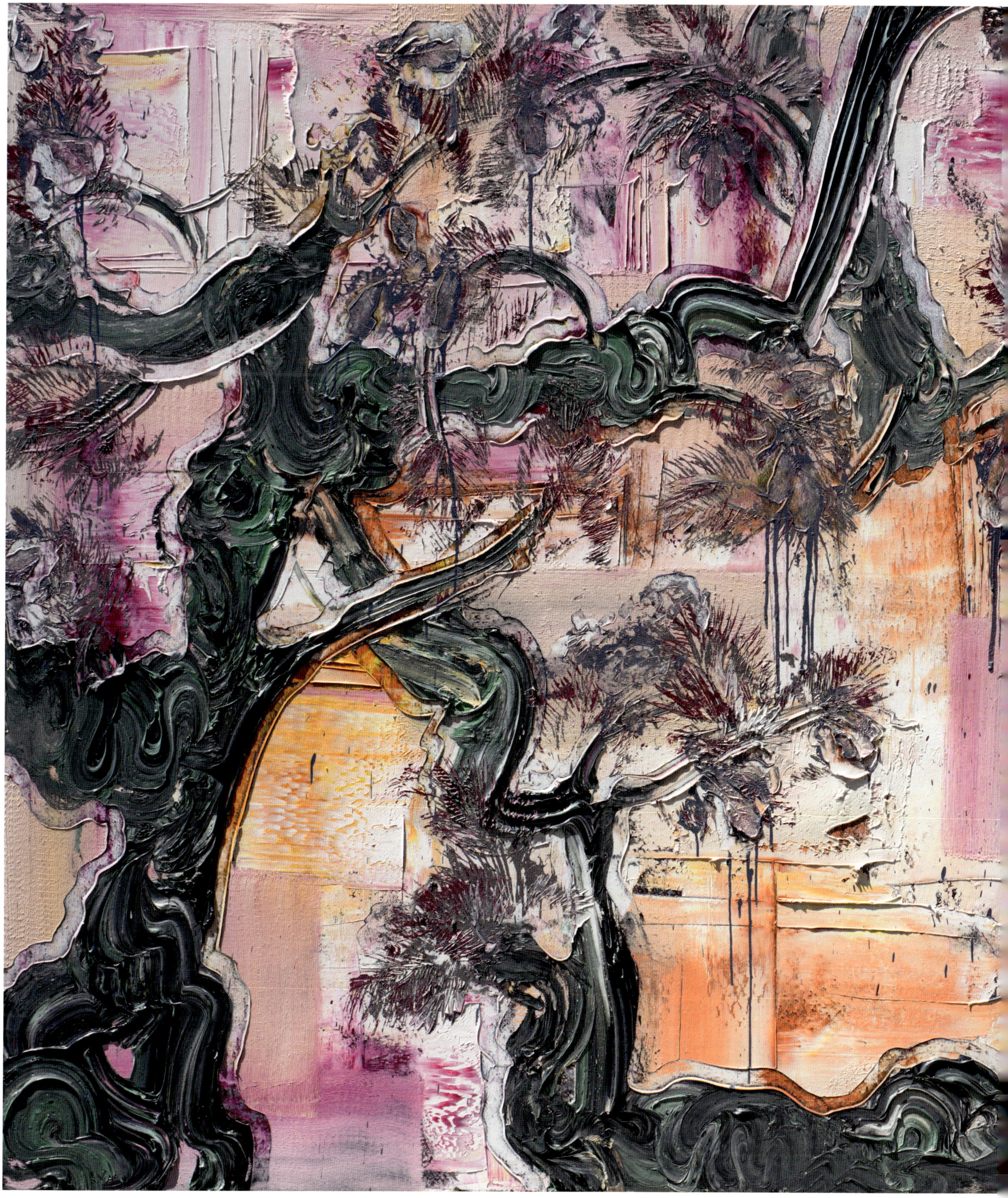

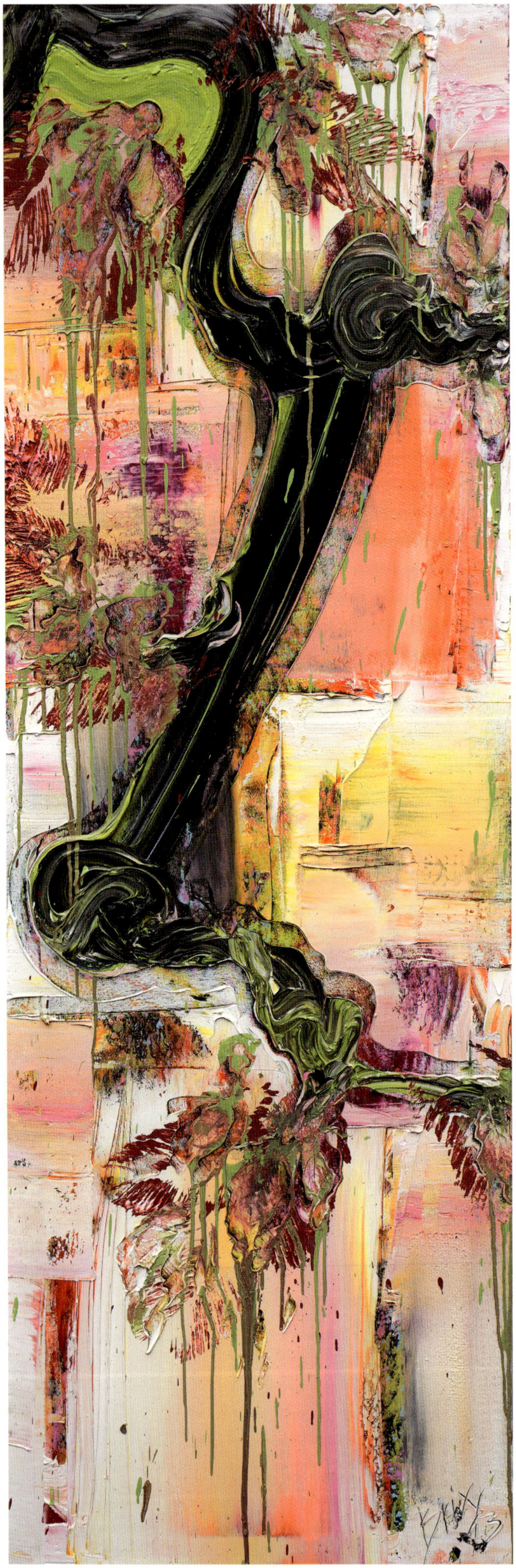

Discover, 2013
180 × 480 cm (zweiteilig)

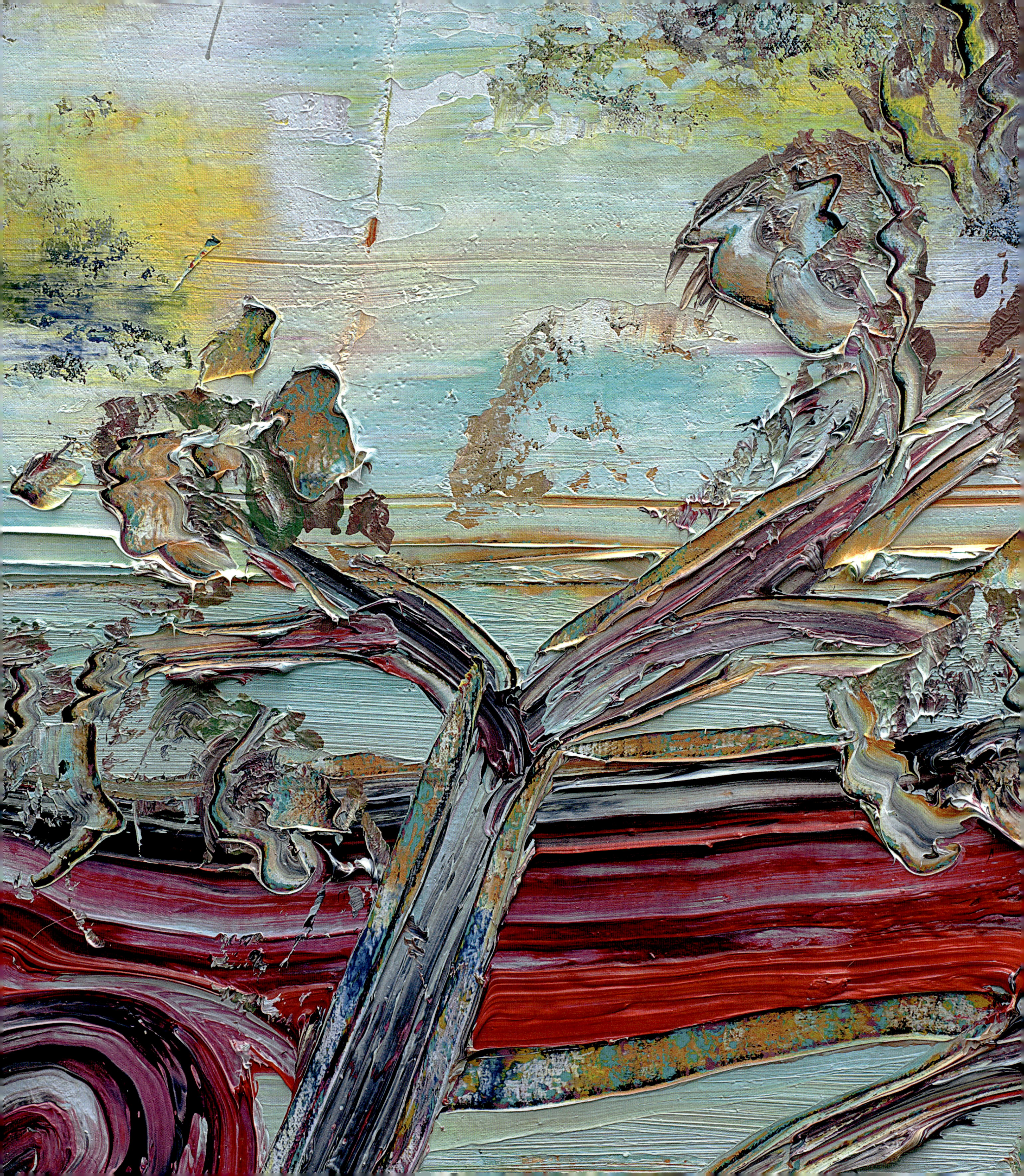

Discover, 2012
180 × 240 cm

130

131

Discover, 2014
70 × 90 cm

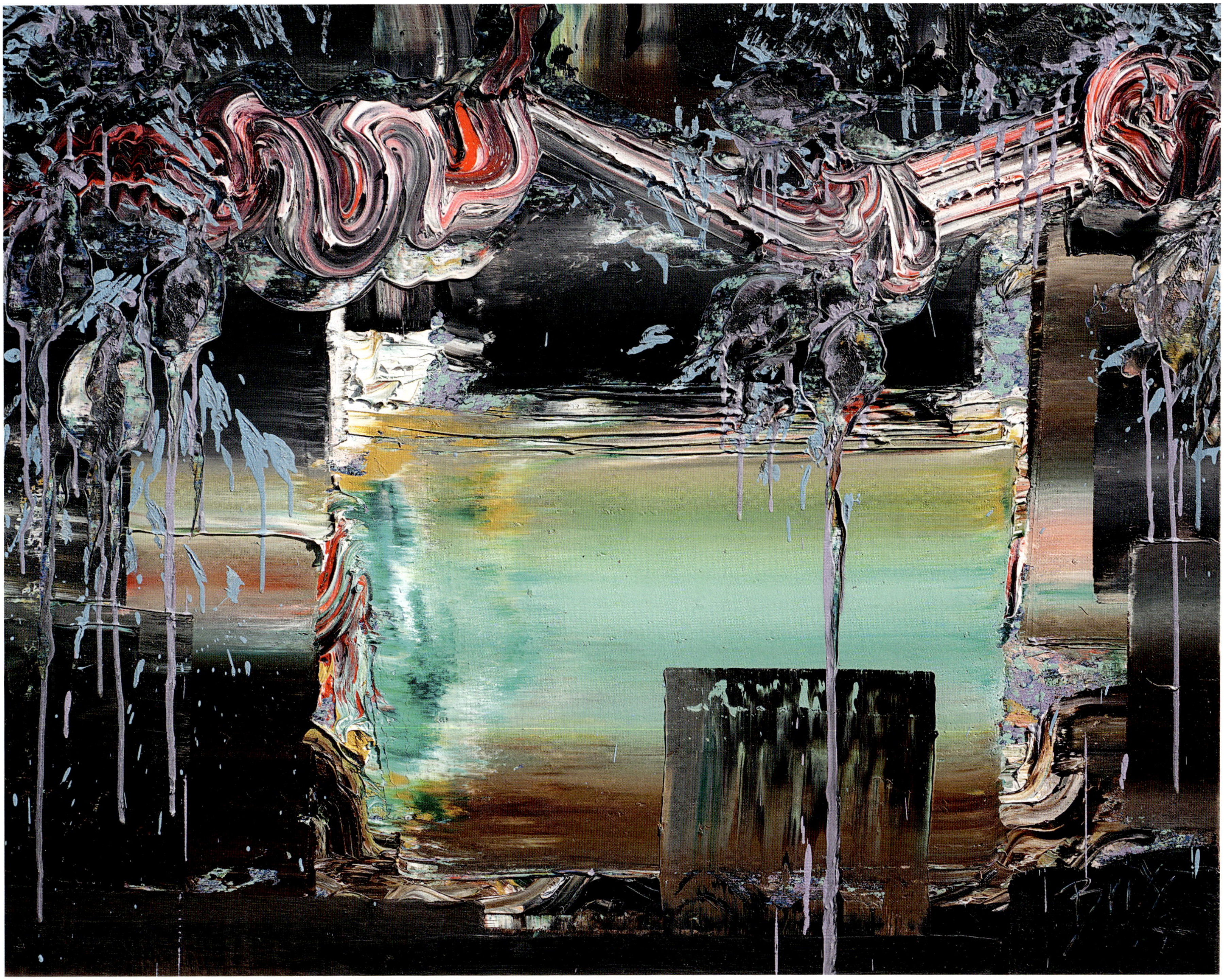

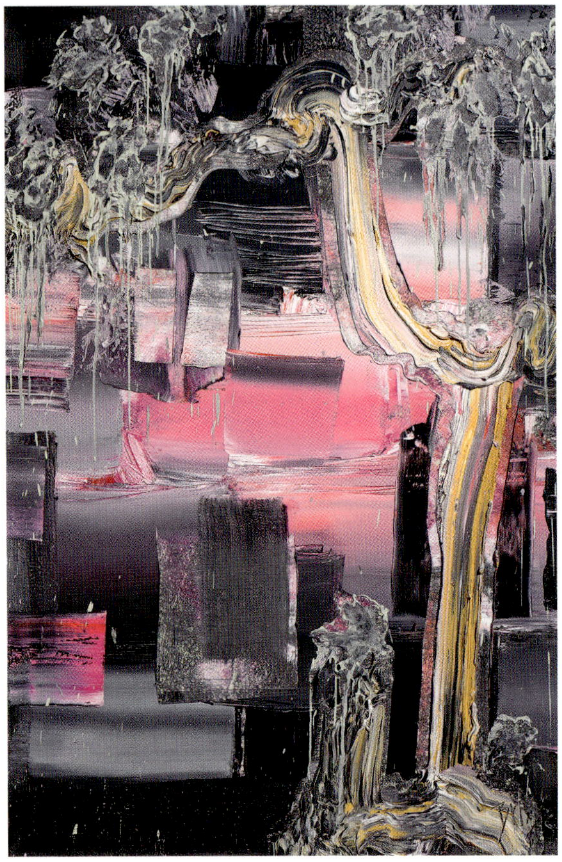
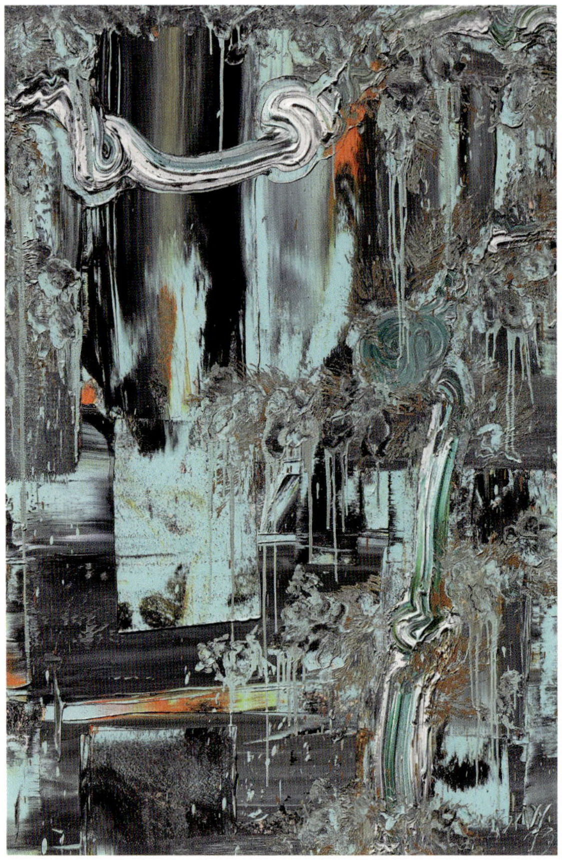
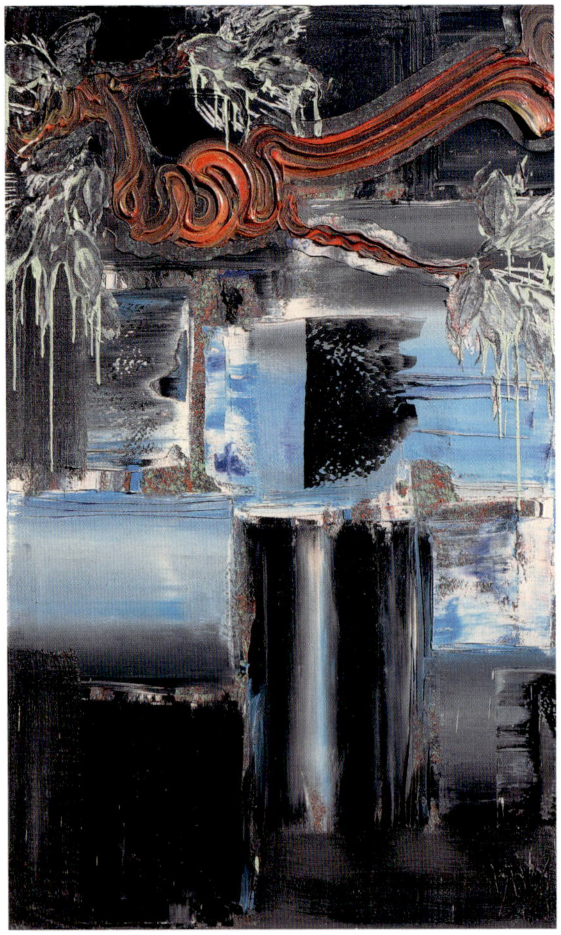
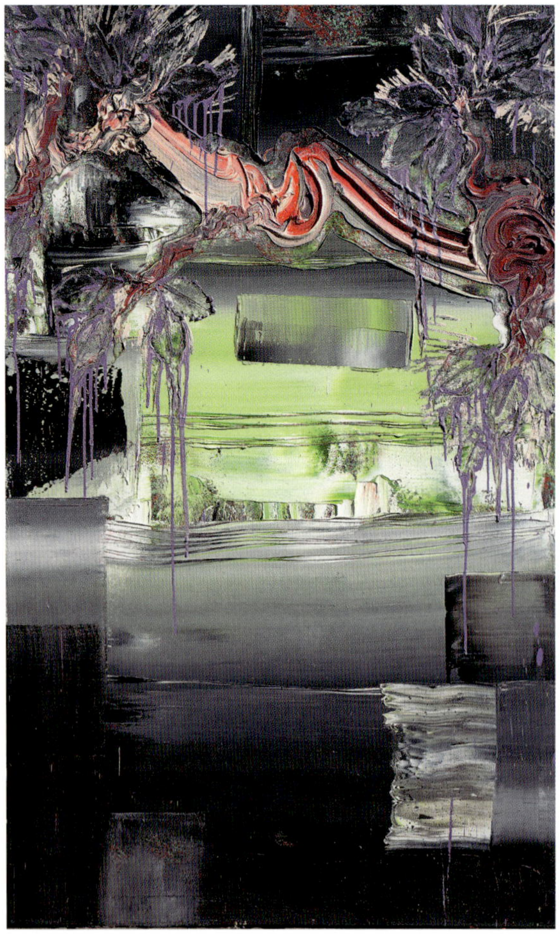

linke Seite oben links |
left page above left
Discover, 2014
180 × 120 cm

linke Seite oben rechts |
left page above right
Discover, 2013
180 × 120 cm

linke Seite unten |
left page below
Discover, 2014
je | each 160 × 100 cm

rechts | right
Discover, 2013
180 × 120 cm

Discover, 2014
je | each 80 × 100 cm

Discover, 2014
100 × 140 cm

Discover, 2012
120 × 300 cm

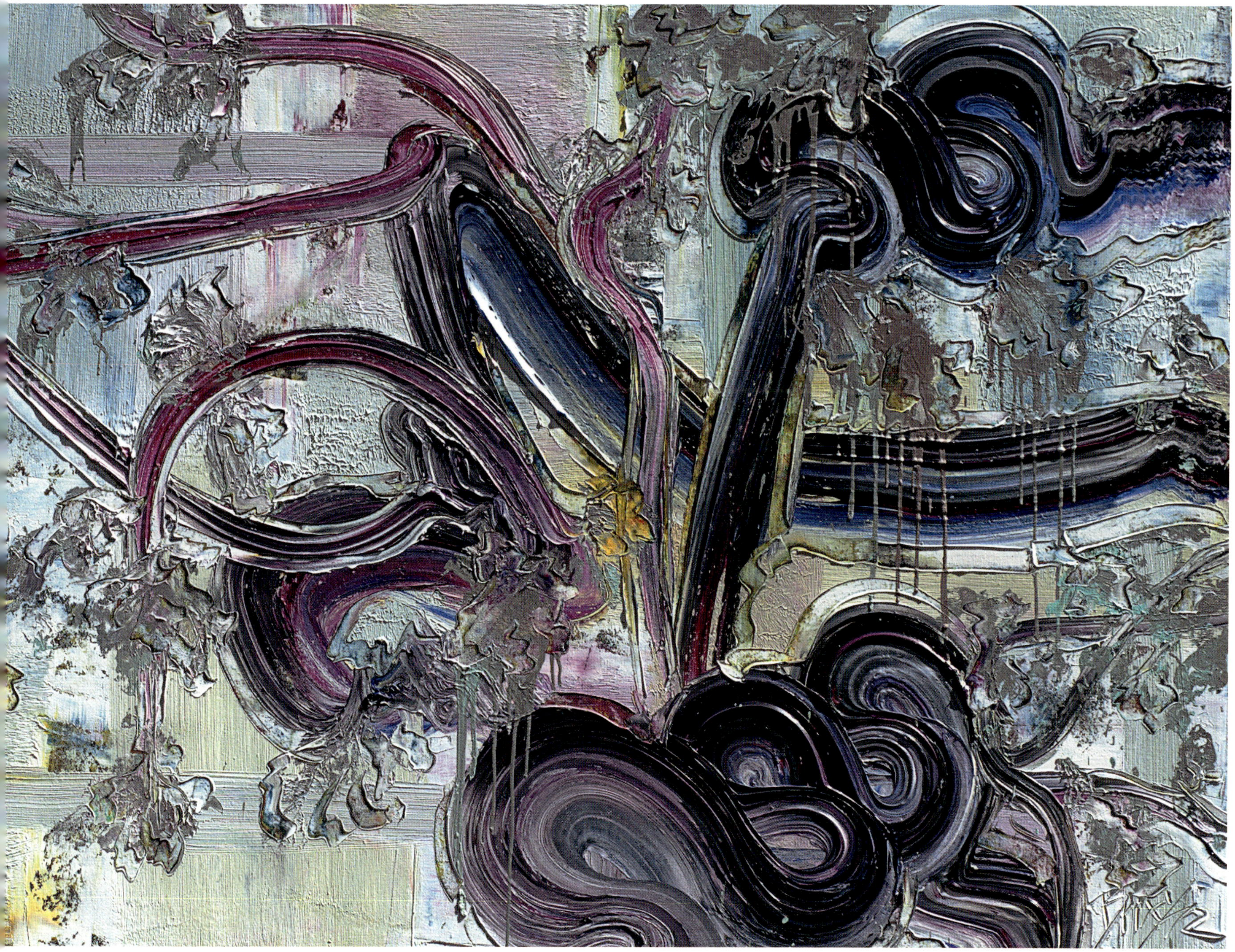

Discover, 2012
160 × 210 cm

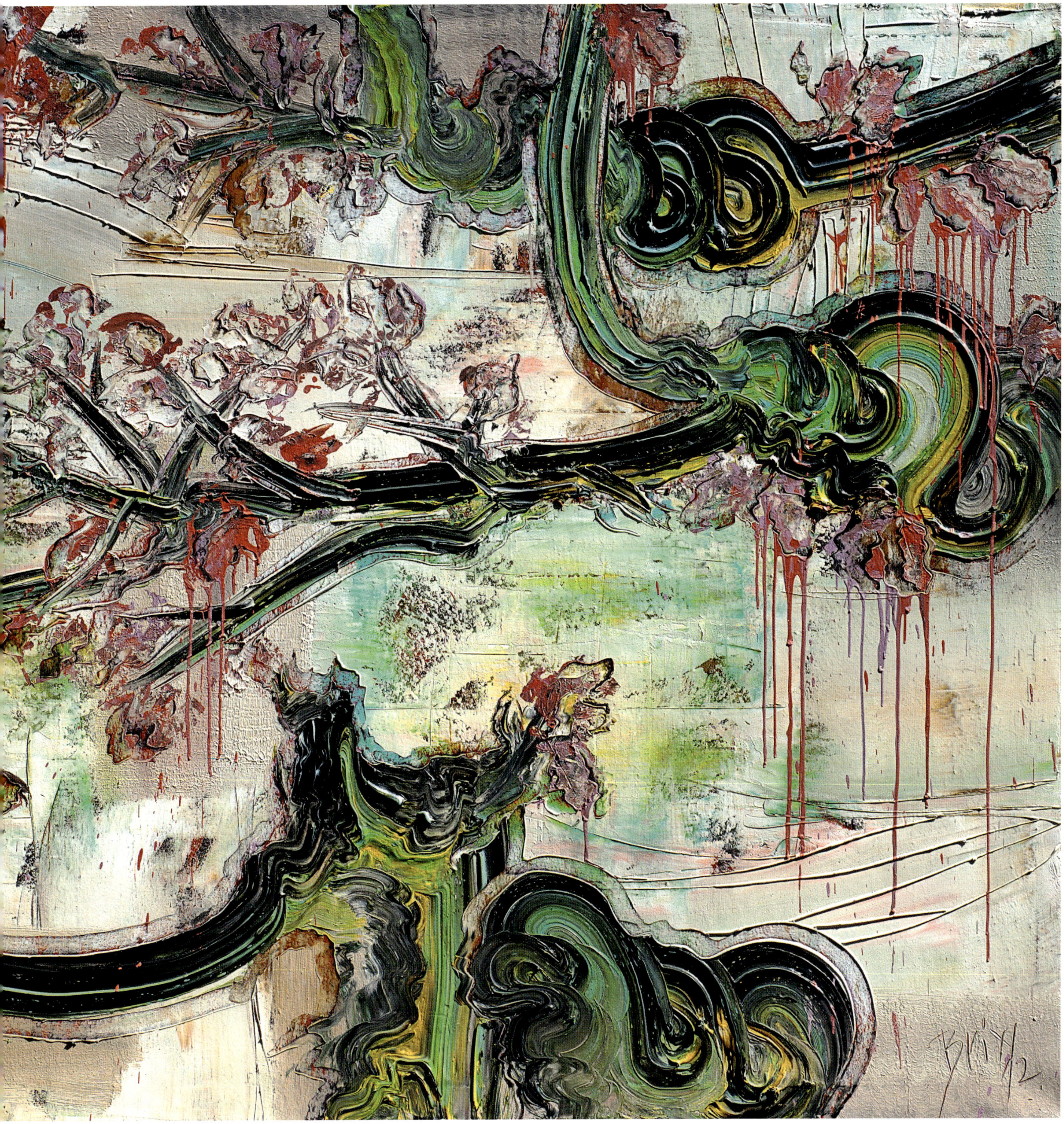

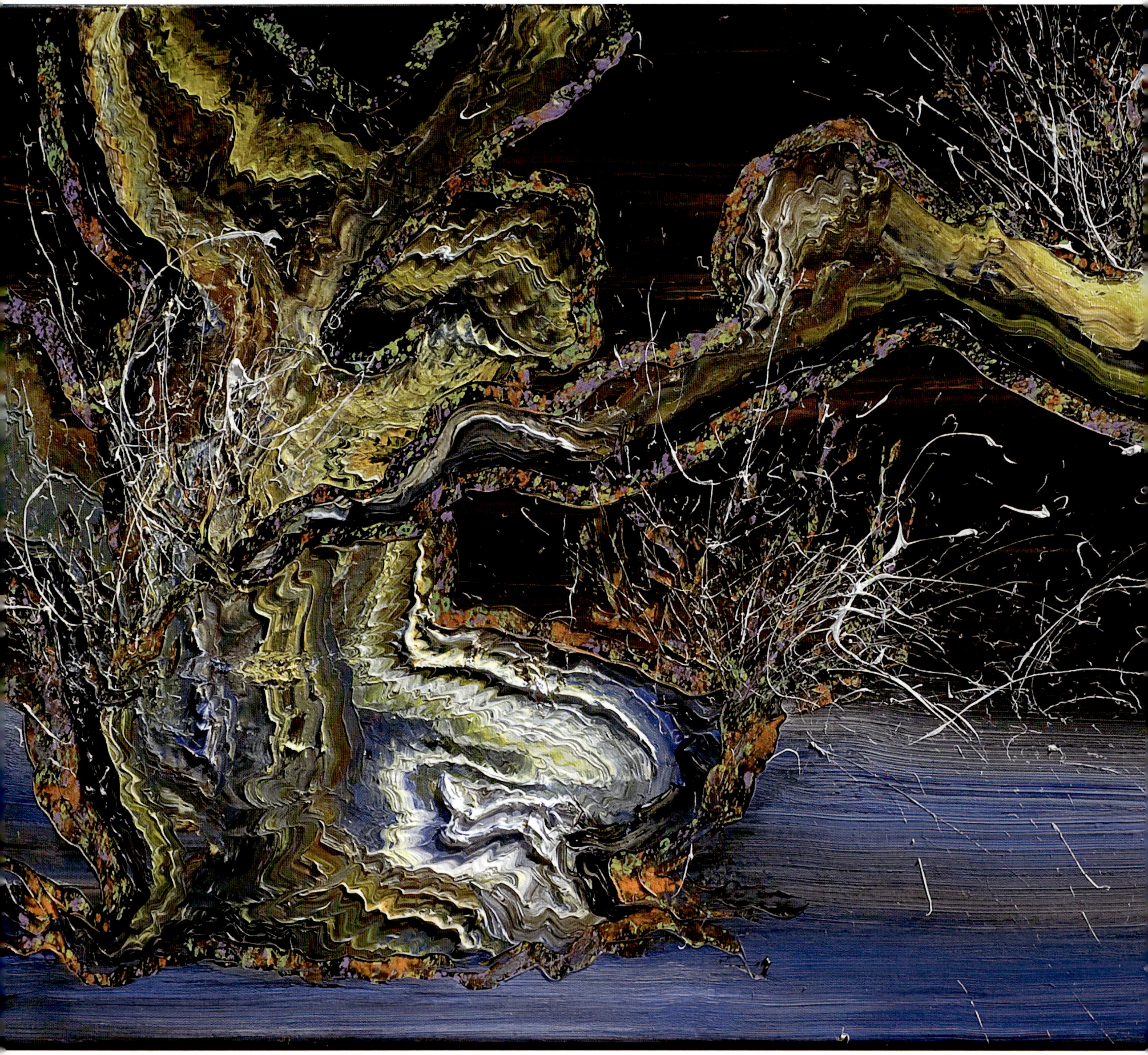

EDEN

Eden, 2011
130 × 480 cm

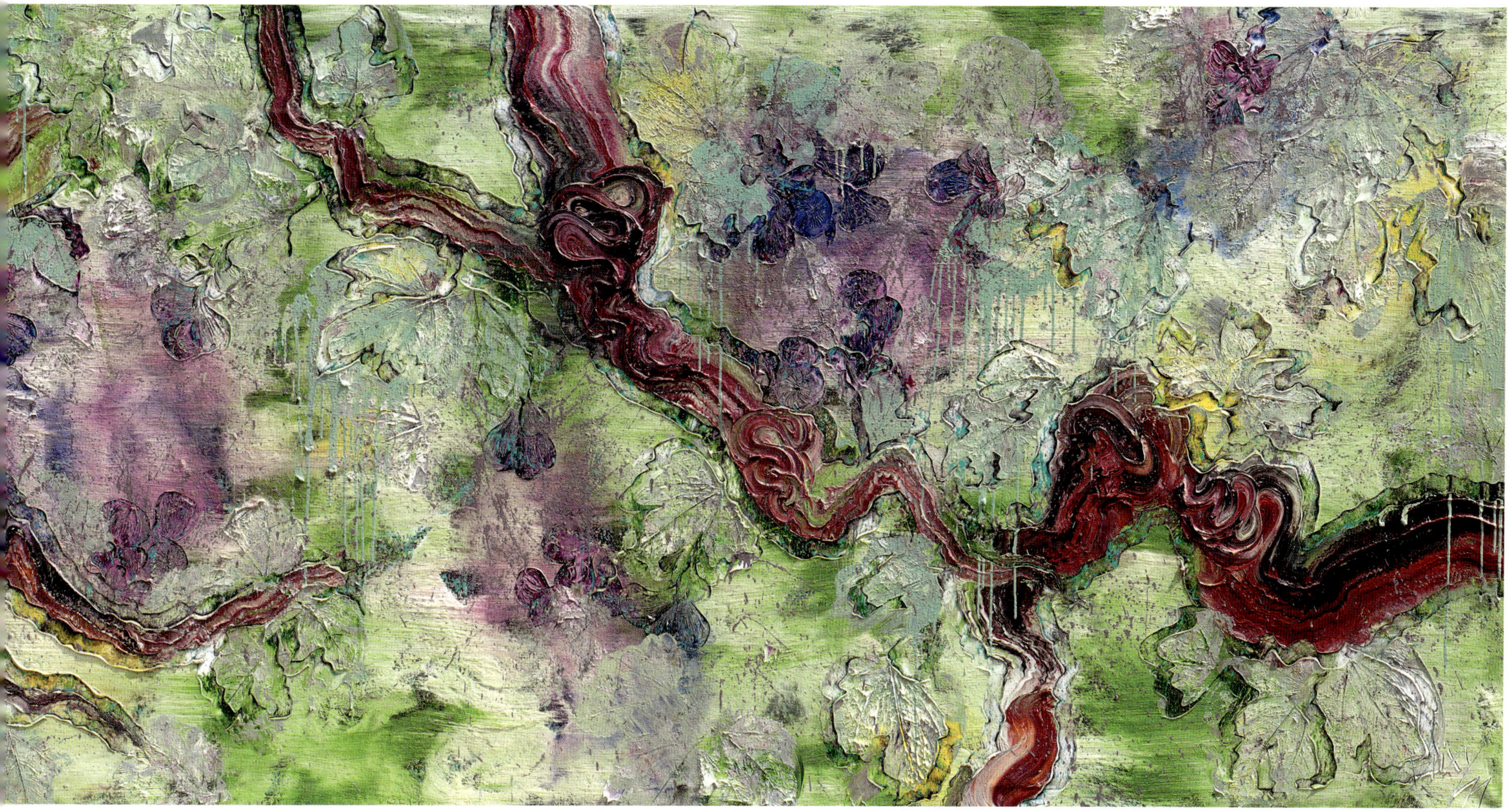

BRIXY IM PARADIES-LABOR

Reinhard Spieler

In den Bildern aus der Serie *Eden* nimmt uns Dietmar Brixy mit ins Paradies. Im extremen Breitformat stellt sich ein kinoartiger Panorama-Eindruck ein – der Betrachter kann mit seinen Augen regelrecht umherwandern in diesem Garten Eden. Wegsam ist dieses Gelände allerdings nicht: Ein undurchdringlicher Farben-Dschungel droht die Sinneswahrnehmung zu überfordern. Üppige Farbschlieren scheinen wie dampfende Wolken durch das Bild zu wabern und dabei ständig in ihren Farben zu changieren. Von verschiedensten Grüntönen über Blau bis hin zu Rosa und Violett reicht das irisierende Farbspektrum. Bizarr geformte Farben-Flüsse durchzucken wie Blitze das bunte Farbnebeldickicht, als gälte es, Energiestöße in dieses noch gestaltlose Urzeit-Paradies zu senden. Sind wir hier Zeugen der ersten Schritte der Genesis? Eines Zustandes noch vor dem eigentlich Garten Eden, noch bevor die Welt aus einer brodelnden Biomasse heraus Form angenommen hat, sich zu blühenden Wiesen, Blumen, Bäumen und Früchten formiert, Gestalt entwickelt? Hinein geraten mitten in eine Bio-Küche, in der sich, scheinbar zufällig, Moleküle zusammenfinden und vage Formen bilden, bis schließlich erste Blätter, Zweige oder Flussläufe entstehen?

Brixy erlaubt uns einen Blick in sein Paradies-Labor. Hier ist nicht der Schöpfer-Gott am Werk, sondern der Maler in seinem Atelier, und es geht nur im übertragenen Sinn um die Erschaffung der Welt, die Entstehung des Gartens Eden. Das Paradies des Malers ist das Bild, und wir blicken hier mitten in die Entstehung von Malerei, in das Werden und Entstehen malerischer Formen. In vielen Schichten wird die Farbe aufgetragen, noch vollkommen formlos wie die erste Ur-Materie. Schritt für Schritt werden Schichten wieder freigelegt, durch Wischen und Kratzen entstehen Formen, und neue, nun bewusst und kontrolliert angelegte Farbverläufe und -spuren. Mit verschiedensten Instrumenten, Pinsel, Spachtel, Kämmen und schließlich mit den Fingern bearbeitet Brixy die

BRIXY'S LABORATORY OF PARADISE

In his *Eden* series, Dietmar Brixy transports us to Paradise. The extremely wide formats create a cinematic panorama effect and allow the viewer's eyes to wander about in this Garden of Eden. However, the landscape is not very gentle: an impenetrable jungle of colors challenges the senses. Rich color blurs seem to wobble through the picture like misty clouds changing color all the time. The iridescent color spectrum ranges from diverse greens to blues, pinks, and violets. Bizarre rivers of color flash through the thick color fog like bolts of lightning as if they endeavored to send jerks of energy through this amorphous primeval paradise.

Are we witnesses to the first steps of Genesis? A stage of existence before the real Garden of Eden was created, before the world took shape from the seething biomass to form flowering meadows, plants, trees, and fruits and become form? Have we tumbled into a bio-kitchen in which molecules link seemingly without aim to create vague shapes at first until they finally turn into leaves, twigs, or rivers?

Brixy allows us to take a look at his laboratory of Paradise. Here, it is not the Creator-God who is at work, but the painter in his studio, and his paintings are only metaphors for the creation of the world, the creation of the Garden of Eden. The painting itself is the painter's paradise, and we are allowed glimpses into the creation of painting, into the birth of pictorial forms. The colors are superimposed in many layers, at the start completely shapeless like the first prime matter. Then, step by step, by wiping and scraping, the layers are uncovered again, forms come into existence, and new tracks and rivers of color appear fully planned and controlled by the painter. The color material is treated with diverse tools – brushes, spatulas, combs and eventually Brixy's fingers. Nature herself is also allowed to become articulate – fig leaves being pressed into the color mass and leaving their traces. In contrast to the biblical story they

Celeste, 2011
130 × 240 cm

Farbmaterie. Auch die Natur selbst kommt noch zu Wort – Feigenblätter werden in die Farbmasse hineingepresst und hinterlassen ihren Abdruck. Entgegen ihrer biblischen Geschichte verbergen sie hier nichts, sondern zeigen sich selbst in ihrer sinnlichen und ornamentalen Fülle.

Durch die reliefartige, pastose Farbschichtung wird der Prozess der Entstehung ablesbar – der Betrachter wird zum Zeugen bei der Entstehung des Bildes. Nicht nur der fertige Garten Eden, sondern vor allem der Prozess seiner Entstehung ist das Thema dieser Bilder. Malerei, so die

do not hide anything, but expose themselves in their sensuous ornamental richness.

By deciphering the relief of the thick layers of color, the process of creation can be traced – the viewer becoming witness to the creation of the painting. It is not only the finished Garden of Eden, but the process of its genesis which is the thematic core of these pictures. Here Dietmar Brixy reveals his basic idea that painting is not a finished product, but an ever-changing process in development, thus becoming an allegory of Nature herself whose never-ending metamorphosis is its only constant.

Whereas the paintings from the Eden series above all show the potential to change and the primeval and unbroken force of the bio or rather color mass, the bamboo pictures reveal a different stage of genesis. Here, the clear linear forms of the bamboo plants structure the amorphous mass of colors. Like an architectural skeleton, they move through the color mists and give order and stringency to the composition mediating between the format and the subject – in the round tondi by curving lines, in the square pictures in a straighter direction. Their relief gives an additional physical stability to the composition and so underlines the concept of a supporting structure.

When looking at Brixy's paintings, Monet comes to mind: he initially turned the luscious thicket of plants into a real garden paradise, before transforming it into shimmering color visions in his grandiose pictures of the water lilies. It seems, however, as if Brixy had moved Monet's gardens further east. The color combinations evoke Asian cultures. Bamboo, in particular, is indigenous to Asia. In Brixy's representations, the home of this plant is experienced directly, the clear purism of the bamboo stems in the paintings reminding us of Chinese or Japanese calligraphy – the expressive formations of branches or rivers in the Eden series incidentally having the same effect, by reminding us in their ornamental structures of Asian landscape paintings as well as the clear spirituality of Zen gardens.

These, die Brixy hier formuliert, ist kein fertiges Produkt, sondern ständig sich verändernder und entwickelnder Prozess – und darin ein Gleichnis zur Natur, die als einzige Konstante die ewige Verwandlung in sich trägt.

Während die Bilder aus der *Eden*-Serie vor allem dieses Verwandlungspotenzial, die urwüchsige und ungebremste Kraft der Bio- oder vielmehr der Farbmasse zeigen, vermitteln die *Bamboo*-Bilder eine andere Genesis-Stufe. Hier strukturieren die klaren, linearen Formen der Bambus-Rohre die ungestaltete Farbmasse. Wie ein architektonisches Gerüst durchziehen sie die Farbnebel und verleihen der Komposition Ordnung und Strenge, vermitteln zwischen den Formaten und der Darstellung – bei den runden Tondi durch gebogene Verläufe, bei den rechteckigen Bildern durch eher orthogonale Ausrichtung. Ihre reliefartige Ausformung gibt der Komposition zusätzlich eine physische Stabilität, die den Eindruck einer tragenden Struktur unterstreicht.

Man kann bei Brixys *Eden*-Bildern an den späten Monet denken, der das überbordende Pflanzendickicht zunächst als paradiesischen Garten in Wirklichkeit angelegt hat, bevor er es dann in seinen grandiosen Seerosenbildern in flirrenden Farbvisionen verwandelte. Doch es scheint, als habe Brixy die Monet'schen Gärten weiter nach Osten verlegt. Nicht nur die Farbkombinationen lösen Assoziationen an asiatische Gefilde aus. Bambus ist vor allem in Asien heimisch. In Brixys Darstellung wird diese Heimat unmittelbar erfahrbar, wenn er die Bambus-Rohre in präzisem Purismus wie chinesische oder japanische Kalligraphien ins Bild setzt – wie im übrigen auch die expressiven Ast- oder Flusslauf-Formationen der Eden-Serie an die ornamentale Linienführung asiatischer Landschaftsbilder und nicht zuletzt auch an die spirituelle Klarheit von Zen-Gärten denken lassen.

So ist Brixys *Eden* ein ebenso individueller wie exotischer Paradiesgarten, der uns nicht nur einen Einblick in den Urzustand der Natur gewährt, sondern vor allem in die Entstehung von Malerei: Malerei als Gewinnung von Form und Gestalt aus reiner Farbmaterie - und aus der Verbindung von malerischen Errungenschaften der beginnenden Moderne mit fernöstlicher Spiritualität.

Thus, Brixy's Garden of Eden is an individual, as well as an exotic paradise garden that gives the viewer a deeper insight, not only into the prime state of the existence of nature, but above all into the birth of painting: painting as the creation of form and substance from color – and the union with pictorial achievements at the beginning of modern painting.

Dusk, 2009
120 × 240 cm

Mission, 2009
180 × 60 cm

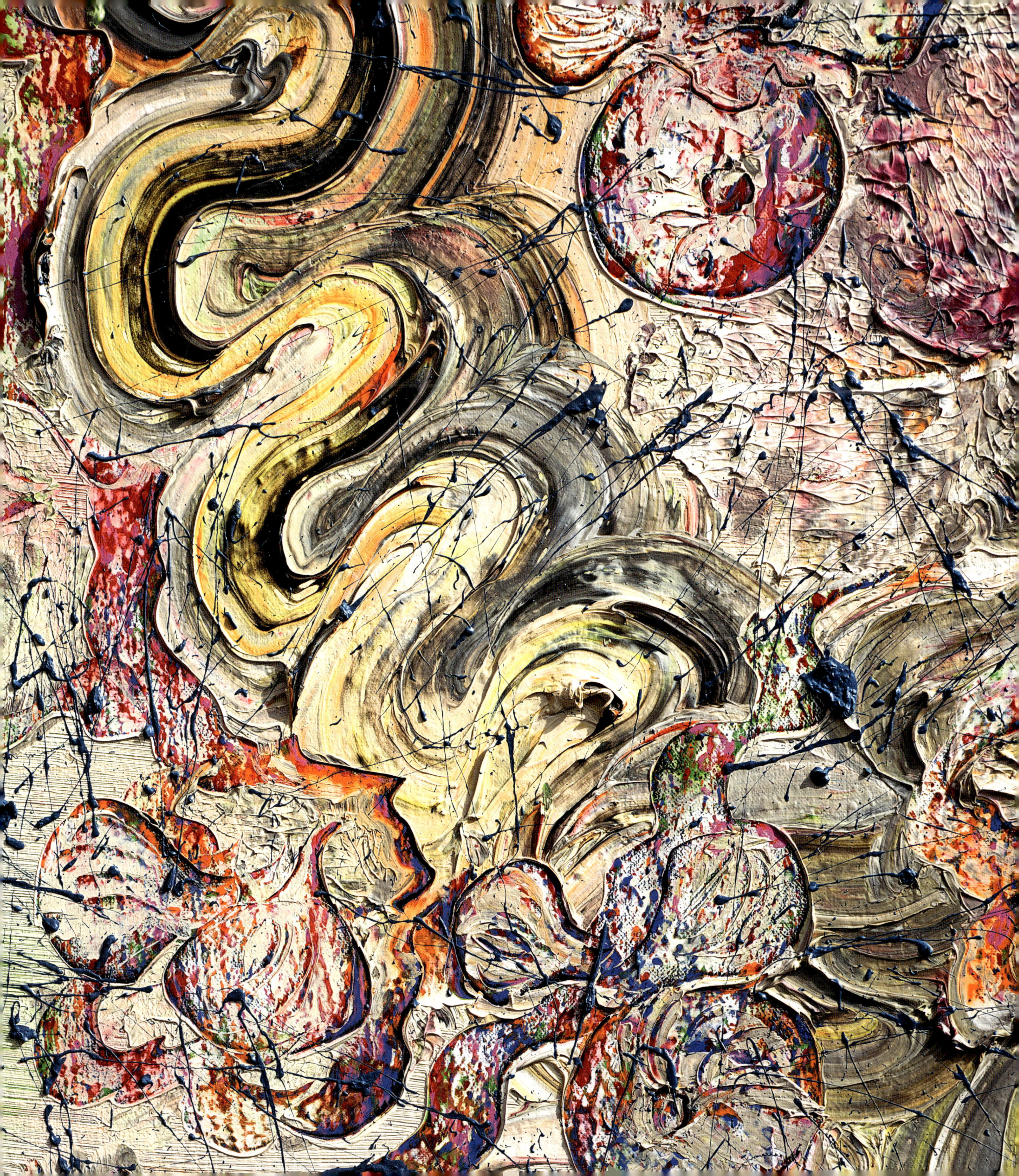

150

151

oben | above
Winter Bamboo Bubble, 2011
Ø 120 cm

rechts | right
Hubba Bubba Bamboo
Bubble, 2011
Ø 160 cm

Moulin Rouge Bamboo
Bubble, 2011
Ø 120 cm

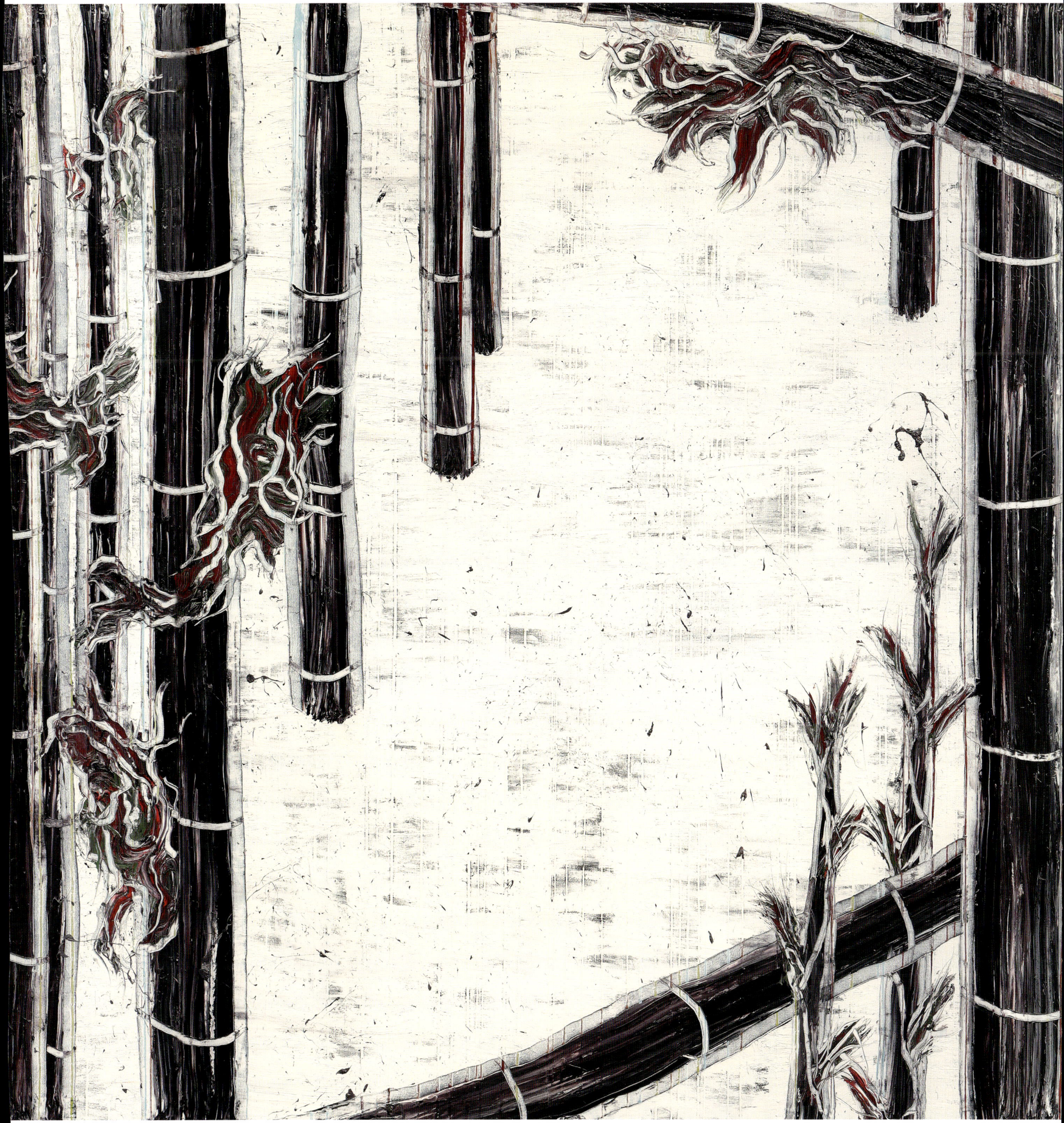

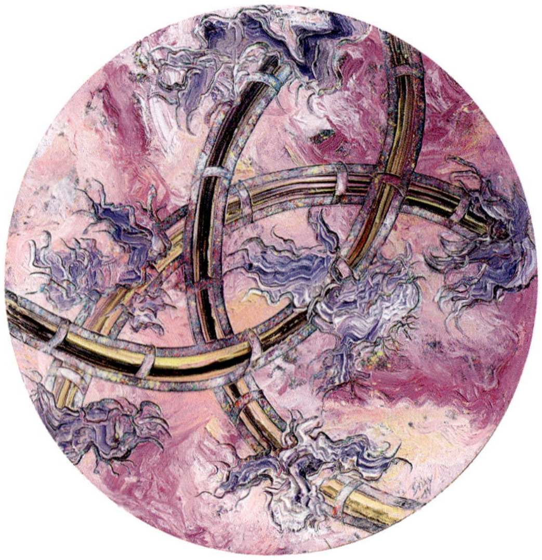

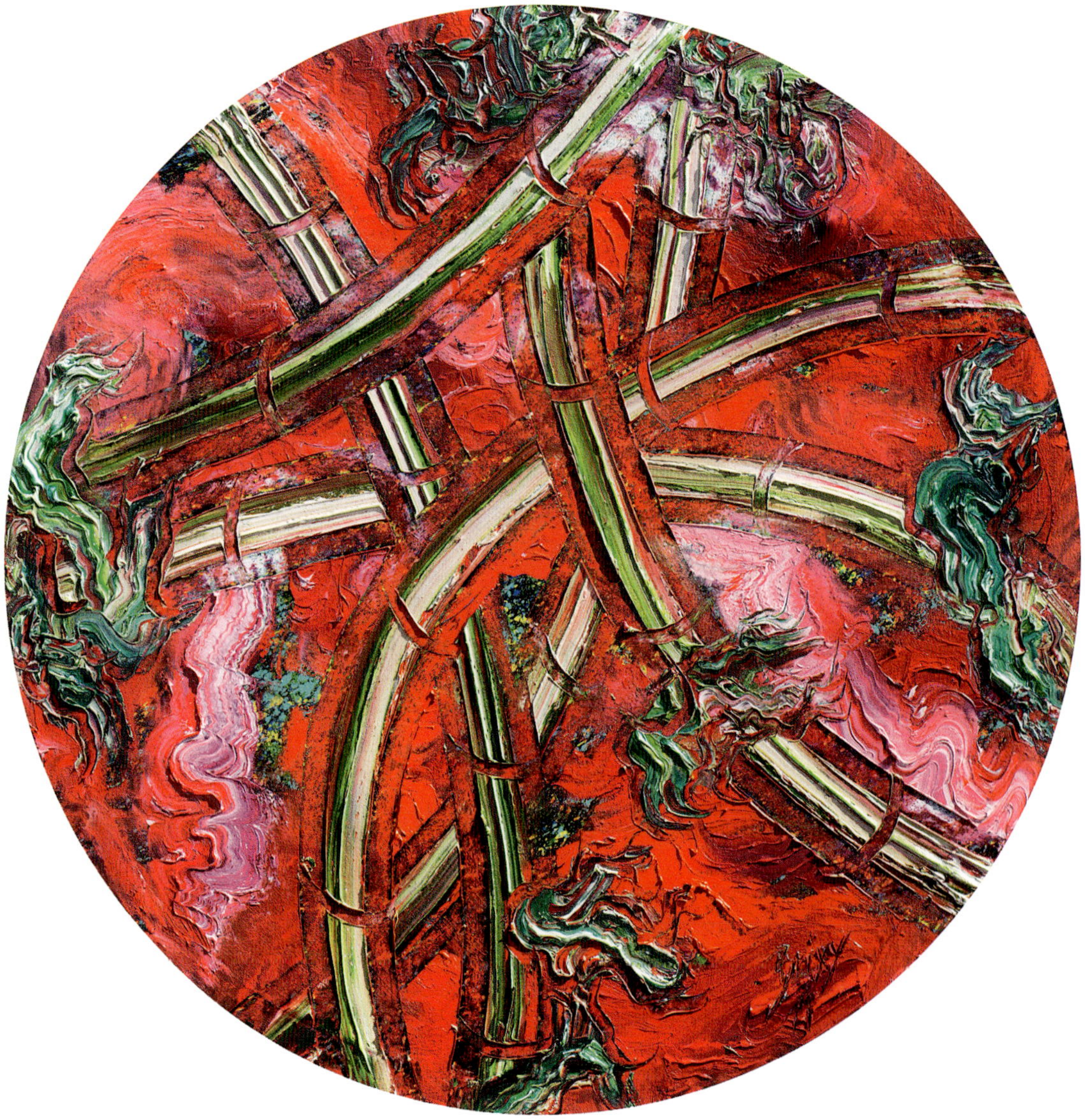

Dreaming Bamboo Bubble, 2006
⌀ 200 cm

Lichtung, 2007
240 × 540 cm (dreiteilig)

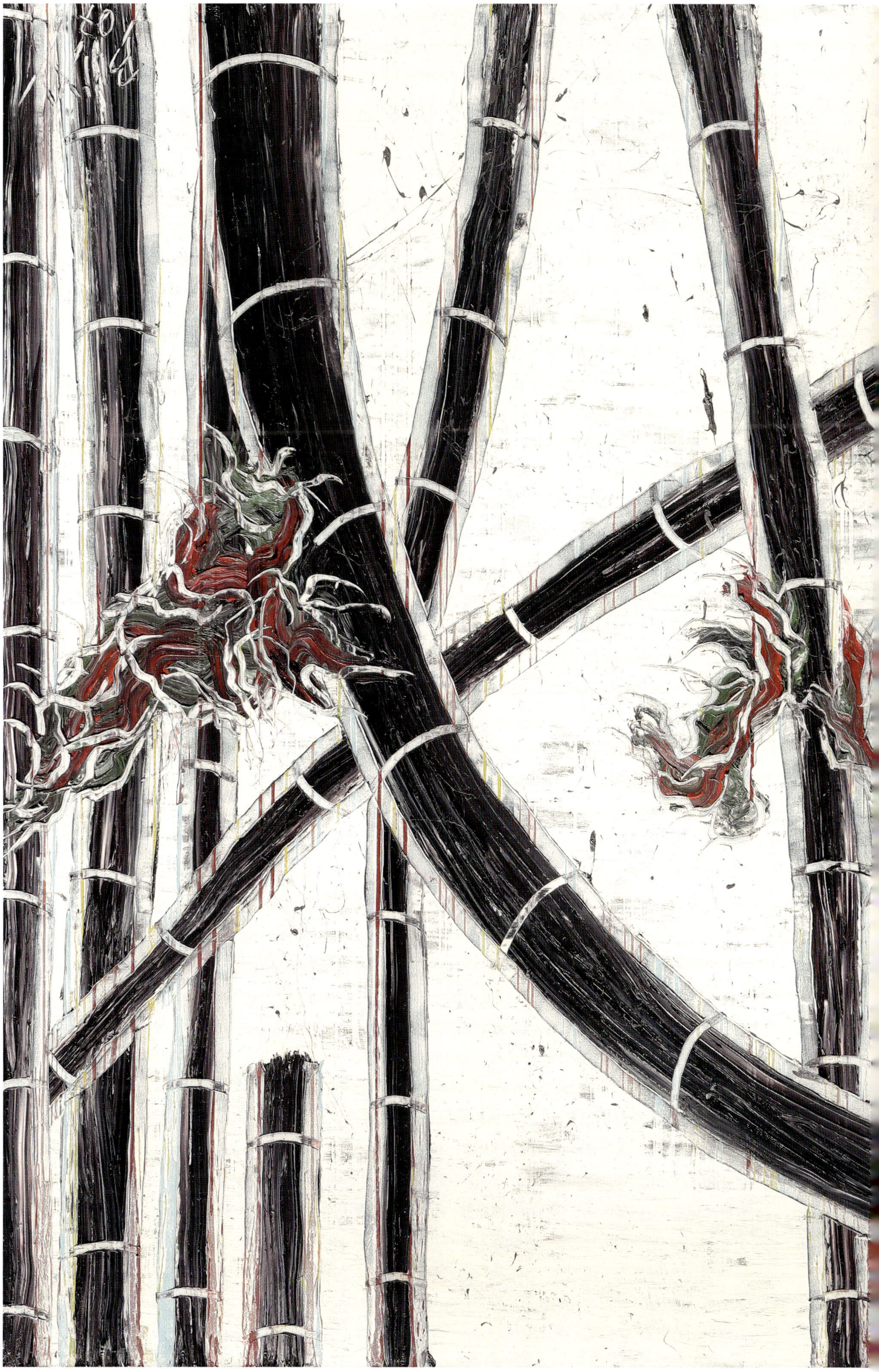

Bambuszauber, 2005
180 × 120 cm

152
153

Sari Lob, 2009
120 × 240 cm

Federspiel, 2004
180 × 240 cm

Hello Darkness, 2007
120 × 240 cm

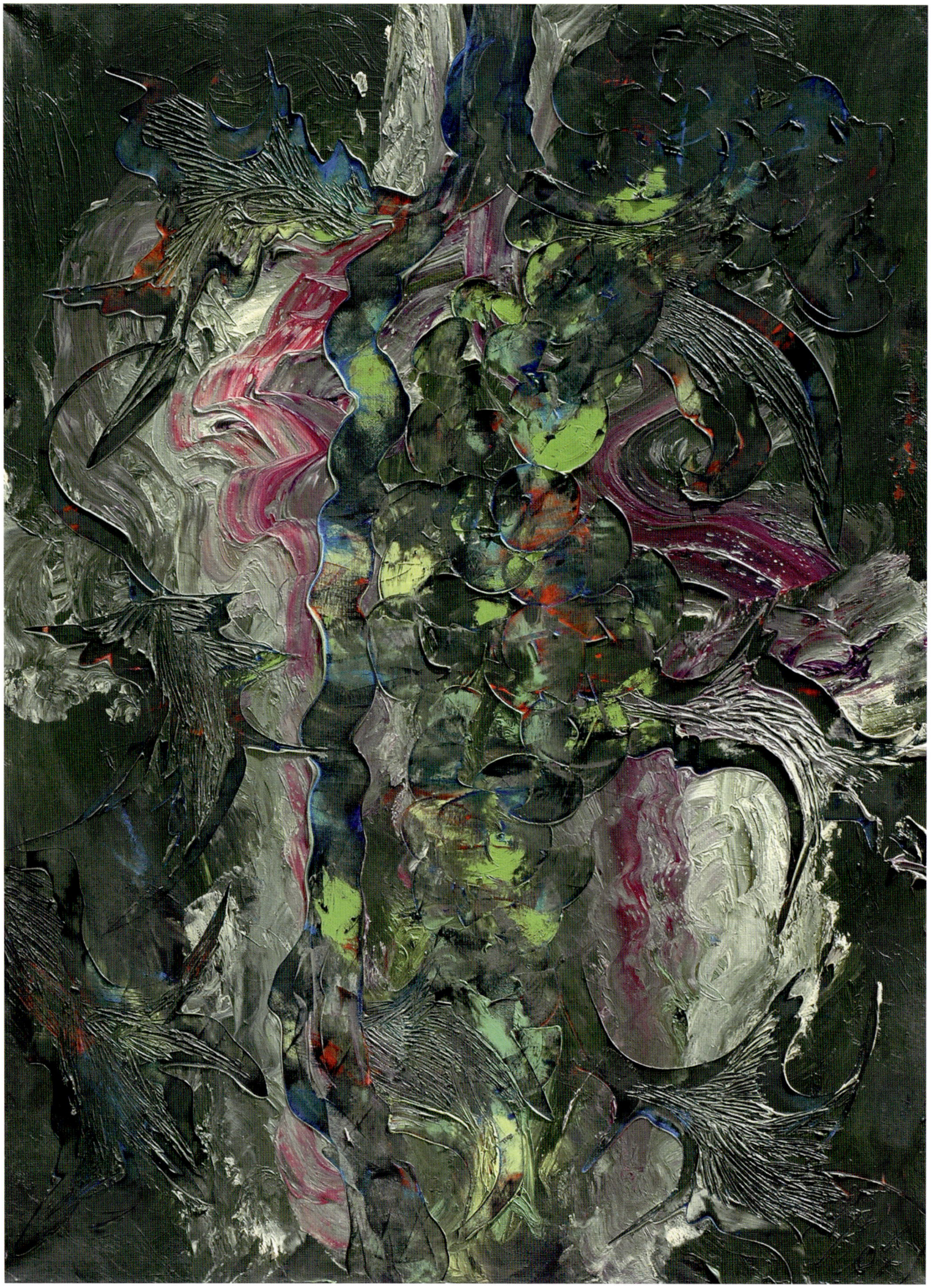

156
157

Anthozyane, 2004
120 × 90 cm

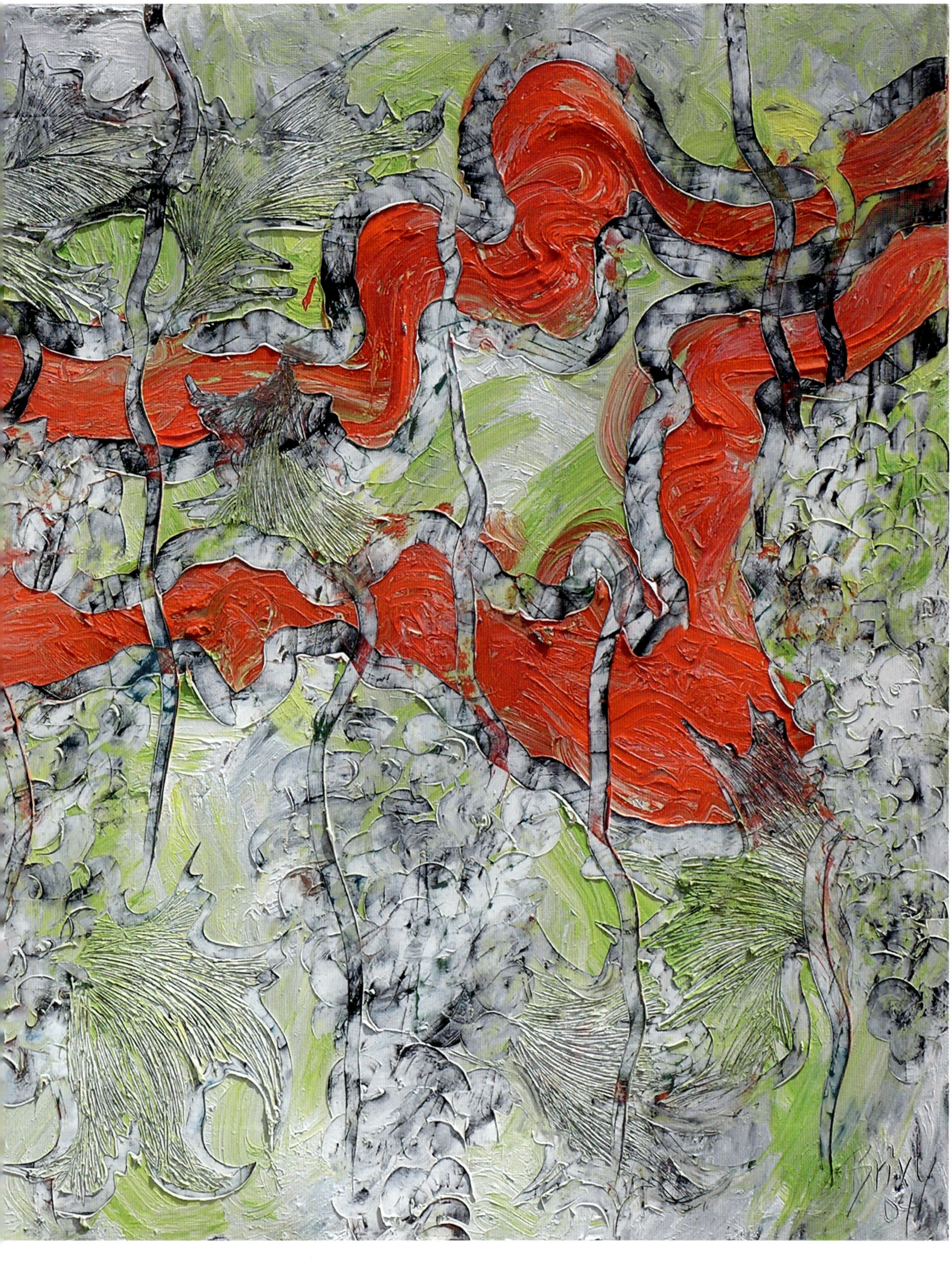

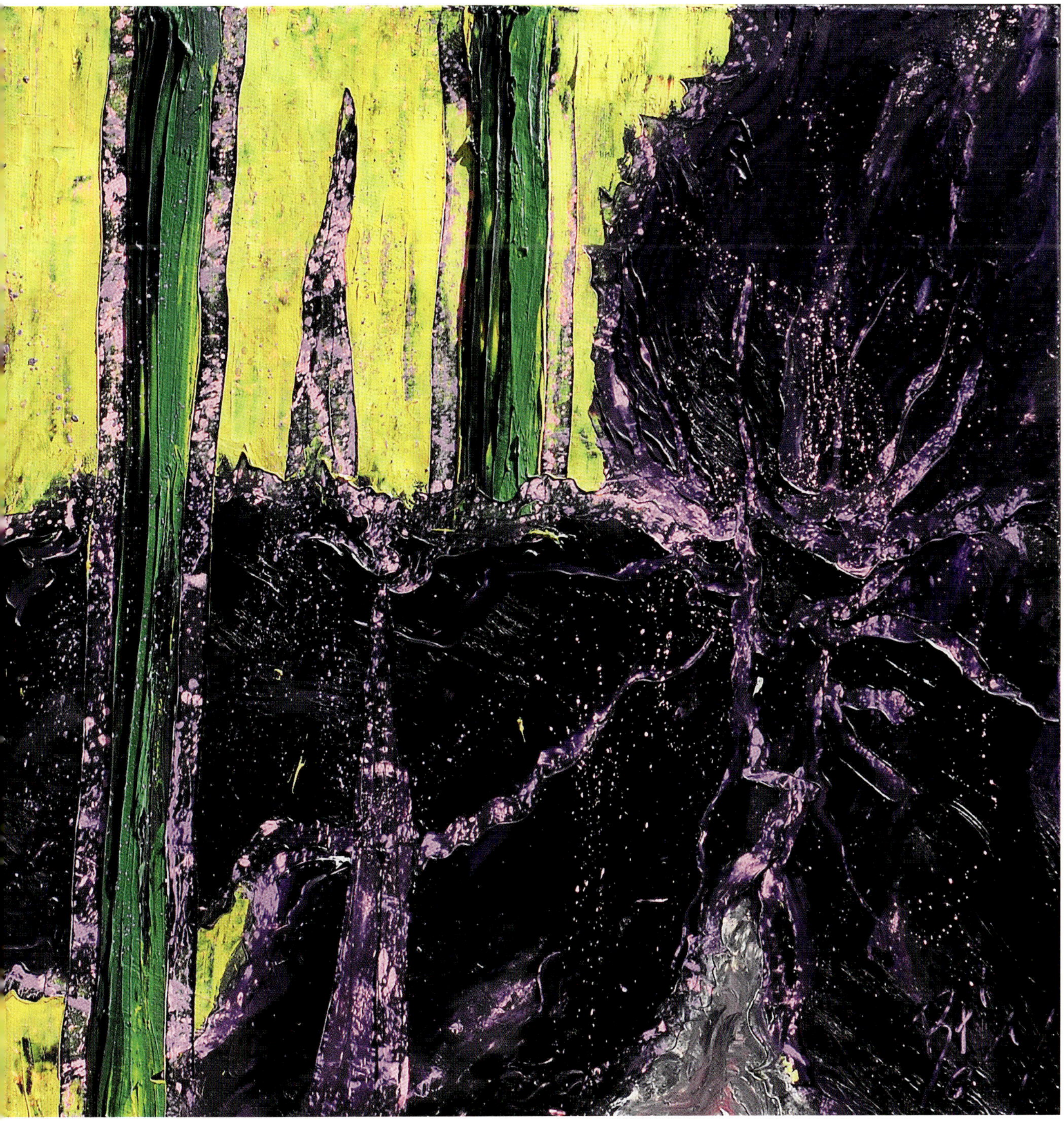

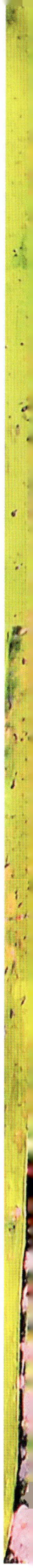

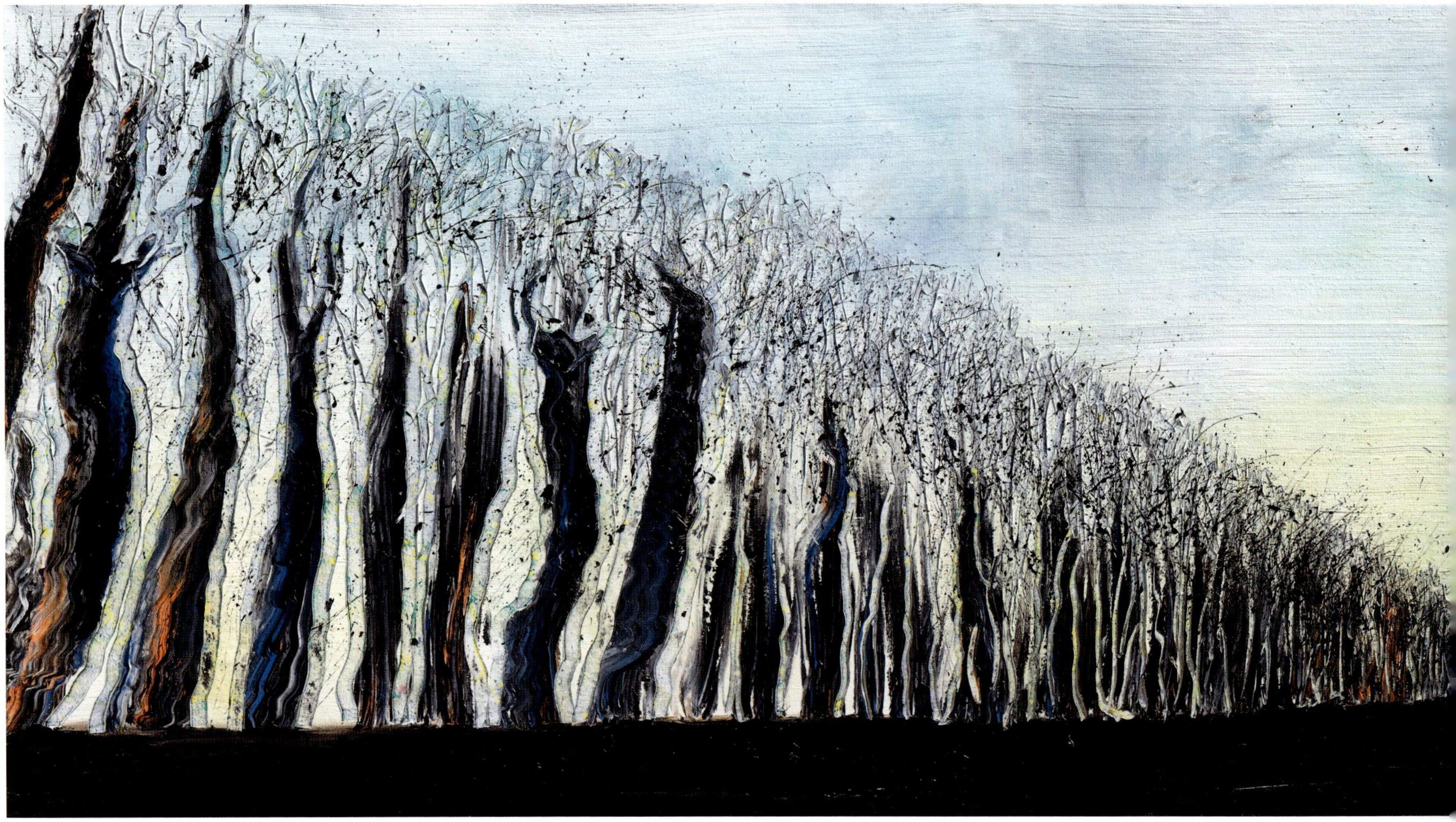

Beyond, 2008
140 × 540 cm (dreiteilig)

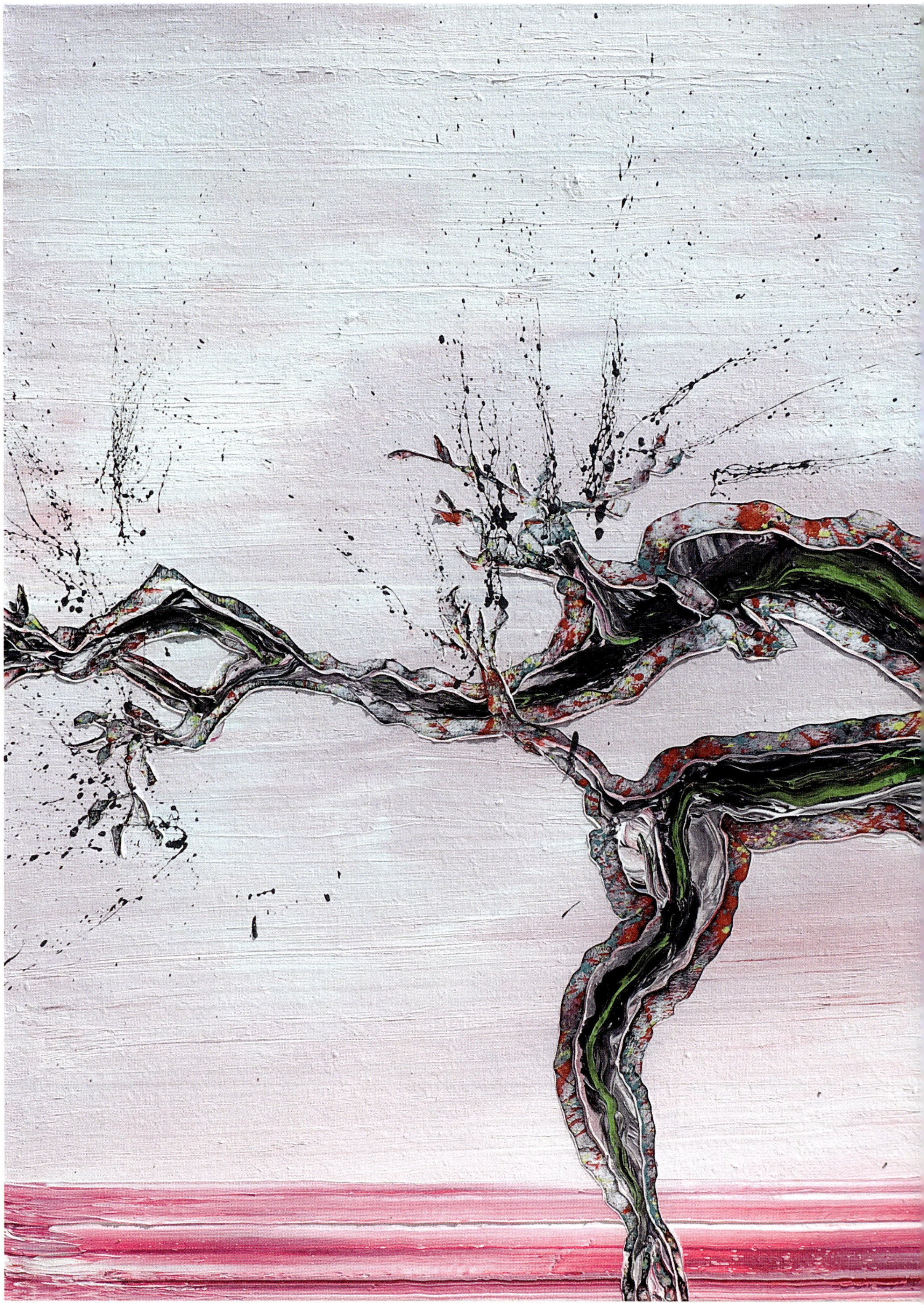

Bosana, 2008
120 × 180 cm

DIS COVER EDEN

Sonderedition | **Special Edition**

Der Künstler fertigte eine auf 50 Exemplare limitierte Sammleredition.
Alle Arbeiten sind gefertigt in Acryl auf Büttenpapier im Format 24 × 17 cm.
Jedes Original ist vom Künstler auf der Rückseite nummeriert und signiert.

The artist has created a collector's edition limited to fifty original artworks.
All works are executed in acrylic on handmade paper measuring 24 × 17 centimeters.
Each original is numbered and signed by the artist on the verso.

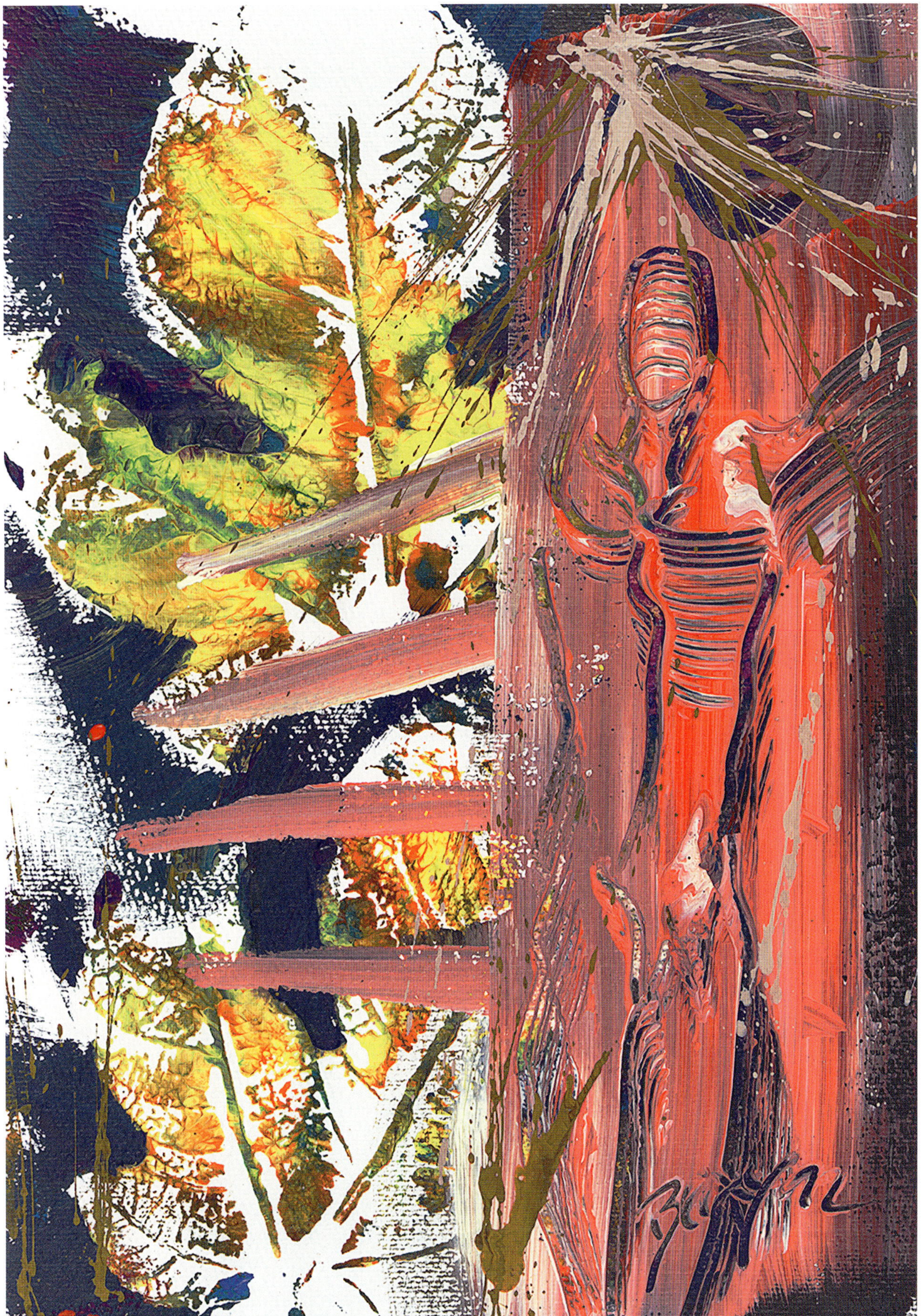

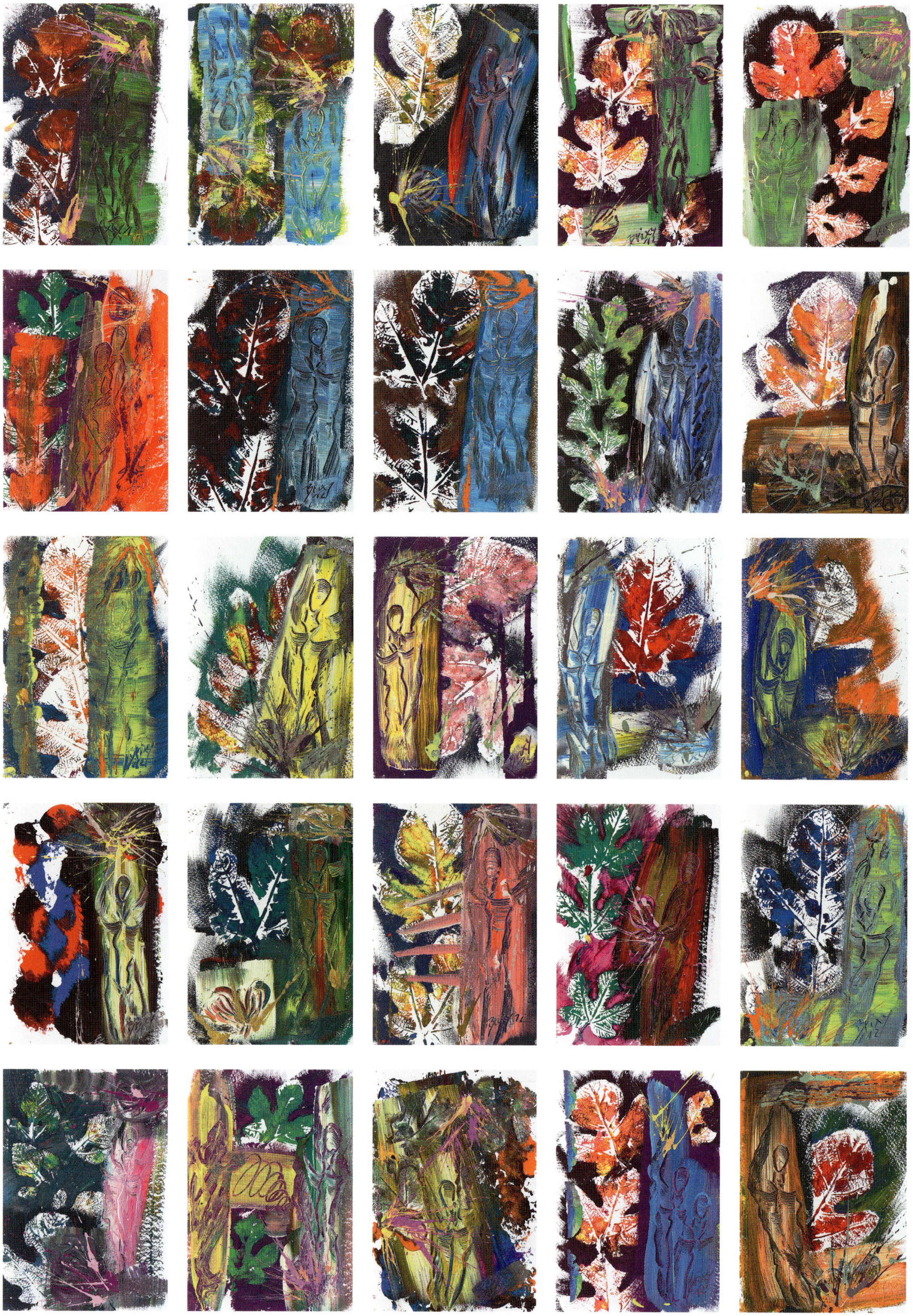

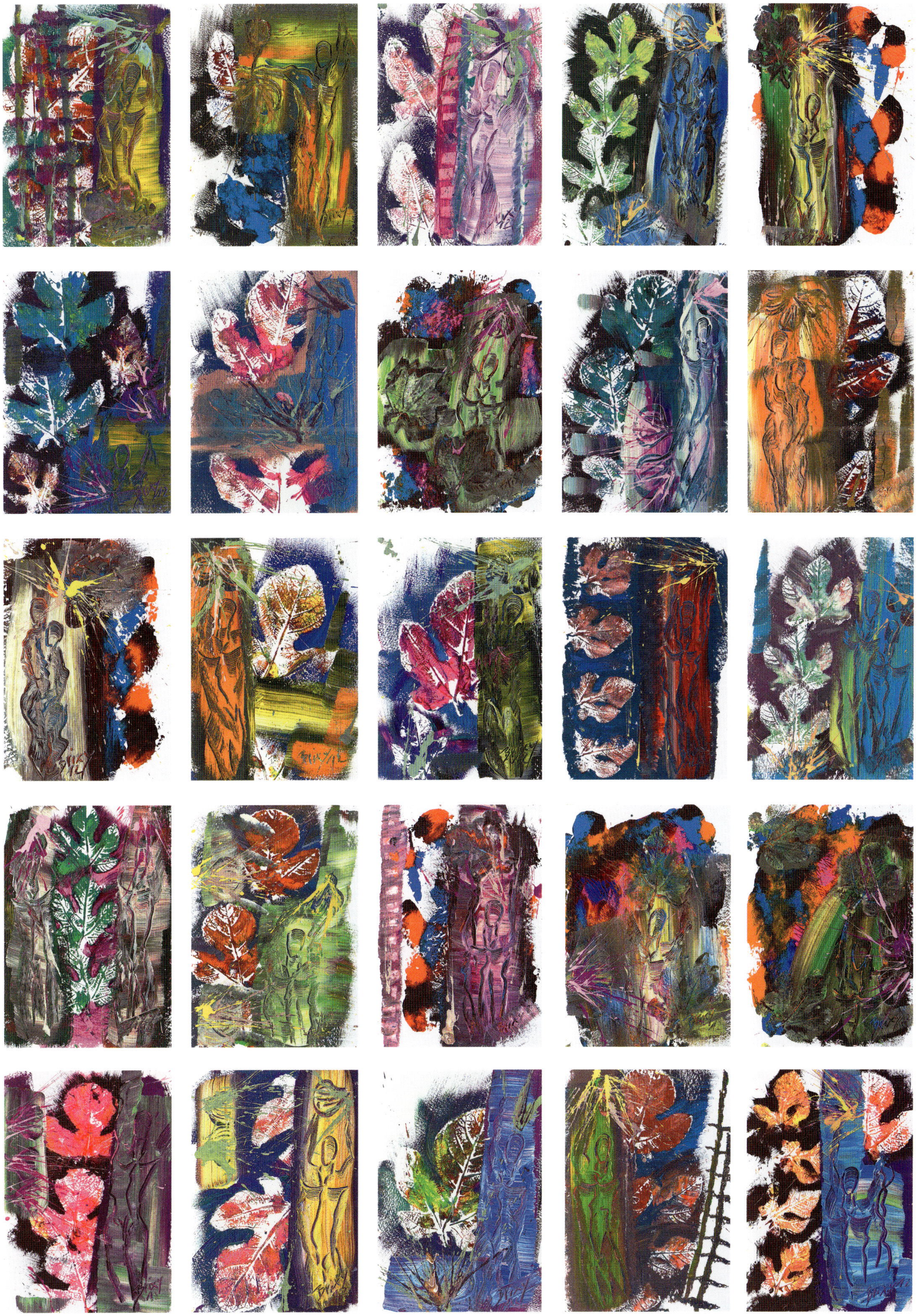

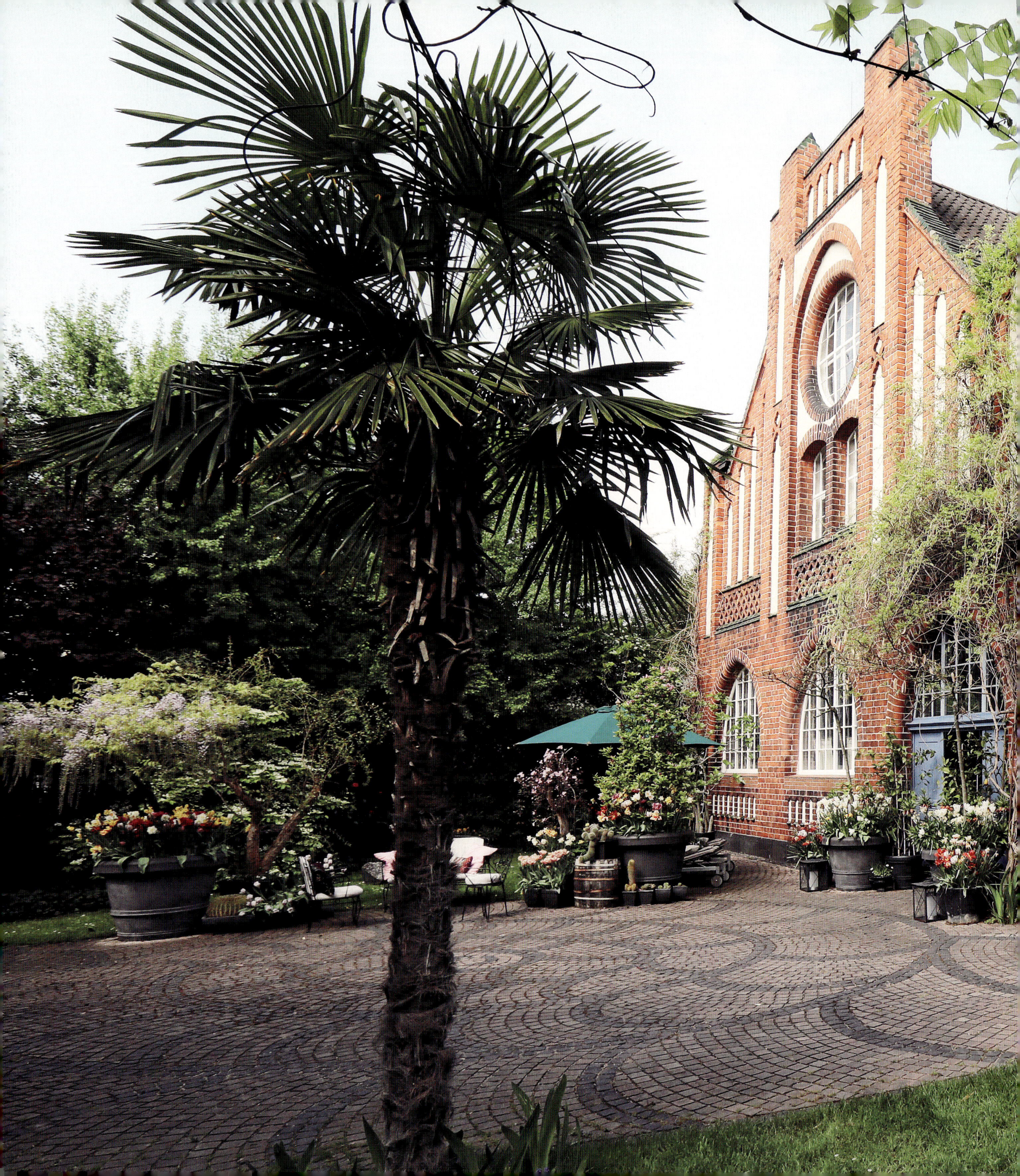

BRIXY'S WORLD

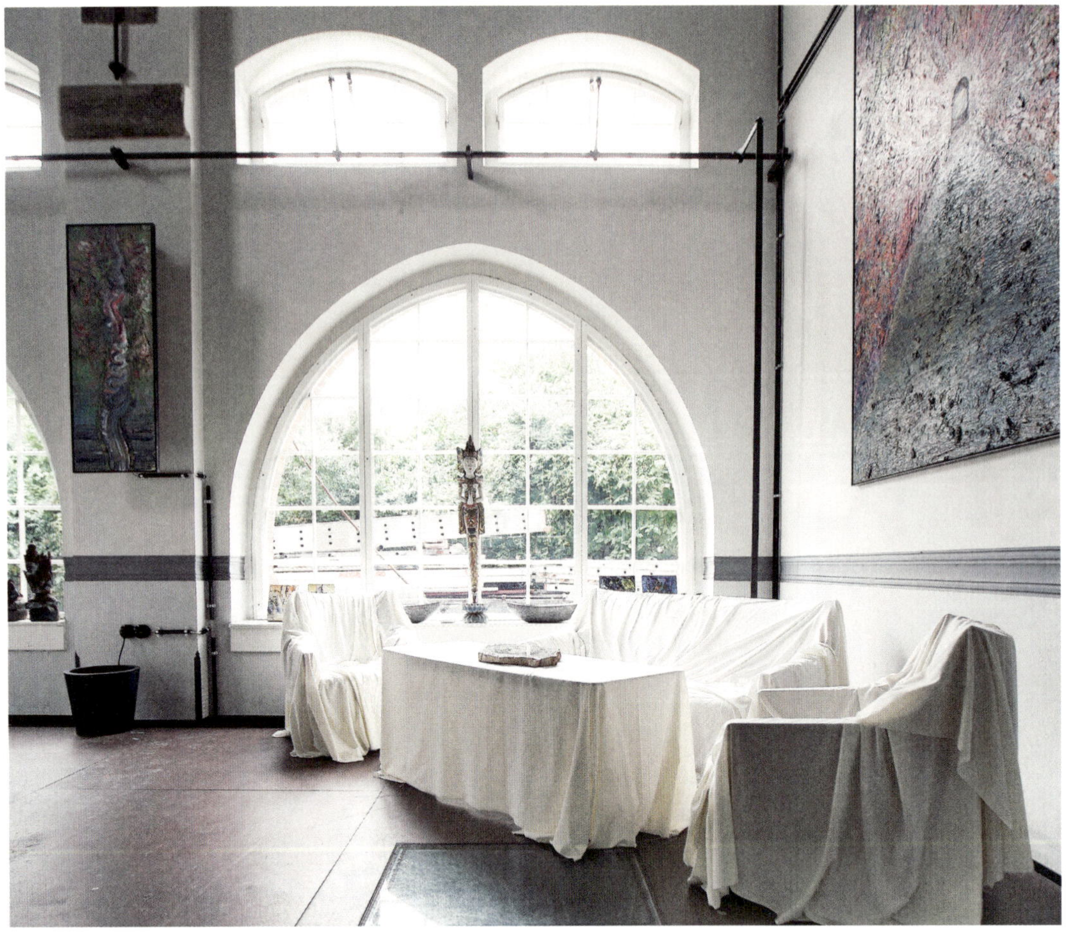

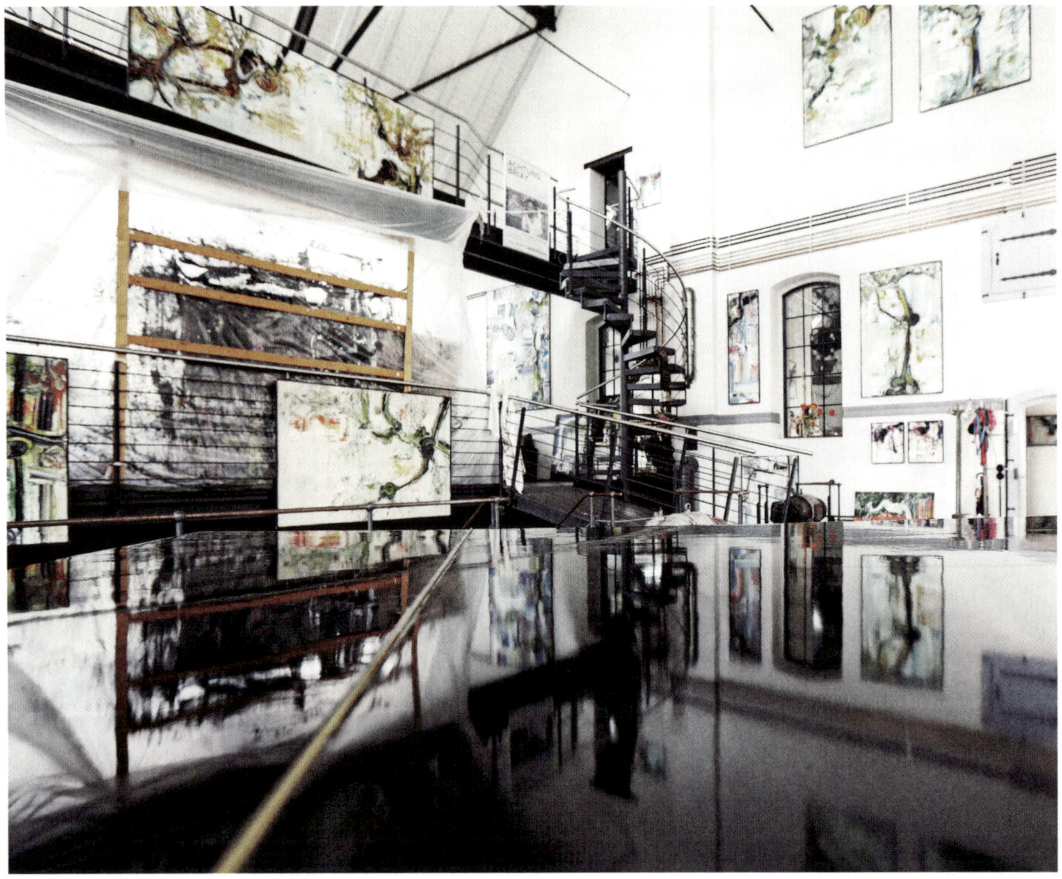

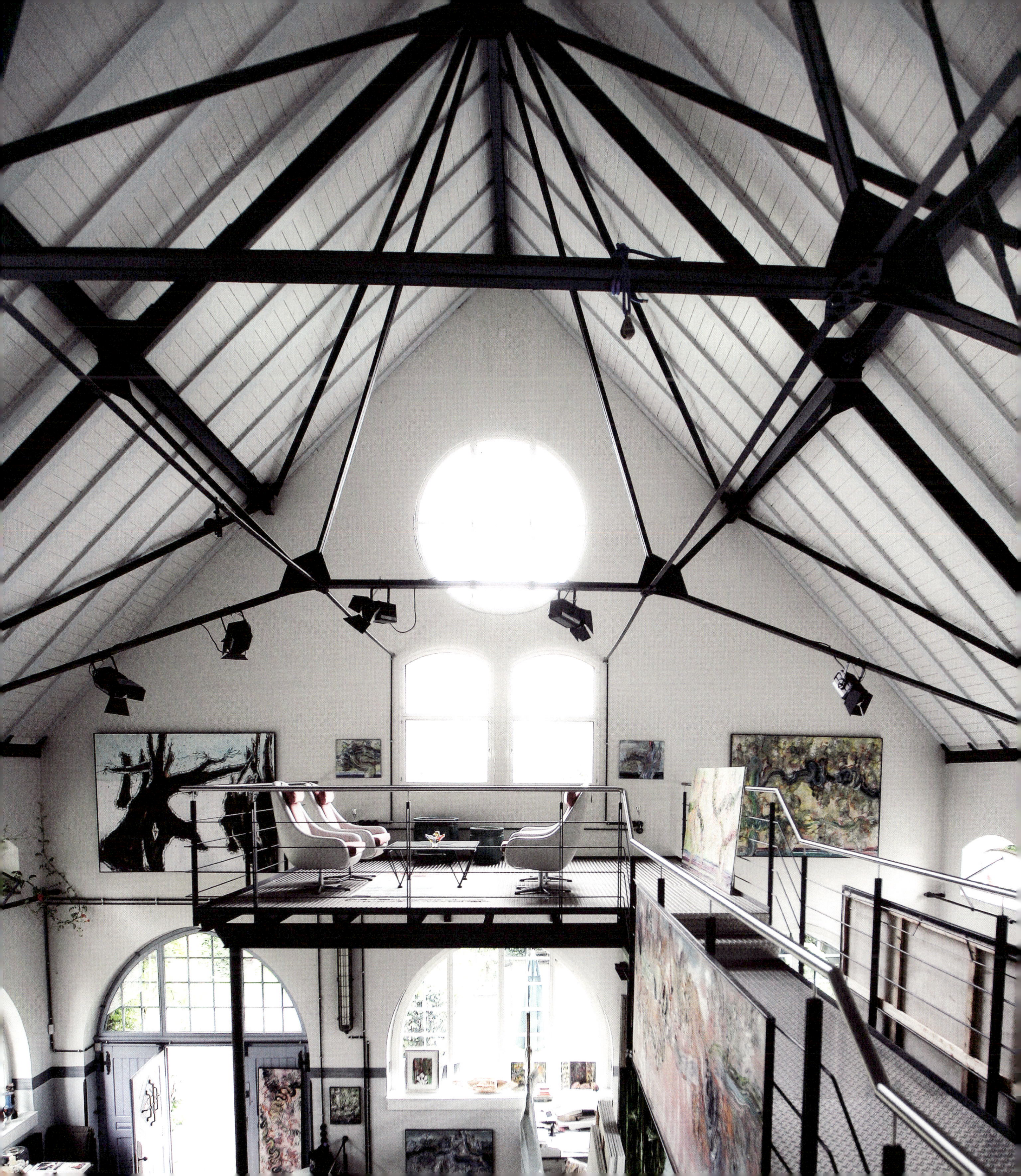

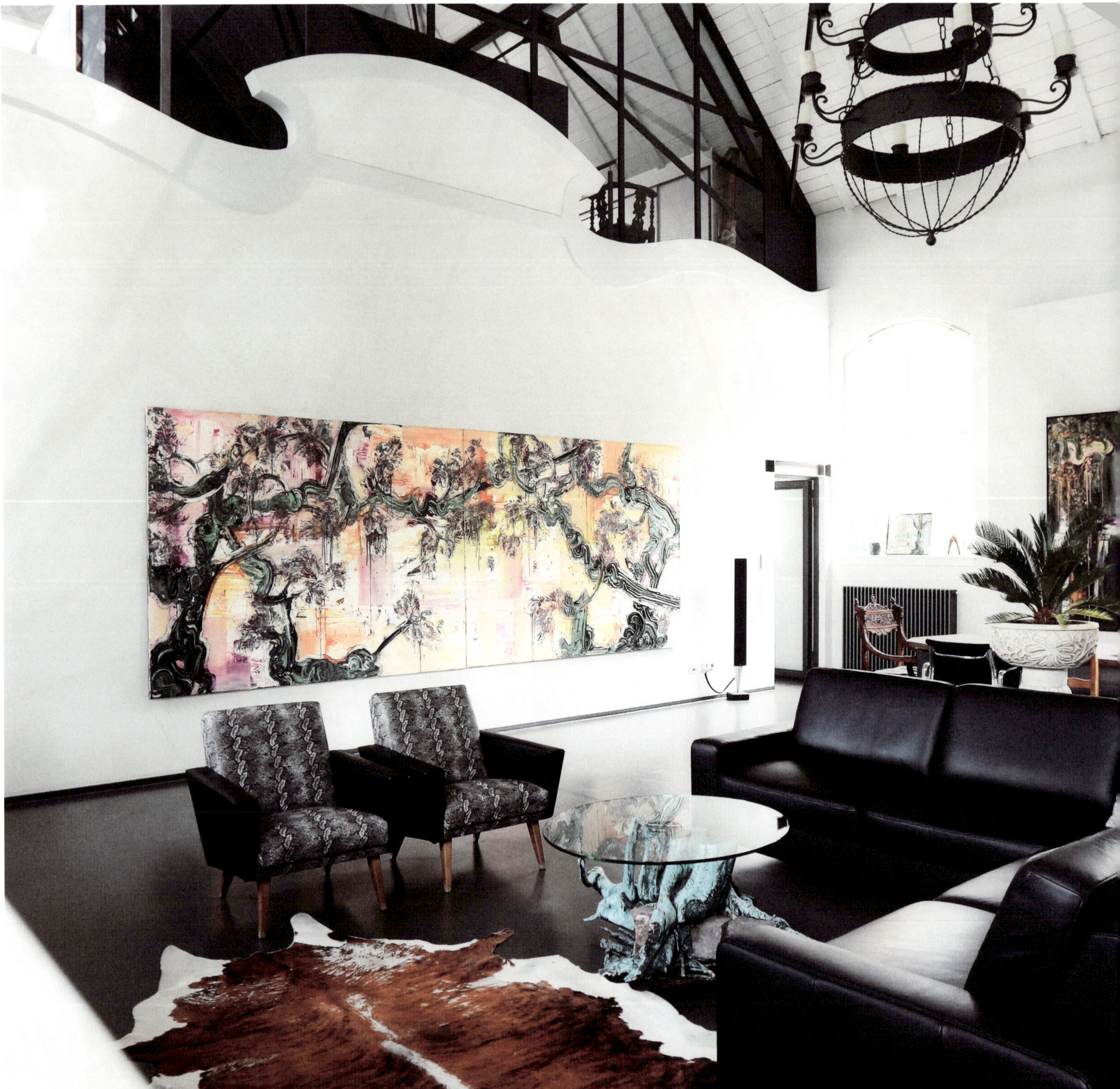

Dieses **Teilhabenlassen** der Menschen draußen an meiner Kunstwelt hier drinnen beflügelt mich – bis ich wieder die Tore schließe für eine Zeit der Reinigung, des **Inwendigwerdens**.

Allowing people "outside" to take part in my art world "in here" also animates me – until I close the gates again for a period of purification and of focusing on that which is inside.

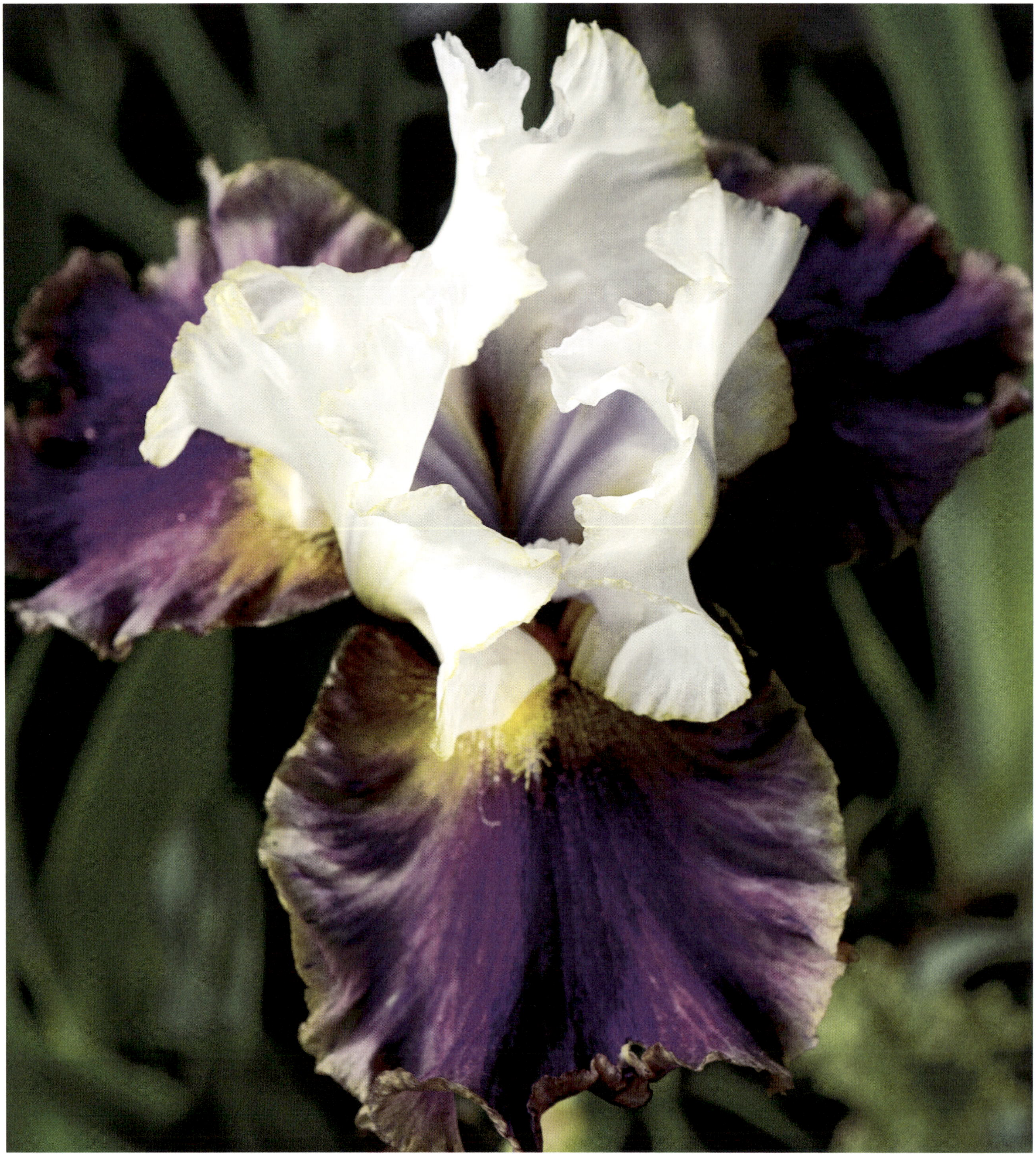

Schwertlilie „Dietmar Brixy"
Iriszüchtung:
Richard Cayeux, Frankreich

Iris "Dietmar Brixy"
Breeder:
Richard Cayeux, France

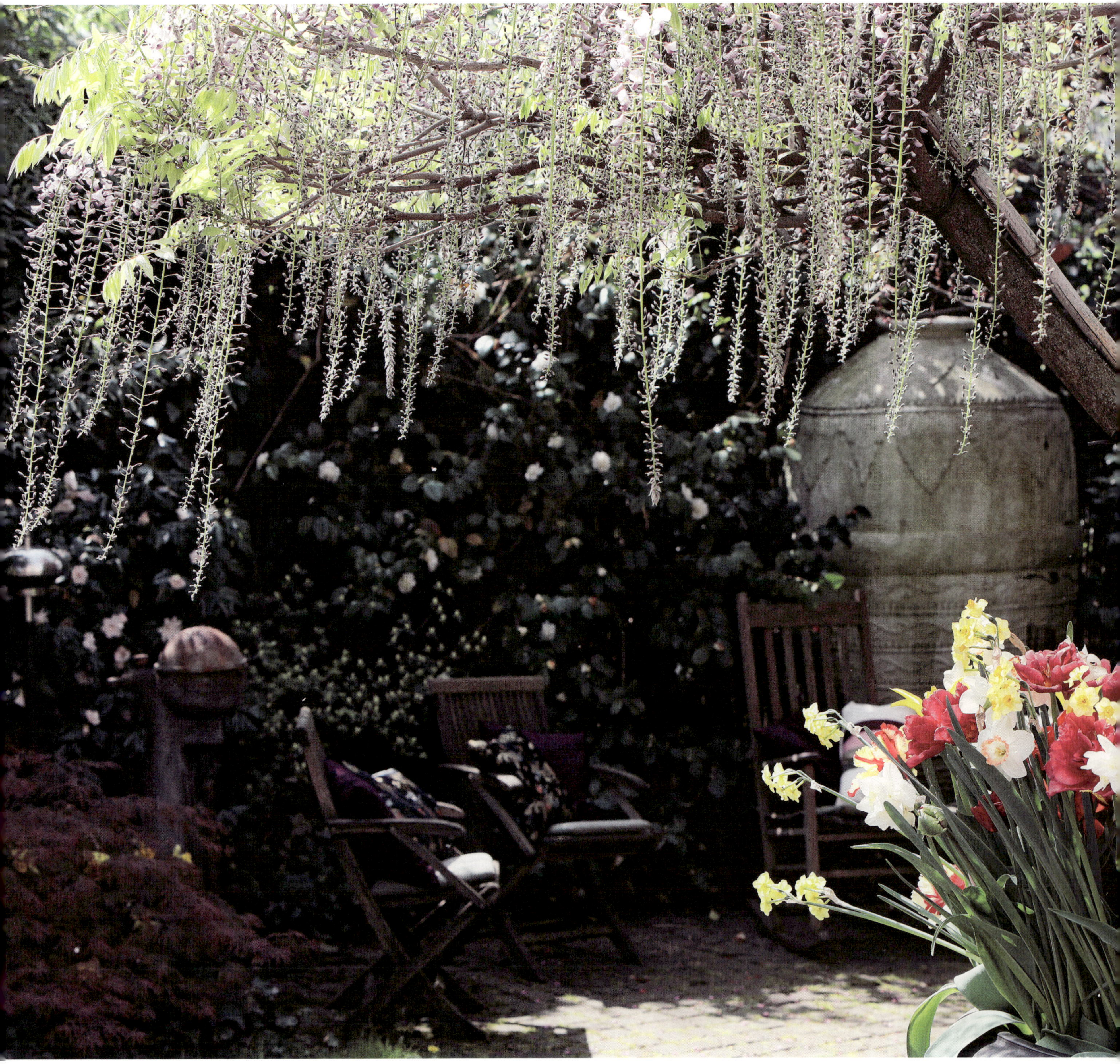

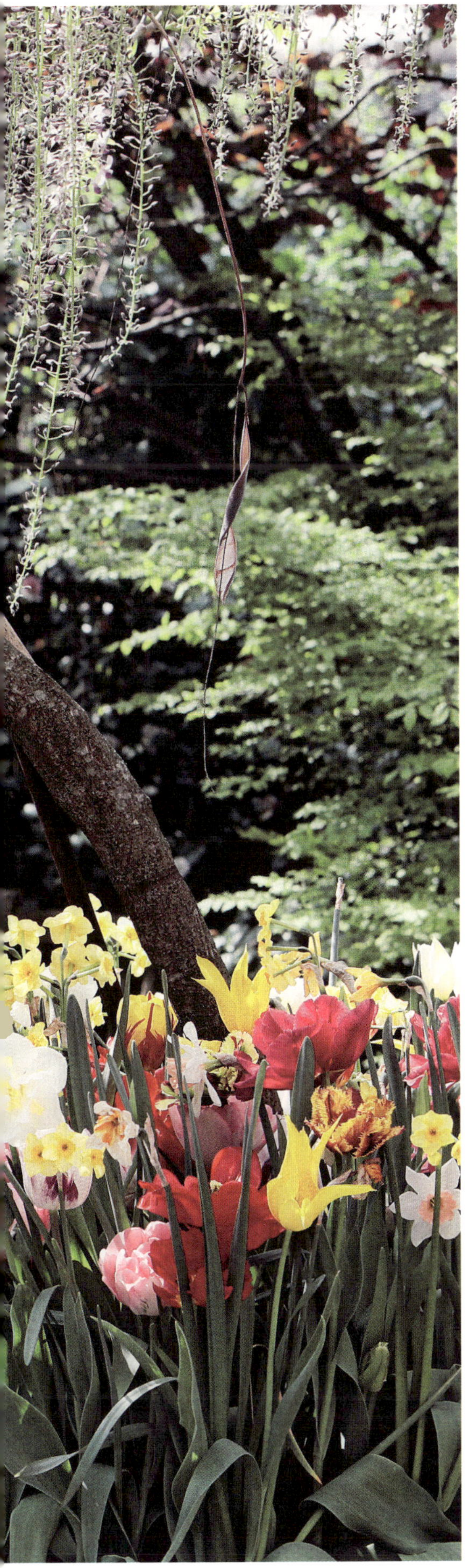

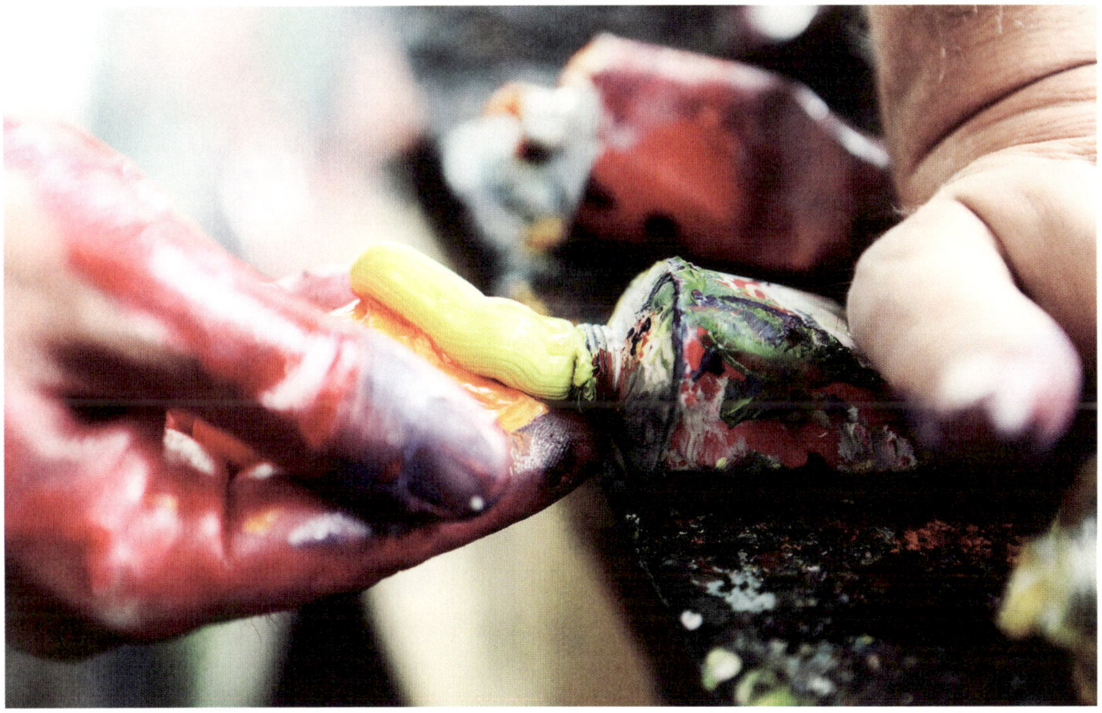

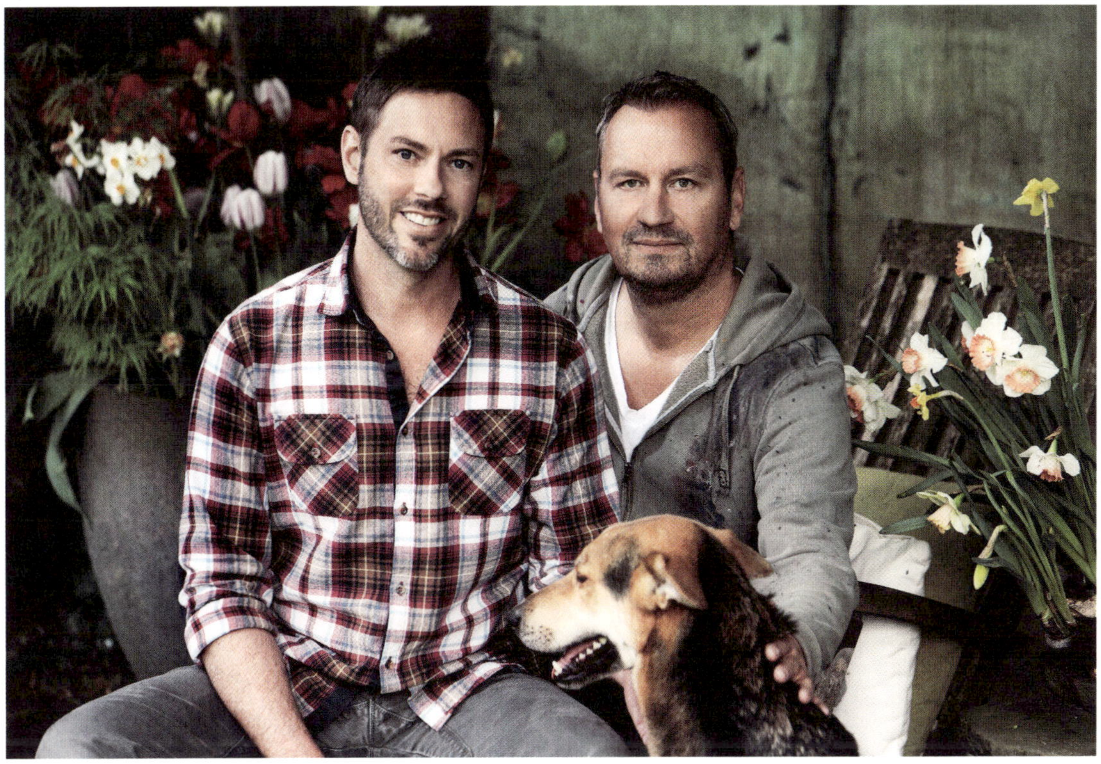

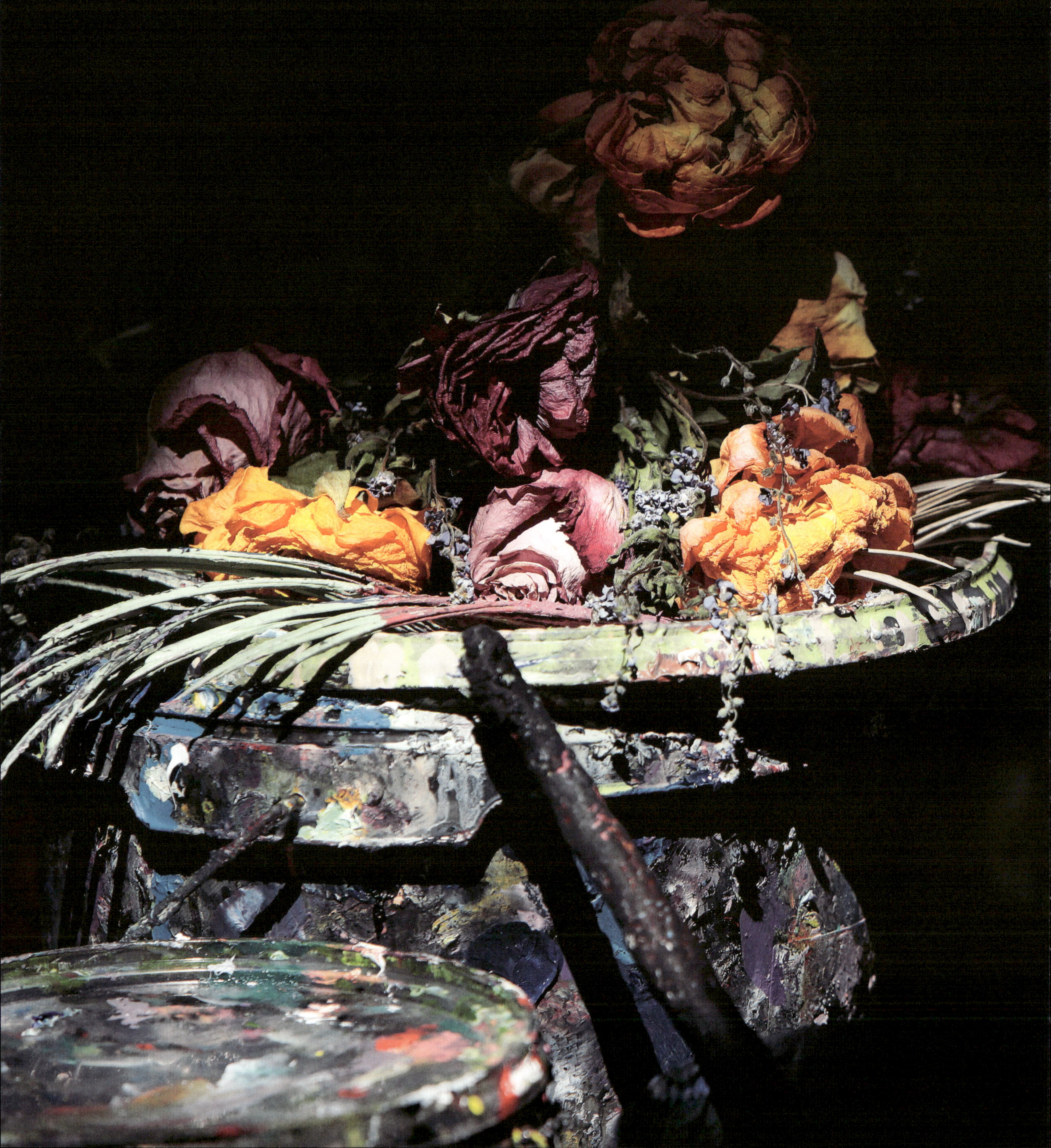

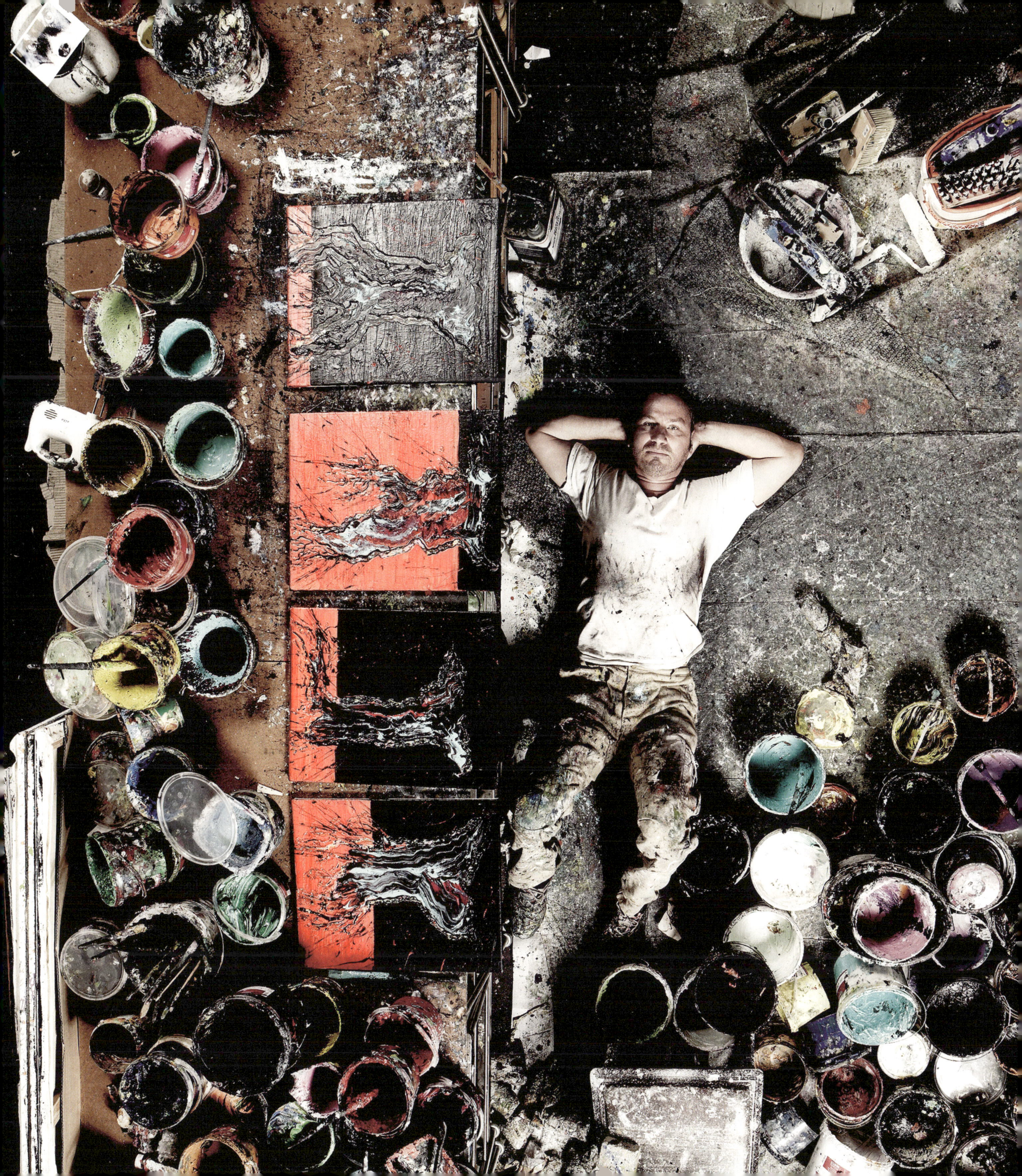

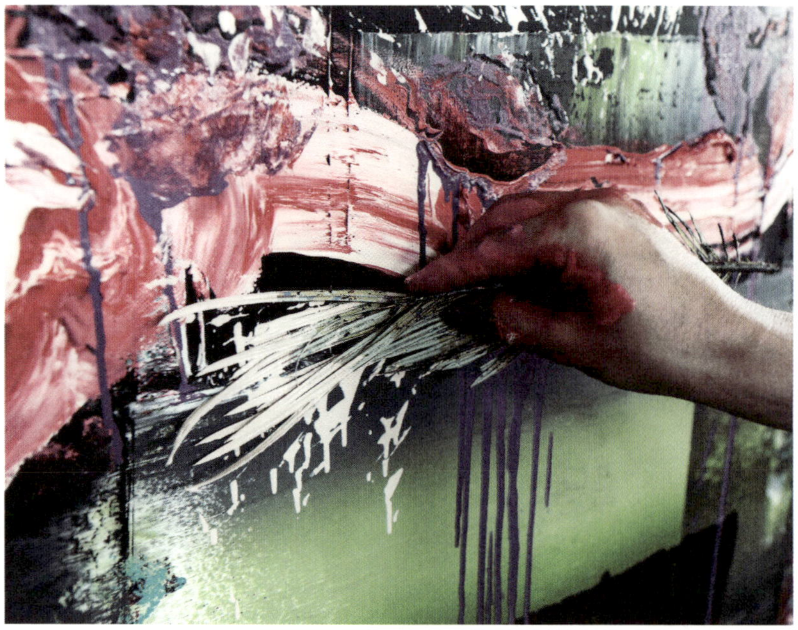
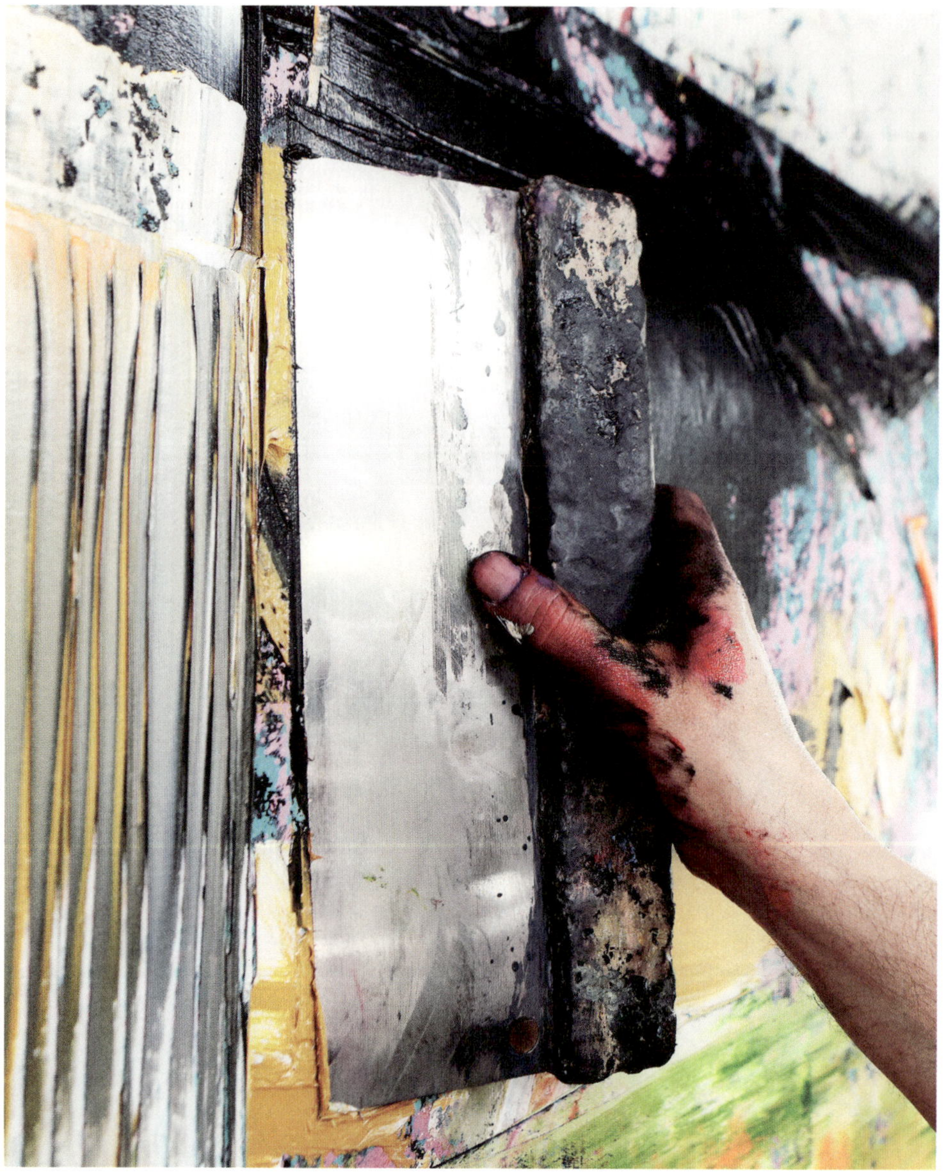
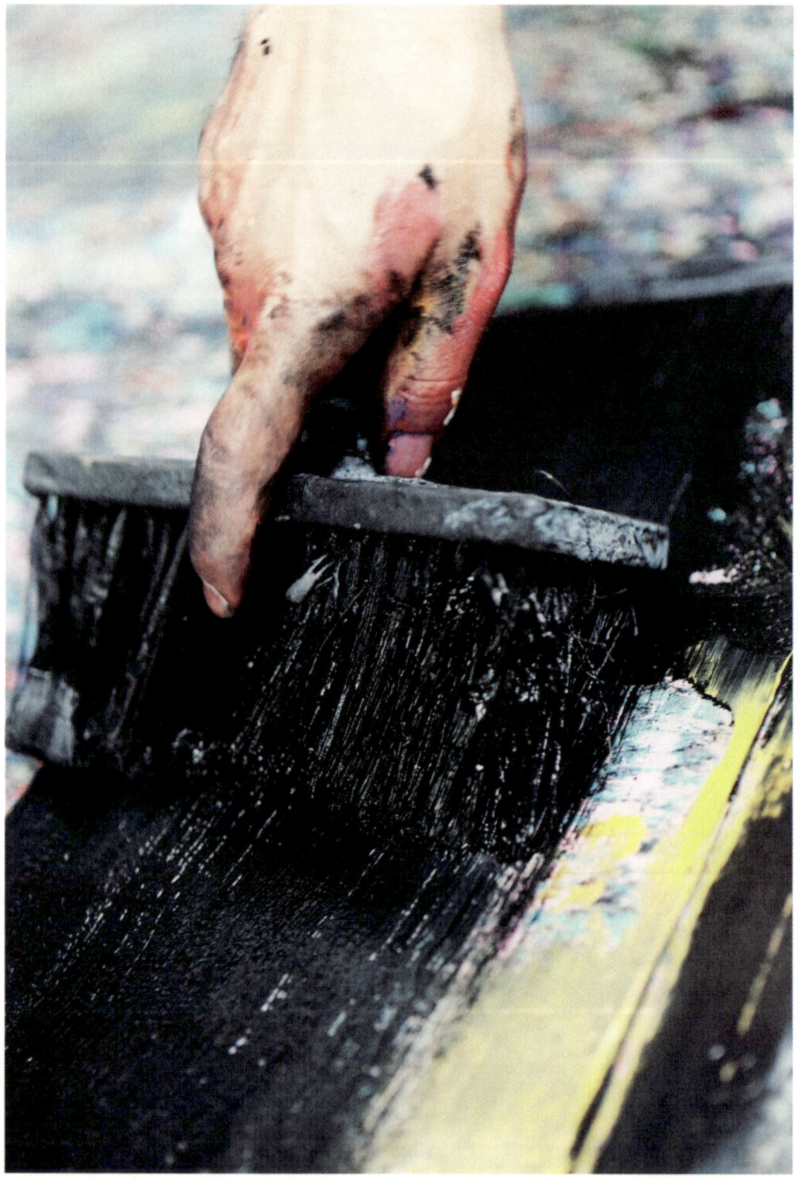
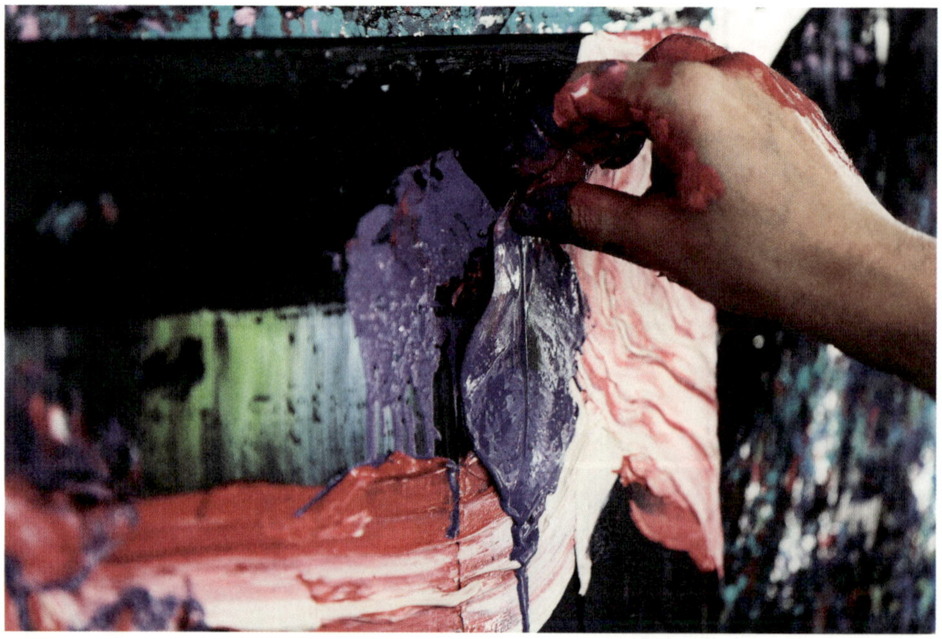

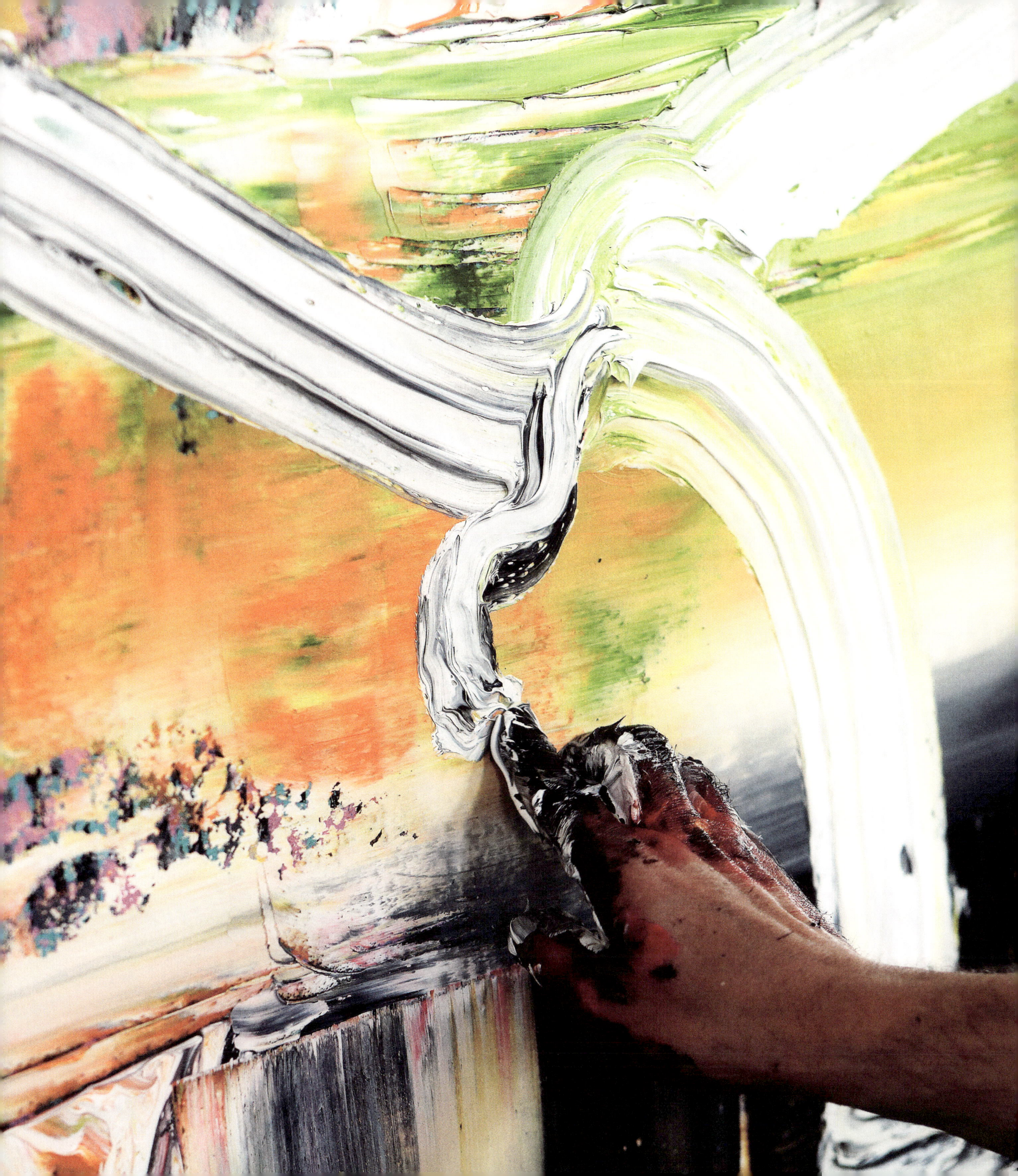

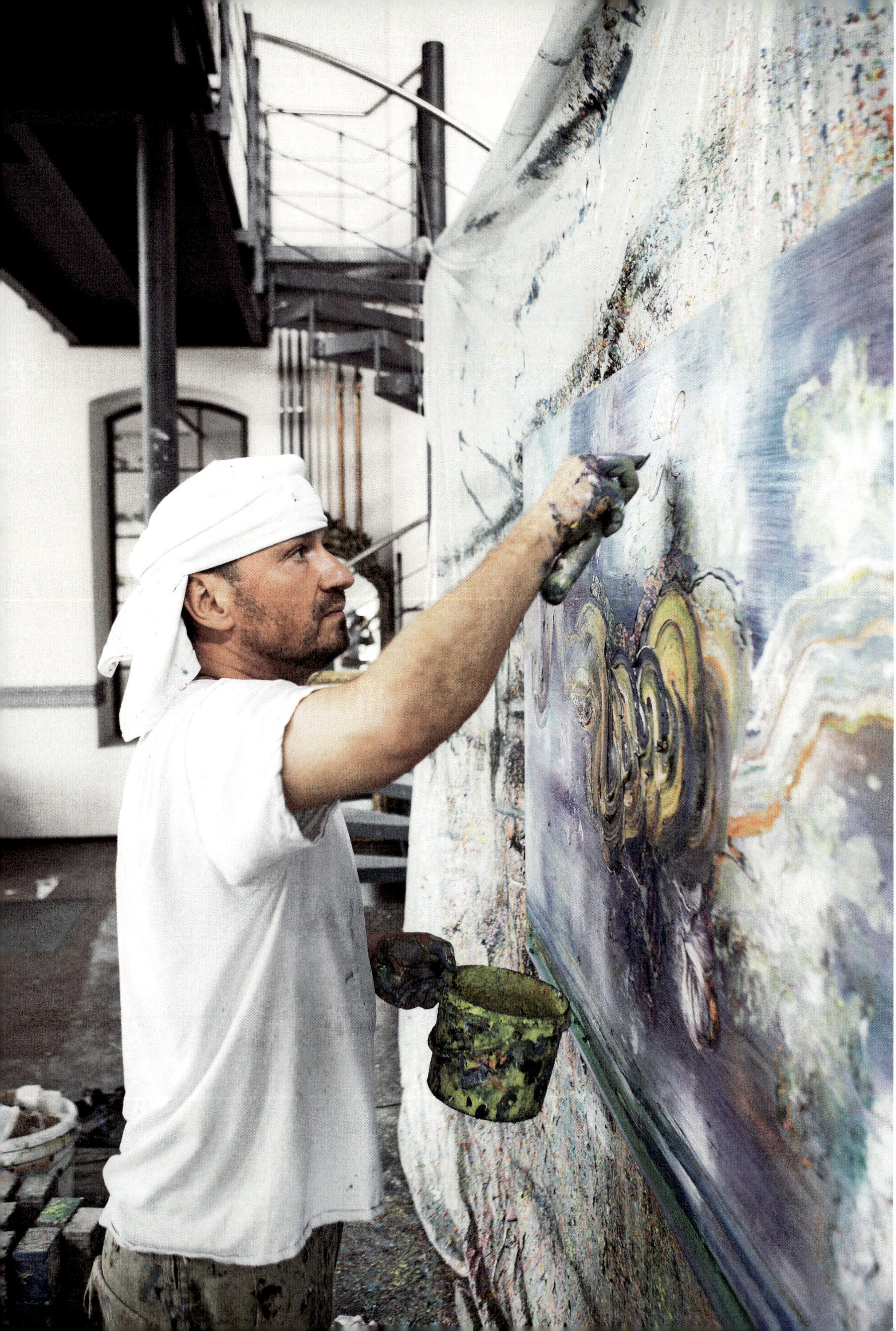

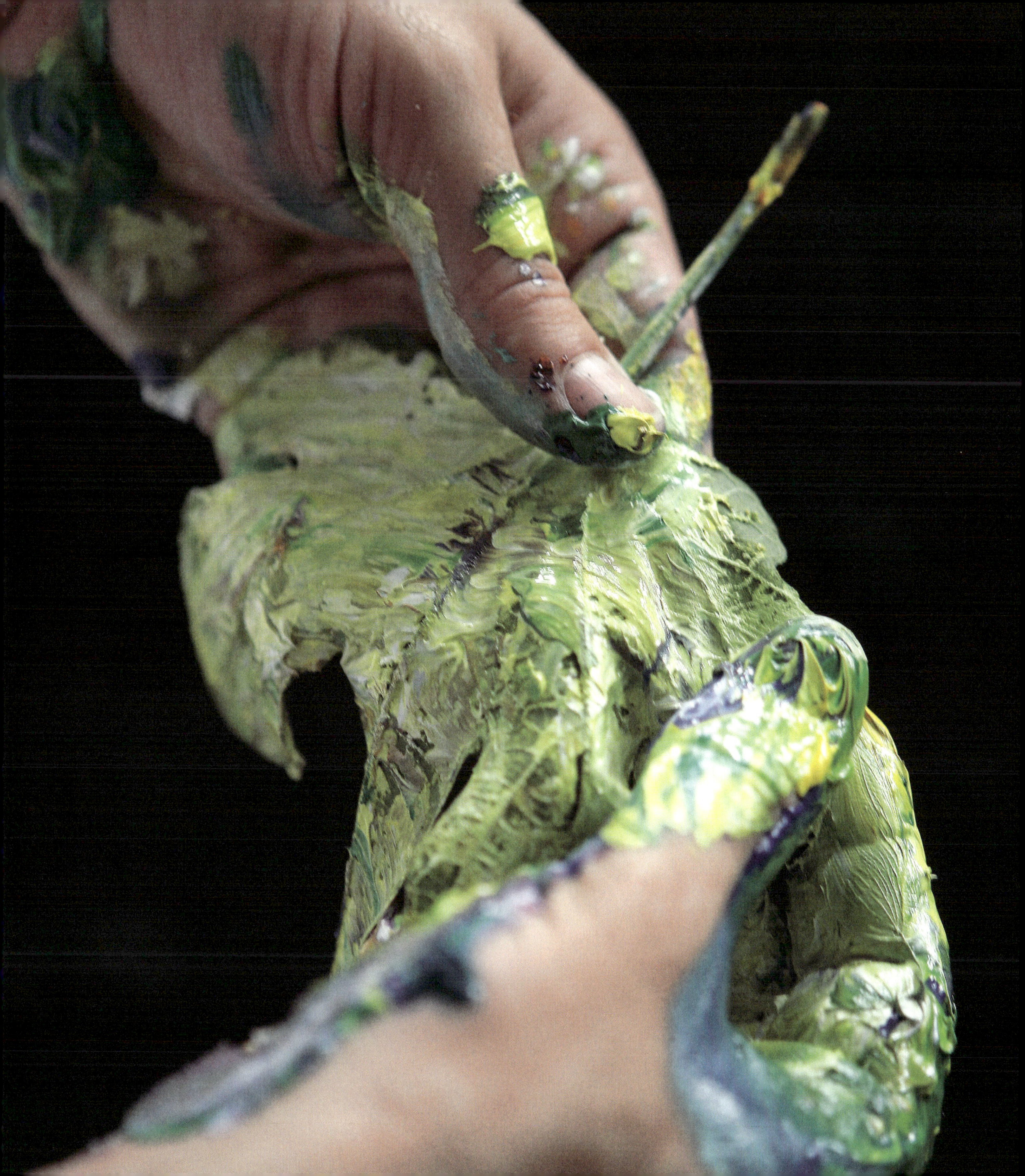

184

185

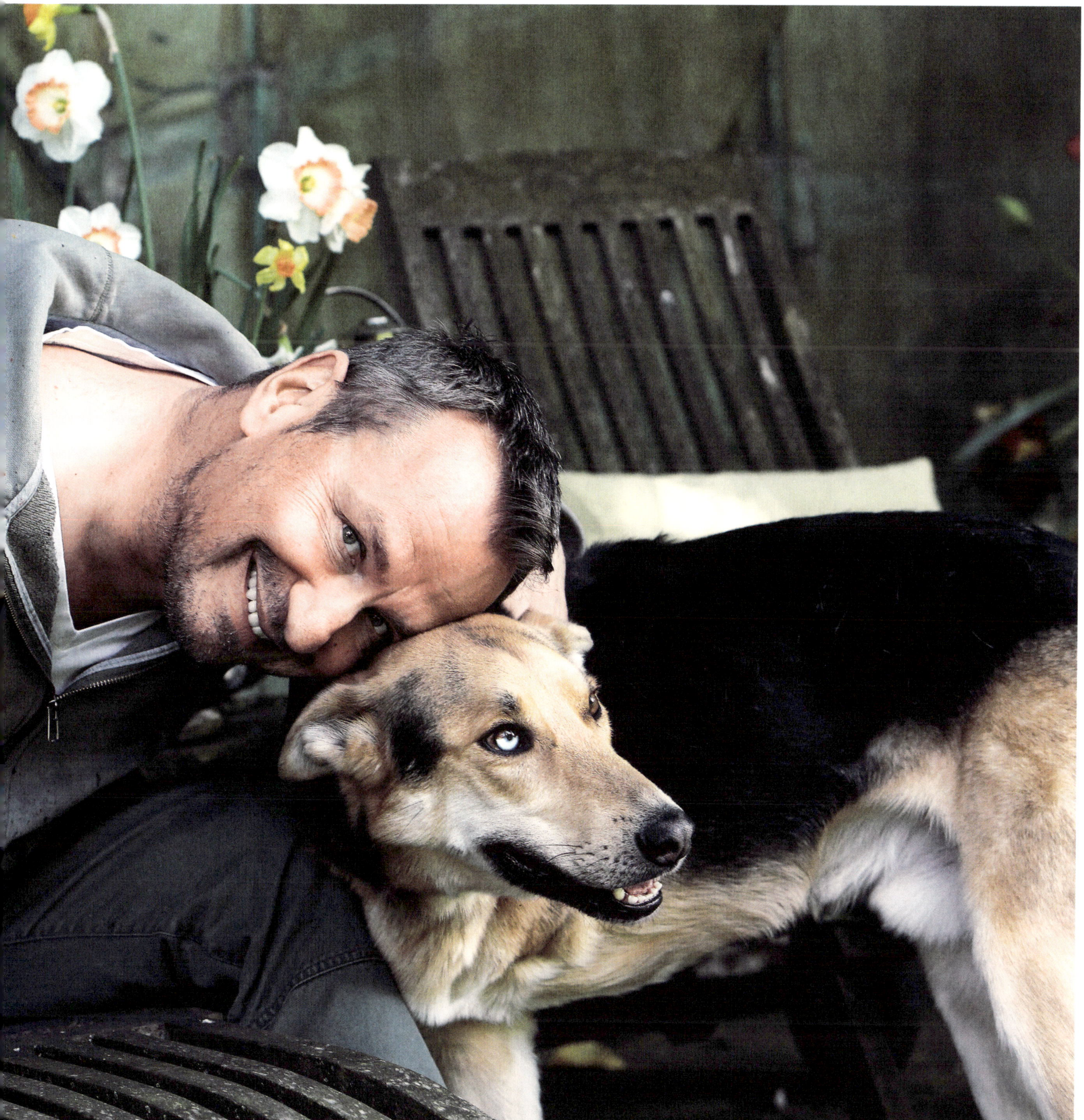

INSPIRATION INBEGRIFFEN
Volker Lehmkuhl

Besondere Gebäude brauchen außergewöhnliche Nutzer, um zu überleben. Ein mehr als 100 Jahre altes Abwasserpumpwerk in Mannheim hatte dieses Glück. Heute profitieren Bauwerk und Besitzer von ihrem Zusammentreffen.

Der Stadtteil Neckarau ist nicht gerade die Schokoladenseite von Mannheim: Industrieareale und Gewerbegebiete bestimmen das Quartier entlang des Rheinufers, im Schatten eines mächtigen Kraftwerks ducken sich Mietshäuser. Hier ein wertvolles Baudenkmal zu vermuten, kommt den wenigsten Besuchern in den Sinn.

Doch wenn sich das breite Eingangstor des ehemaligen Abwasserpumpwerks öffnet, bleibt den meisten erst einmal der Mund offen stehen: Ein elf Meter hoher, aufwändig verzierter Backsteinbau erstreckt sich über eine Länge von 35 Metern, seine halbrunden Bogenfenster erinnern eher an eine Kirche als an einen Industriebau. Im sorgfältig gepflegten Garten wachsen Kamelien, Bambus, Iris und Magnolien. Hier sollen bis 1986 stinkende Kloaken geflossen sein? Den Kontrast zwischen anrüchiger Nutzung und edlem Erscheinungsbild erklärt Mathias Henrich: „Wasserwerke waren vor 100 Jahren in etwa das, was heute gläserne Autofabriken sind" – High-Tech-Architektur in zeitgemäßem Design. Der Denkmal erfahrene Architekt hat die Umnutzung des Industrieareals geplant und begleitet.

Denkmal statt Doppelhaushälfte

Zu verdanken ist die Rettung des 1903 errichteten Gebäudes aber dem Künstler Dietmar Brixy. Der Mannheimer ist in der Nachbarschaft aufgewachsen und war als Jugendlicher Dutzende Male am Abwasserpumpwerk vorbeigeradelt. Schon als Student an der Kunstakademie faszinierte ihn das Gebäude. „Das Pumpwerk ist gerade durch den Kontrast zwischen seiner Lage und seinem neogotischen Stil ein einzigartiges Bauwerk, das mich als kreativen Menschen seit jeher interessiert hat", sagt der heute 53-Jährige. Doch damals, als Student oder junger Künstler, war für ihn unvorstellbar, einmal die enormen Kosten stemmen zu können, die der Umbau eines 700-Quadratmeter-Baus verschlingt.

INSPIRATION INCLUDED

Special buildings call for extraordinary users if they are to survive. A wastewater pumping station in Mannheim, which is more than one hundred years old, was fortunate enough to find one. Today, both the architectural structure and the owner benefit from their encounter.

The district of Neckarau is by no stretch of the imagination Mannheim's prettiest area. Industrial estates and business parks characterize this area on the banks of the Rhine, and blocks of flats cower in the shadow of an imposing power station. Few visitors will suspect that this location is home to a valuable historic monument. And yet, when the wide entrance gate of the former wastewater pumping station opens, visitors are astonished to find an eleven-meter-high, elaborately decorated brick building that spans a length of thirty-five meters. Its half-round arched windows are more reminiscent of a church than they are of an industrial structure. Camellias, bamboo plants, irises, and magnolias grow in a lovingly maintained garden. Can it be true that stinking sewers ran through the property until 1986?

Mathias Heinrich explains the contrast between the ignoble use and the sophisticated appearance thus: "One hundred years ago, waterworks were similar to what glass-walled car-production plants are to the present day" – high-tech architecture in a contemporary design. The architect, who specializes in historic monuments, planned and supervised the repurposing of the industrial estate.

A Monument Instead of a Semi-detached House

Credit for the salvation of the building constructed in 1903 must go to the artist Dietmar Brixy, however. The resident of Mannheim grew up in the neighborhood and cycled past the wastewater pumping station many times when he was a boy. He was already

Auch andere hatten sich seitdem an dem Objekt verhoben, eine zwischenzeitlich geplante Nutzung als Erlebnisgastronomie war an den Einsprüchen der Nachbarschaft gescheitert. Als das Denkmal geschützte Pumpwerk später aber erneut zum Verkauf stand, hatte sich Brixys Situation deutlich verbessert. Er hatte sich nach Jahren des Reisens und Arbeitens einen festen Kundenstamm erarbeitet, dessen Begeisterung für die farbenfrohen, meist expressiven Bilder den finanziellen Spielraum für eine Investition dieser Größenordnung machbar erscheinen ließ. Letztlich siegten Faszination und Mut zum Risiko über Vernunft.

Einst Dampfstrahler statt Pinsel

Mit dem Kauf begann eine intensive Arbeitsbeziehung zwischen dem Gebäude und seinem neuen Eigentümer. Dietmar Brixy und zahlreiche Freunde schafften tonnenweise Müll und Schutt aus dem verwahrlosten Areal, schlugen lose Putzteile ab, schrubbten und bürsteten die Maschinen und Pumpen in der Arbeitshalle.

Eine besondere Entdeckung war der sorgfältig aus Klinkern gemauerte Abwasserkanal, der sich nach seiner Trockenlegung und einer aufwändigen Reinigung per Dampfstrahler

fascinated by the building when he was a student at the art academy. "It is precisely because of the contrast between its location and its neo-Gothic style that the pumping station is a unique architectural structure that has always interested me as a creative person," says the artist, who is now fifty-three years old. At the time, when he was a student and a young artist, he could not have imagined that he might one day be able to raise the money to pay for the substantial cost for the repurposing of the 700-square-meter building.

Others had met their Waterloo when attempting to take on the property. Its planned use as a site of experience-gastronomy had been thwarted by the objections of local residents. When the pumping station, a listed historic monument, later reappeared on the market, Brixy's situation had markedly improved. After years of traveling and working, he had developed an established client base, whose enthusiasm for his colorful and generally expressive paintings appeared to provide the financial buffer necessary for an investment on this scale. In the end, fascination and the courage to take risks trumped reason.

Once a Steam Blaster in Place of a Paintbrush

An intense working relationship between the building and its new owner began once the sale had been completed. Dietmar Brixy and numerous friends removed tons of rubbish and rubble from the run-down site, knocked off loose pieces of plaster, and scrubbed and brushed the machines and pumps in the work hall.

The wastewater canal, carefully constructed from brick, was a particularly significant discovery. It presented itself in remarkably good condition after it had been drained and painstakingly cleaned using a steam blaster, transmitting special acoustics and an

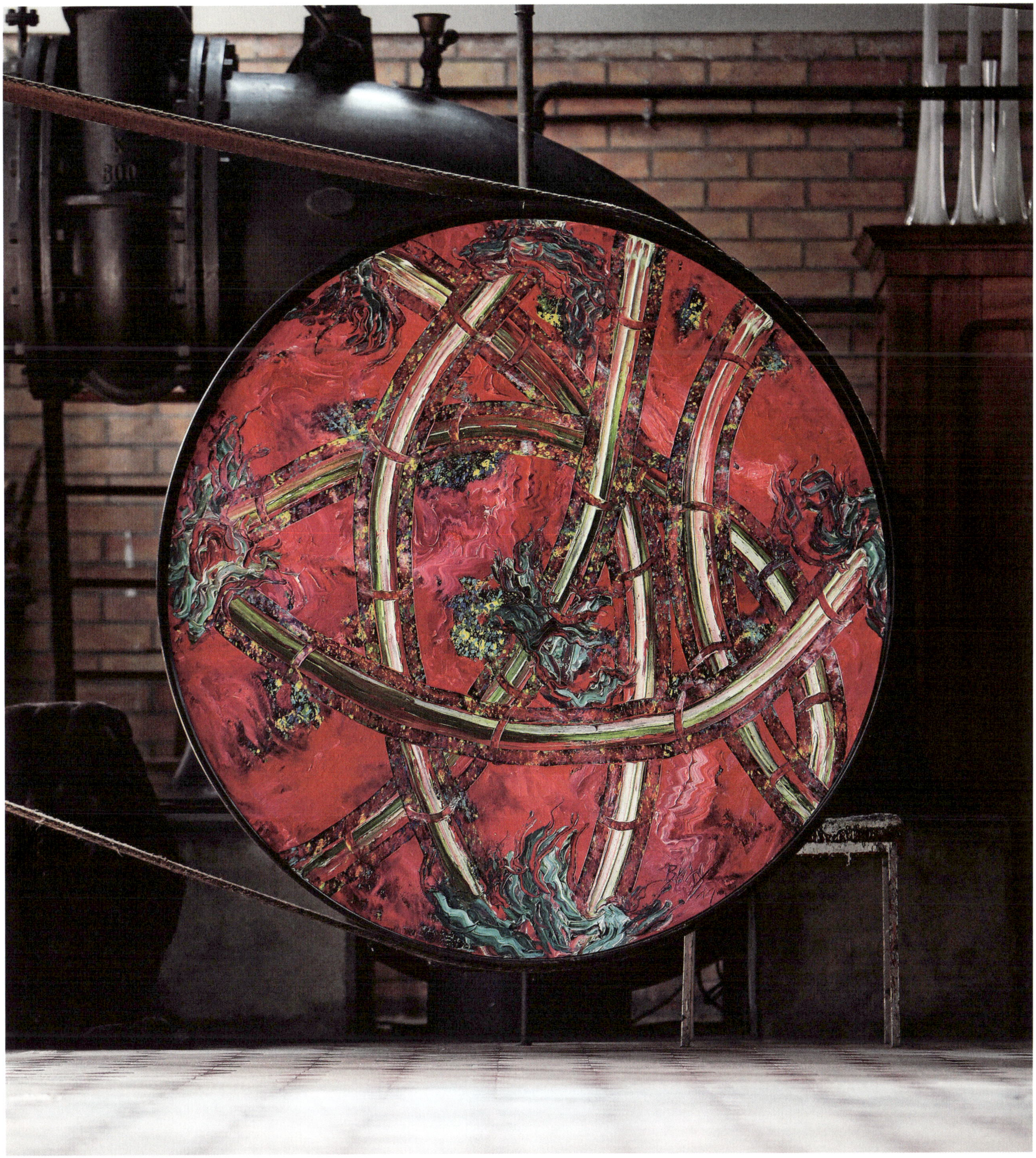

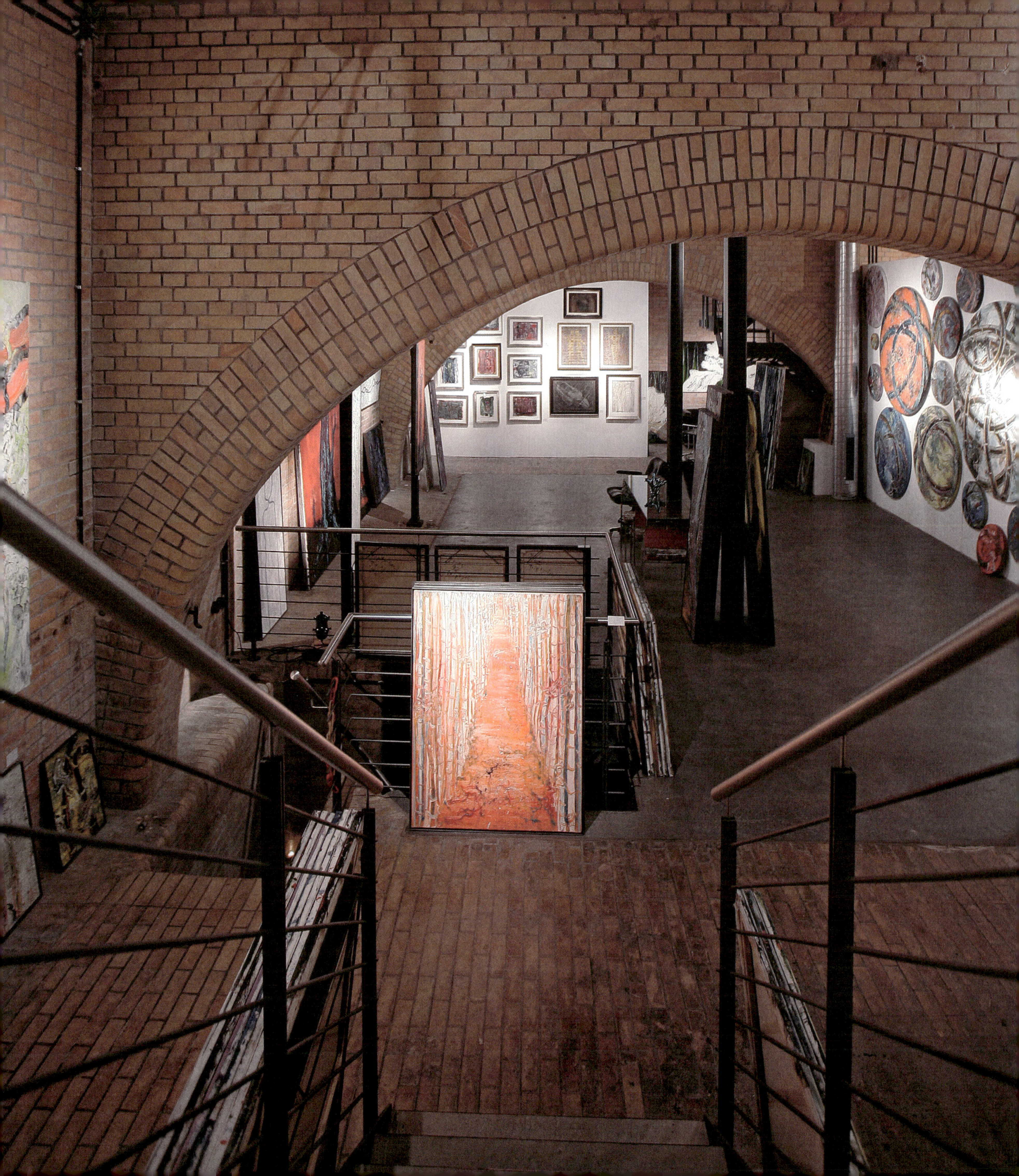

in einem erstaunlich guten Zustand präsentiert und eine ganz besondere Akustik und Atmosphäre vermittelt. Heute dient er als Weinlager und temporäre Ausstellungsfläche. Parallel zu den Aufräumarbeiten lief die Abstimmung mit der Denkmalpflege und Bauamt über die notwendigen Veränderungen. Denn um das Pumpwerk überhaupt zum Wohnen und Arbeiten nutzen zu können, waren Eingriffe in die Bausubstanz unumgänglich.

„Unser Grundsatz war aber immer, das Pumpwerk so wenig wie möglich zu verändern, um seinen Charakter zu bewahren", erläutert Architekt Henrich. Die meisten Diskussionen gab es um die Schließung der Abwassergrube im heutigen Wohnteil. „Ohne die neue Decke über dem ehemaligen Becken für den Schmutzfangrechen hätten wir die Sache vergessen können", erzählt Brixy. Heute verschließt eine dünne Betonschicht auf Stahlelementen die Grube. Wie alle nachträglichen Einbauten könnte sie aber jederzeit ohne großen Aufwand wieder zurückgebaut werden.

Entstanden ist ein fast 100 Quadratmeter großer Wohnraum an den sich die Küche anschließt. Im Luftraum über der Küche und den Nebenräumen trennen große Glasflächen ein Büro und auf der anderen Seite einen Schlafraum sowie ein Bad ab. Ansonsten reicht der Blick frei bis zum Dachfirst, dessen ehemals offene Lüftungsschlitze mit neuen, elektrisch angetriebenen Fenstern geschlossen wurden.

Der anthrazitfarben beschichtete Estrich und die weiß verputzten Wände halten sich farblich zurück. Umso mehr kommen die expressionistischen Gemälde von Dietmar Brixy zur Geltung, einige davon in metergroßen Formaten. Intensive Farben und Motive aus der Natur bestimmen die vielschichtigen Werke. Wer genau hinschaut erkennt Vögel, Geckos und Schmetterlinge zwischen Bambus, Blättern und Blüten.

Kreativität statt Kloake

Entstanden sind diese Bilder in der früheren Maschinenhalle des Pumpwerks. Wo einst Pumpen Fäkalien und andere Abwässer fauchend, schmatzend und ratternd in den Rhein beförderten, arbeitet Dietmar Brixy heute auf einer nachträglich eingebauten stählernen Bühne, die wie ein überdimensionaler Tisch in dem 17 Meter hohen Raum steht.

„Die Lichtverhältnisse durch Bogenfenster rundum sind ideal. Und ich kann jederzeit in den Garten sehen", freut sich der Maler. Mit welcher Sorgfalt und Liebe zum Detail die für den profanen Zweck der Abwasserentsorgung gebauten Räume ausgestattet wurden, zeigen der gut erhalten Terrazzoboden und die schönen Fliesen im Maschinensaal, die lediglich einer intensiven Reinigung bedurften. Wände und Dach präsentierten sich auch nach über 100 Jahren in gutem Zustand.

---

unmistakeable atmosphere. Today, it serves as wine storage and a temporary exhibition space.

The clean-up efforts took place alongside coordination of the necessary changes with the government departments charged with the preservation of historic monuments and with the building authorities. This was because in order to make use of the pumping station as a space for living and working, changes to the fabric of the building were unavoidable.

"But our guiding principle was always that we would make as few changes to the pumping station as possible in order to safeguard its character," the architect Mathias Heinrich explains. The main subject of discussion was the closing of the sewage pit in what are now the living quarters. "We would have had to abandon the entire project without the new cover on the pit for the bar screen," as Brixy says. Now a thin layer of concrete on steel elements seals the pit. Like all recent structures, it could be removed again easily at any time.

This has resulted in a living area that is almost one hundred square metres in size, which abuts the kitchen. In the space above the kitchen and the adjoining rooms, large sheets of glass separate an office on the one side, and the sleeping area and bathroom on the other. Other than that, the view extends unhindered to the roof ridge, whose formerly open ventilation slits have been closed with new, electrically operated windows.

The colors of the anthracite-colored floors and the white plastered walls are subdued. This allows the expressionistic paintings of Dietmar Brixy to take center stage, some of them in meter-long formats. Intense colors and subjects drawn from nature characterize the multilayered works. Attentive viewers will discover birds, geckos, and butterflies among bamboo plants, leaves and blossoms.

Nur an einer Stelle musste nachträglich ein Wanddurchbruch geschlossen werden. Die dafür notwendigen Ziegel im ungewöhnlichen, so genannten Klosterformat aufzutreiben, bedeutete wochenlange Recherche. Schließlich wurden die Klinker von einer norddeutschen Ziegelei anhand eines Musters nachgebrannt. Gut erhalten waren auch die Fenster in der Pumpenhalle, auch wenn in der Zeit des Leerstands alle Glasscheiben zu Bruch gegangen waren. Ihre hölzernen Rahmen mussten lediglich aufgearbeitet und gestrichen werden. Um die Wärmedämmung zu verbessern, montierten die Restaurateure eine zweite, innenliegende Scheibe samt Rahmen auf die alten Fensterflügel. Nicht mehr zu retten waren die Fenster im Bereich der ehemaligen Kläranlage. Sie wurden nach Vorgaben der Denkmalschützer komplett neu angefertigt und eingebaut. Da auch das Dach nachträglich von innen mit einer Dämmung aus Hartschaumplatten gegen Wärmeverlust geschützt wurde, sind die lichtdurchfluteten Räume nun ohne weiteres zu beheizen, ohne dass die Kosten ins Unermessliche steigen. An Ort und Stelle blieben die großen Pumpen und Motoren, die das Atelier ein Stück weit zum technischen Museum machen. Verbunden mit ledernen Treibriemen scheinen sie nur darauf zu warten, ihre Arbeit wieder aufzunehmen. Dazwischen stehen fertige und halbfertige Bilder, ein Sofa, ein Flügel. „So viel Platz zu haben, ist natürlich wie ein Geschenk", sagt Dietmar Brixy, der regelmäßig Kunstfreunde aber auch die Öffentlichkeit in sein Atelier einlädt. „Noch wichtiger ist aber die Inspiration, die vom Pumpwerk und dem Garten drum herum ausgeht und die mich jeden Tag aufs Neue anregt und beflügelt", betont der Künstler.

Dass die Reaktivierung des Pumpwerks ein finanzieller Kraftakt war, verhehlt Brixy nicht. Rund eine Million Euro hat er investiert, erarbeitet in Form von Gemälden, die jetzt auch bei Sammlern in den USA oder China hängen. Geholfen haben aber auch Zuschüsse der Denkmalpflege und von Stiftungen. Zudem fand sich nach kurzer Suche auch eine Bank, die das ungewöhnliche Objekt und seinen kreativen Besitzer vertrauenswürdig genug für einen Kredit fand. Somit bekam der Umbau auch eine wirtschaftlich solide Basis, auch wenn bei Dietmar Brixys Entscheidung, sich das Denkmal zu eigen zu machen, mehr die Emotion als die Vernunft eine Rolle gespielt hatte.

Creativity Where Once There Were Sewers

These paintings were created in what was the machine hall of the pumping station. Where once pumps dispatched excrement and other wastewater into the Rhine amidst a din of hissing, smacking, and groaning, Dietmar Brixy today works on a steel stage, which was recently added and looks like an oversized table under the seventeen-meter-high ceiling.
"The lighting conditions through arched windows all around are ideal. And I can see into the garden whenever I like," the painter enthuses. The care and attention to detail with which the building serving the mundane purpose of wastewater disposal was furnished are reflected in the well-preserved terrazzo ground and the beautiful tiles in the machine hall. These needed nothing more than intensive cleaning. The walls and roof presented themselves in good condition even after one hundred years. A wall breakthrough had to be closed in just one place. Several weeks of research were necessary in order to track down the necessary tiles in the unusual so-called monastery format. Finally, the bricks were fired by a north-German brickyard according to a specimen. The windows in the pump hall were also in good condition, despite the fact that all of the glass panes had been broken during the period of vacancy. It was merely necessary to recondition and paint their wood frames. The restorers mounted a second, inner pane along with a frame on the old casements to improve the thermal insulation.

The windows of the former sewage treatment plant were beyond salvation. They were produced from scratch and fitted according to specifications by specialists in the preservation of historical monuments. Because the roof was also fitted with an insulating layer of expanded plastic slabs to prevent the loss of heat, the light-filled spaces can now easily be heated without generating astronomical costs.

The pumps and motors, which transform the studio into a technical museum of sorts, have remained in place. Connected by leather drive belts, they appear to be ready to start work again at any moment. They are interspersed with finished and half-finished paintings, a sofa, and a grand piano. "It is of course a gift to have so much space," says Dietmar Brixy, who regularly invites art lovers as well as the general public into his studio. "The inspiration that emanates from the pumping station and the garden that surrounds it, and which inspires and animates me every single day, is even more important, though," the artist emphasizes.

Brixy does not conceal the fact that the reactivation of the pumping station involved a considerable financial effort. He invested approximately one million euros, having earned the money with paintings that are now the property of collectors in the USA and China. Grants from the historic-monument-preservation authorities and foundations also played their part, however. And after a short search, a bank was found that considered the unusual property and its creative owner trustworthy enough to merit a loan. This provided a solid economic basis for the repurposing, whereby Dietmar Brixy's decision to make the monument his own was based more on emotion than on reason.

BIOGRAFIE | BIOGRAPHY

1961 in Mannheim geboren   **1985–1991** Studium an der Staatlichen Akademie der Bildenden Künste in Karlsruhe bei den Professoren Wilhelm Loth, Michael Sandle, Harald Klingelhöller, Katharina Fritsch, Werner Pokorny und Elisabeth Wagner   **1988** Jahresausstellung Akademie der Bildenden Künste, Karlsruhe (1. Preis)   **1989** Stipendium der Stadt Mannheim (Aufenthalt in Polen, Krakau)   **seit 1991** freischaffender Künstler, lebt und arbeitet in Mannheim

1998 Förderpreis des Ludwig-Roos-Fonds   **2001–2003** Sanierung und denkmalgerechter Umbau des neugotischen „Alten Pumpwerks Neckarau" (1903 entworfen u. errichtet nach Plänen des Mannheimer Stadtbaudirektors Richard Perry) zum Wohnhaus und Atelier, mit einer kunstvoll gestalteten Gartenlandschaft   **2004** gewinnt der Künstler als Bauherr des neuen Alten Pumpwerks den Denkmalschutzpreis der Württemberg Hypo, des Schwäbischen Heimatbundes, des Landesvereins Badische Heimat, der Denkmalstiftung Baden-Württemberg   **2008** „WELDE Kunstpreis" (Gewinner Publikumspreis)   **seit 2004** finden im Alten Pumpwerk Mannheim Neckarau jährliche Ausstellungen aktueller eigener Arbeiten von Dietmar Brixy statt, die für Kunstinteressierte vom Geheimtipp zum Pflichttermin geworden sind: u. a. **2004** „Weinlese",   **2005** „Roots",   **2006** „Runde Sache",   **2007** „Grow",   **2008** „Beyond",   **2009** „Eden",   **2010** „Seven",   **2012** „Discover",   **2013** „Achtung Brixy",   **2014** „Ten – Zehn Jahre Kunst im Alten Pumpwerk"

Mal- und Studienreisen in das europäische Ausland (seit 2003 regelmäßig auf die Kanareninsel La Palma, wo seit 2009 seine Papierarbeiten zur Serie „Eden" entstehen und fortgesetzt werden) sowie u. a. auch nach Malaysia, Mexiko und Bali sowie auf die Seychellen und in die USA.

1961 **Born in Mannheim**   1985–1991 **Studied at the Staatliche Akademie der Bildenden Künste in Karlsruhe, as a student of professors Wilhelm Loth, Michael Sandle, Harald Klingelhöller, Katharina Fritsch, Werner Pokorny, and Elisabeth Wagner**   1988 **Annual exhibition of the Akademie der Bildenden Künste, Karlsruhe (first prize)**   1989 **Scholarship awarded by the city of Mannheim (sojourn in Poland, Krakow)**   Since 1991 **Independent artist, lives and works in Mannheim**
1998 **Recipient of the Förderpreis award of the Ludwig-Roos-Fonds**   2001–2003 **Restoration and conversion into a home and studio with an artfully designed garden landscape of the Neo-Gothic Altes Pumpwerk Neckarau pumping station (designed and erected in 1903 according to the plans of Mannheim's director of town planning Richard Perry) in accordance with monument preservation guidelines**   2004 **The artist was awarded the monument preservation prize of the Württemberg Hypo, the Schwäbischer Heimatbund, the Landesverein Badische Heimat, and the Denkmalstiftung Baden-Württemberg for the work he commissioned as owner of the new Altes Pumpwerk pumping station**   2008 **WELDE Kunstpreis award (recipient of the audience award)**   Since 2004 **Annual exhibitions of Dietmar Brixy's work have taken place at the Altes Pumpwerk Mannheim Neckarau. They have developed from an insider's tip into must-see events for art enthusiasts, including:** 2004 **"Weinlese,"** 2005 **"Roots,"** 2006 **"Runde Sache,"** 2007 **"Grow,"** 2008 **"Beyond,"** 2009 **"Eden,"** 2010 **"Seven,"** 2012 **"Discover,"** 2013 **"Achtung Brixy,"** 2014 **"Ten – Zehn Jahre Kunst im Alten Pumpwerk"**
Painting and study sojourns **in other European countries (since 2003: regular trips to the Canary Island of La Palma, where his works on paper, which are part of the "Eden" series, have been created and continued since 2009) and in Malaysia, Mexico and Bali, as well as on the Seychelles and in the USA, among other places.**

AUSSTELLUNGEN | EXHIBITIONS

2009–2014 (Auswahl|selection), Einzel- (EA) u. Gruppenausstellungen (GA)|solo and group shows

2014 CONTEXT ART MIAMI mit „Art from Berlin" (Galerie Tammen & Partner, Berlin); Contemporary Istanbul mit Galerie Tammen & Partner, Berlin; Art Market Budapest, International Contemporary Art Fair; Altes Pumpwerk Neckarau, „Ten – Zehn Jahre Kunst im Alten Pumpwerk" (EA) und special guests: Anke Eilergerhard, Detlef Waschkau (Galerie Tammen & Partner, Berlin); Galerie Cornelia Kamp, Sylt, „Discover. Brixy" (EA); Stadtgalerie Mannheim „20 Jahre Welde Kunstpreis" (GA), Galerie Tammen & Partner, Berlin, „Discover. Brixy" (EA); art KARLSRUHE mit Galerie Tammen & Partner (one artist show); R-House/White Porch Gallery, Wynwood Arts District, Miami, USA „Discover Brixy" (EA), Badischer Kunstverein, Mitgliederausstellung (GA)

2013 R-House/White Porch Gallery, Wynwood Arts District, Miami, USA, „Brixy Launch USA"(EA); CONTEXT ART MIAMI Brixy bei „Art from Berlin" mit Galerie Tammen & Partner (one artist show); Contemporary Istanbul mit Galerie Tammen & Partner (one artist show); Altes Pumpwerk Neckarau, „Achtung Brixy" (EA) und special guests: Marion Eichmann, Lothar Seruset (Galerie Tammen & Partner, Berlin); art studio fael, Hannover, „Discover. Brixy" (EA); Galerie Biesenbach, Köln, „Summer of Paper" (GA); White Porch Gallery, Provincetown, USA, „Discover. Brixy" (EA), Wasserturm Mannheim – Friedrichsplatz, „Lange Nacht d. Museen, 13", Brixy-Schau im Wahrzeichen der Stadt Mannheim (EA), Galerie Arrigoni, Baar/Zug, CH (EA), „Discover. Brixy"; art KARLSRUHE mit Galerie Tammen & Partner (one artist show); Kunsträume Zermatt, CH, „Discover. Brixy" (EA); Tammen & Partner, Berlin, „Jahresendausstellung" (GA)

2012 Galerie Tammen & Partner, Berlin, „Weihnachtsausstellung" (GA); Kunstverein Worms, „Denk mal an Wagner" (GA); Altes Pumpwerk Neckarau, „Discover" (EA) und special guest: Herbert Mehler (Galerie Tammen & Partner, Berlin); Galerie Tammen & Partner, Berlin, „Eden in Berlin" (EA); art KARLSRUHE mit Galerie arthea, Mannheim (one artist show)

2011 Badischer Kunstverein, „Weihnachtsausstellung" (GA); Klinikum Ludwigshafen, „Neue Arbeiten" (EA); Sparkasse Heidelberg, „Eden" (EA); Brixy verhüllt eine Bauruine in Mannheim Stadt mit einer 400 m²-Plane (Werkausschnitt: „Rapture", a.d. Serie „Ripe & Juicy"); ART. FAIR 21 Köln mit Galerie arthea, Mannheim (one artist show); art KARLSRUHE mit Galerie arthea, Mannheim (one artist show); Commerzbank Hamburg (GA)

2010 Altes Pumpwerk Neckarau, „Seven" (EA); Kunstverein Schwetzigen, „Animal Art" (GA); Kunstverein Schwetzingen (EA) und Kunstverein Worms (EA), „Ripe & Juicy" in Orangerie Schloss Schwetzingen (EA); art KARLSRUHE mit Galerie arthea & lauth, Mannheim (one artist show)

2009 Altes Pumpwerk Neckarau, „Eden" (EA); Besuch von Staatsminister Bernd Neumann im Alten Pumpwerk Neckarau; Schillertage Mannheim (Projekt-Arbeit)

seit 1995 Präsentation in Galerien (Auswahl) | since 1995 presentation in galleries (selection)

arthea. Galerie am Rosengarten, Mannheim (EA); Galerie Monika Beck, Homburg (EA); Galerie Peter Breuer, Zwickau (EA); el-ga-le-rie, Karlsruhe (EA); Galerie Angelo Falzone, Mannheim (EA u. GA); Galerie Française, München (EA); Galerie Heufelder - Koos, München (EA); Galerie Saby Lazi, Stuttgart (EA); Galerie Tammen & Partner, Berlin (EA u. GA); Galerie Vigny, München (EA); Galerie Weisses Haus, Wuppertal (EA); Galerie Zulauf, Freinsheim (EA u. GA); Galerie Zezhong, Beijing, China (EA); Pfalzgalerie, Kaiserslautern (GA)

seit 1995 Präsentation in Institutionen, Museen, Kunstvereinen (Auswahl) | since 1995 presentation in institutions and museums

Commerzbank Mannheim (GA); Commerzbank Hamburg (GA); Volksbank, Weil der Stadt (EA); Fruchthallen, Kaiserslautern (GA); Galerie der Hoechst AG, Frankfurt (EA); Hochschule Pforzheim (GA); Kulturstiftung Rhein-Neckar-Kreis e.V., Dilsberg (GA); Landesgartenschau Hockenheim (GA); Badischer Kunstverein, Karlsruhe (GA); Mannheimer Kunstverein, in den Räumen der BGN, Mannheim (EA u. GA); Kunstverein Schwetzingen (EA u. GA); Kunstverein Worms (EA); Nationaltheater Mannheim (GA); Museum Baden, Solingen-Gräfrath (GA); Museum für Technik + Arbeit, Mannheim (GA); Reißmuseum, Mannheim (GA); Wilhelm-Hack-Museum, Ludwigshafen (GA); Salon d' Automne International de Luneville, Frankreich (GA)

seit 1999 Messebeteiligungen (Auswahl) | since 1999 art fairs

ART.FAIR 21, Köln; ART Frankfurt; ART Innsbruck; art KARLSRUHE; Biennale Internazionale Dell'Arte Contemporanea, Florenz; Contemporary Istanbul, Context art Miami, Vienna Art, Wien

Arbeiten im öffentlichen Raum u. Sammlungen (Auswahl) | works in public collections

AIDAbella Passenger Ship (vermittelt durch Samuelis Baumgarte Galerie, Bielefeld; Thema: „Ferne Welten"); Altes Rathaus Mannheim, Trausaal (Triptychon „Gefunden", Öl/Nessel, je 240×120 cm, erworben von der Vetter-Stiftung, Müller-Stiftung u. Kanzlei Rittershaus, Mannheim); Gartenhallenbad Mannheim Neckarau (Schenkung an die Stadt Mannheim durch Gerda Brand); GKM (Großkraftwerk) Mannheim (Auftragsarbeit: „Energiegeladener Brixyscher Kosmos", Öl/Nessel, 180×960 cm)

Ankäufe für d. Regierungspräsidium Karlsruhe; Sammlung Insider Technologies GmbH, Kaiserslautern sowie Werke in zahlreichen Sammlungen in Deutschland, der Schweiz, den USA, Südafrika, China.

AUTOREN | AUTHORS

Dr. Melanie Klier, geboren 1970 in Gräfelfing, studierte Germanistik, Kunstgeschichte und Theaterwissenschaften an der Ludwig-Maximilians-Universität München. Sie arbeitete lange am Lehrstuhl für Neuere deutsche Philologie sowie als freie Kulturjournalistin (Süddeutsche Zeitung, Münchner Merkur) sowie beim Bayerischen Rundfunk für Film und Hörfunk. Sie ist als Kunstbuchautorin (u. a. Prestel, Dumont, DOM publishers), freie Artreferentin und Laudatorin für die Gegenwartskunst tätig. www.klartextkunst.de

Volker Lehmkuhl, Jg. 1963, ist Fachjournalist für alle Themen rund um Bauen, Sanieren, Erneuerbare Energien und Denkmalschutz. Aufgewachsen in Mannheim-Pfingstberg und Ladenburg kennt er Mannheim-Rheinau und die Neckarau aus Schüler- und Studentenjobs. Die Welt des Dietmar Brixy und das ehemalige Pumpwerk lernte er bei der Berichterstattung über den Denkmalschutzpreis Baden-Württemberg kennen, für den er seit 2000 die Presse- und Öffentlichkeitsarbeit macht.

Dr. Ulrike Lorenz – Seit 2009 Direktorin Kunsthalle Mannheim; 2004–2008 Direktorin Kunstforum Regensburg; 1992–2004 Direktorin Kunstsammlung Gera/Otto-Dix-Haus; Studium Kunstwissenschaft Universität Leipzig/Promotion Bauhaus-Universität Weimar zum Avantgarde-Architekten Thilo Schoder; Ausstellungen und Publikationen zur Klassischen Moderne (Otto Dix, Bauhaus, Brücke) und zeitgenössischen Kunst

Dr. Reinhard Spieler, 1964 in Rotenburg an der Fulda geboren, seit 2014 Direktor des Sprengel Museums in Hannover. Zuvor war er seit 2007 Direktor des Wilhelm-Hack-Museums in Ludwigshafen am Rhein. Reinhard Spieler studierte Kunstgeschichte, Klassische Archäologie und Neuere deutsche Literatur in München, Berlin und Paris. Neben seiner Museums- und Ausstellungstätigkeit hat er Lehraufträge an der Kunstakademie Düsseldorf sowie an den Universitäten Düsseldorf, Bern und Heidelberg wahrgenommen.

Werner Tammen, geboren 1952 in Poggenburg/Friesland. Gelernter Verlagskaufmann in Wilhelmshaven, Lehramtsstudium Deutsch/Geschichte zum 1. Staatsexamen in Berlin. Dort noch während des Studiums Gründung der ersten „Galerie Am Chamissoplatz" (legendär für Comix, Karikatur und Cartoon), heutige Galerie für zeitgenössische Kunst Galerie Tammen & Partner, Teilnahme an nationalen und internationalen Messen, seit 1994 Vorsitzender des Landesverbandes Berliner Galerien (LVBG)

Christoph Tannert, geboren 1955 in Leipzig, ist Kunsthistoriker und Autor zahlreicher Kunstpublikationen. Als Kurator, Projektleiter und Geschäftsführer ist er am Künstlerhaus Bethanien in Berlin tätig. Seine hauptsächlichen Arbeitsgebiete sind Ausstellungsorganisation und Kunstkritik im Bereich der Gegenwartskunst. Christoph Tannert lebt in Berlin.

Dr. Melanie Klier, **born in 1970 in Gräfelfing, studied German language and literature, art history, and drama at Ludwig Maximilian University Munich. She worked for many years in the Faculty of Modern German Philology and as an independent journalist on the subject of culture (*Süddeutsche Zeitung, Münchner Merkur*). She also worked in film and radio for Bayerischer Rundfunk. She is the author of art books (including Prestel, Dumont, DOM publishers), and works as an independent art lecturer and consultant.   www.klartextkunst.de**

Volker Lehmkuhl, **born in 1963, is a journalist who specializes in all subjects relating to construction, redevelopment, renewable energy sources, and monument conservation. Having grown up in Mannheim-Pfingstberg and Ladenburg, he knows Mannheim-Rheinau and the Neckarau from jobs he took on as a schoolboy and student. He was introduced to the world of Dietmar Brixy and the former pumping station while covering the Denkmalschutzpreis Baden-Württemberg award. He has been in charge of press relations and public relations for the award since 2000.**

Dr. Ulrike Lorenz **Since 2009: director of Kunsthalle Mannheim; 2004–2008: director of Kunstforum Regensburg; 1992–2004: director of Kunstsammlung Gera/Otto-Dix-Haus; Studied fine art at the University of Leipzig/doctorate at the Bauhaus University Weimar on the subject of the avant-garde architect Thilo Schoder; Exhibitions and publications on classic modernism (Otto Dix, Bauhaus, Brücke) and contemporary art**

Dr. Reinhard Spieler, **born in 1964 in Rotenburg an der Fulda, has been the director of the Sprengel Museum in Hannover since 2014. Before that, he was director of the Wilhelm-Hack-Museum in Ludwigshafen am Rhein from 2007. Reinhard Spieler studied art history, classical archaeology, and modern German literature in Munich, Berlin, and Paris. In addition to his work for museums and exhibitions, he has taught at Kunstakademie Düsseldorf and at the universities of Düsseldorf, Bern, and Heidelberg.**

Werner Tammen **was born in 1952 in Poggenburg in Friesland. He trained as a publishing manager in Wilhelmshaven and studied for a teaching degree in German and history, completing the First State Exam in Berlin. While a student there, he founded the first Galerie Am Chamissoplatz (legendary for comics, caricatures and cartoons), now the contemporary art gallery Galerie Tammen & Partner. He participates in national and international fairs; and has been the head of the Landesverband Berliner Galerien (LVBG) since 1994.**

Christoph Tannert, **born in 1955 in Leipzig, is an art historian and the author of numerous art publications. He works at the Künstlerhaus Bethanien in Berlin as curator, project coordinator and director. His main fields of activity are exhibition organization and art criticism in the sphere of contemporary art. Christoph Tannert lives in Berlin.**

TAMMEN & PARTNER GALERIE

Impressum | Imprint

© Art Identity GmbH, 2014
© für die Texte bei den Autoren | texts by kind permission
of the authors
© alle Werke | all images Dietmar Brixy, 2014
© alle Fotos | all images, Christian Dammert, Peter Schlör, 2014

Alle Rechte vorbehalten – insbesondere das Recht auf Vervielfältigung und Verbreitung sowie Übersetzung. Kein Teil dieses Werkes darf in irgendeiner Form ohne schriftliche Genehmigung des Verlags reproduziert oder unter Verwendung elektronischer Systeme verarbeitet, vervielfältigt und verbreitet werden.

All rights reserved. No part of this publication may be reproduced, translated, stored in a retrieval system, or transmitted in any form or by any means, electronic, mechanical, photocopying, or recording or otherwise, without the prior permission of the publisher.

Umschlagabbildung | Cover illustration
Detail *Discover*, 2014, 120 × 180 cm

Herausgeber | Editor
Jürgen Krieger

Englische Übersetzung | English translation
Jane Michael, Prof. Dr. Elke Platz-Waury

Gestaltung | Design
zwischenschritt, Rainald Schwarz
Liquid, Augsburg (Cover)

Herstellung | Production
zwischenschritt, Rainald Schwarz, München
Beata Nemesszeghyová, print service

Litho | Origination
Reproline mediateam, München

Druck und Bindung | Printing and binding
TBB, a.s. | Banská Bystrica

Die Deutsche Nationalbibliothek verzeichnet diese Publikation in der Deutschen Nationalbibliografie; detaillierte bibliografische Daten sind im Internet über http://dnb.d-nb.de abrufbar.

The Deutsche Nationalbibliothek lists this publication in the Deutsche Nationalbibliografie; detailed bibliographical data is available on the Internet at http://dnb.d-nb.de

EDITION BRAUS Berlin GmbH
Prinzenstraße 85
D-10969 Berlin

www.editionbraus.de

ISBN: 978-3-86228-109-1

… Alla hopp!